W9-BFX-895

Modern Language Association of America

Approaches to Teaching World Literature

Joseph Gibaldi, Series Editor

29. Richard K. Emmerson, ed. *Approaches to Teaching Medieval English Drama*. 1990.
30. Kathleen Blake, ed. *Approaches to Teaching Eliot's* Middlemarch. 1990.
31. María Elena de Valdés and Mario J. Valdés, eds. *Approaches to Teaching García Márquez's* One Hundred Years of Solitude. 1990.
32. Donald D. Kummings, ed. *Approaches to Teaching Whitman's* Leaves of Grass. 1990.
33. Stephen C. Behrendt, ed. *Approaches to Teaching Shelley's* Frankenstein. 1990.
34. June Schlueter and Enoch Brater, eds. *Approaches to Teaching Beckett's* Waiting for Godot. 1991.

Approaches to Teaching Beckett's *Waiting for Godot*

Edited by

June Schlueter

and

Enoch Brater

The Modern Language Association of America
New York   1991

Library of Congress Cataloging-in-Publication Data

Approaches to teaching Beckett's Waiting for Godot / edited by June
    Schlueter and Enoch Brater.
       p.   cm.—(Approaches to teaching world literature ; 34)
    Includes bibliographical references and index.
    ISBN 0-87352-541-8 (cloth) ISBN 0-87352-542-6 (paper)
    1. Beckett, Samuel, 1906–   En attendant Godot.   2. Beckett,
Samuel, 1906–   —Study and teaching.   I. Schlueter, June.
II. Brater, Enoch.   III. Series.
PQ2603.E378E617   1991
842'.914—dc20   91-2356

Cover illustration of the paperback edition: Brian Bedford as Vladimir and
Edward Atienza as Estragon in the 1984 Stratford Festival production of *Waiting
for Godot*. Photo by David Cooper. Courtesy of the Stratford Festival, Ontario,
Canada.

Published by The Modern Language Association of America
10 Astor Place, New York, New York 10003-6981

CONTENTS

PREFACE TO THE SERIES

In *The Art of Teaching* Gilbert Highet wrote, "Bad teaching wastes a great deal of effort, and spoils many lives which might have been full of energy and happiness." All too many teachers have failed in their work, Highet argued, simply "because they have not thought about it." We hope that the Approaches to Teaching World Literature series, sponsored by the Modern Language Association's Publications Committee, will not only improve the craft—as well as the art—of teaching but also encourage serious and continuing discussion of the aims and methods of teaching literature.

The principal objective of the series is to collect within each volume different points of view on teaching a specific literary work, a literary tradition, or a writer widely taught at the undergraduate level. The preparation of each volume begins with a wide-ranging survey of instructors, thus enabling us to include in the volume the philosophies and approaches, thoughts and methods of scores of experienced teachers. The result is a sourcebook of material, information, and ideas on teaching the subject of the volume to undergraduates.

The series is intended to serve nonspecialists as well as specialists, inexperienced as well as experienced teachers, graduate students who wish to learn effective ways of teaching as well as senior professors who wish to compare their own approaches with the approaches of colleagues in other schools. Of course, no volume in the series can ever substitute for erudition, intelligence, creativity, and sensitivity in teaching. We hope merely that each book will point readers in useful directions; at most each will offer only a first step in the long journey to successful teaching.

Joseph Gibaldi
Series Editor

PREFACE TO THE VOLUME

As the first twentieth-century play to be included in the Approaches to Teaching World Literature series, Samuel Beckett's *Waiting for Godot* reasserts its place in the history of dramatic literature. Taught in a range of contexts and from a variety of approaches, the play offers opportunities to beginning and seasoned teachers alike.

This volume, like the others in the Approaches series, is concerned primarily with undergraduate teaching. In keeping with the series format, part 1 presents materials, including an essay on editions and productions, by June Schlueter; commentary on required and recommended student readings, assembled from responses to questionnaires on teaching the play; and essays on the instructor's library and audiovisual materials, by Enoch Brater.

Part 2, "Approaches," contains a prologue by Ruby Cohn and twenty essays arranged in five categories. Following the essays are a list of contributors and other survey participants, a bibliography of works cited, and an index of names.

Collaborations can be difficult, but this one, happily, has been full of collegiality and mutual respect. We are grateful to all those who participated in the survey, to those who contributed essays, to Lafayette College for photocopying assistance, and to the MLA for its guidance throughout the project.

JS and EB

Part One

MATERIALS

Editions and Productions

En attendant Godot was published in 1952 by Les Editions de Minuit, Paris. *Waiting for Godot*, published by Grove Press, New York, appeared in 1954. The first British edition of the play was published by Faber and Faber in 1956. But particular passages of that volume were censored by the lord chamberlain. Subsequent single-volume Faber editions of the play print Beckett's original and uncensored text. The Faber edition of *Samuel Beckett: The Complete Dramatic Works* (1986), however, uses the censored text, an obvious error on the publisher's part. Teachers of *Godot* will notice, too, that there are several minor discrepancies between the American and British editions of the play. These result not only from the censor's demands but from differences between British and American English, not to mention careless proofreading on both sides of the Atlantic (for a discussion of this matter, see Zeifman).

The American and English editions contain changes initiated by Beckett as well as modifications suggested by Roger Blin, director of the first Paris production in 1953. Now in its eighty-seventh printing, the Grove Press edition retains the peculiar pagination of the first American text: only verso pages are numbered. Since Grove Press has never permitted reprintings, the only American anthology containing *Waiting for Godot* is the press's own: *Nine Plays of the Modern Theater*, edited by Harold Clurman (originally *Seven Plays of the Modern Theater*, 1962). The British anthology *Samuel Beckett: The Complete Dramatic Works* does not reflect the changes included in the single English-language texts. A trilingual edition of the play, *Warten auf Godot. En attendant Godot. Waiting for Godot*, contains the French and English texts on the two-column left-hand pages and the German text, in larger typeface, on the right-hand pages.

Blin's premiere of *En attendant Godot* took place on 5 January 1953, at the Théâtre Babylone, Paris. The English version premiered at the Arts Theatre Club, London, on 3 August 1955, under the direction of Peter Hall. Alan Schneider's unhappily received American premiere, at the Coconut Grove Playhouse in Miami, Florida, took place on 3 January 1956; the New York premiere, directed by Herbert Berghof at the John Golden Theatre, followed on 19 April of that year. The quarter century since the Paris opening has seen numerous revivals, in French, English, German, and other languages. Especially notable are the San Francisco Actor's Workshop production at San Quentin prison on 19 November 1957, directed by Herbert Blau; the German production at the Schiller Theater, Berlin, in April 1975, directed by Beckett; the National Theatre of Great Britain production, which opened on 25 November 1987, directed by Michael Rudman and based on the Actor's Workshop and Schiller Theater productions; New York's Lincoln Center production, directed by Mike Nichols, which opened exactly a year later; and the Dublin Gate Theatre production, directed by Walter Asmus, which opened on 30 August 1988. The year 1988 also saw two all-female versions, produced against Beckett's wishes, one at the Haarlem Toneelschuur Theater, the other at the Denver Center Theatre Company.

Required and Recommended Student Readings

One-third of the respondents to the MLA survey on teaching *Waiting for Godot* expressed resistance to collateral reading for undergraduates. For some, assigning secondary sources is not part of their pedagogy regardless of text; for others, the avoidance of such materials is specific to Beckett. Teachers want students to encounter *Godot* themselves, to work through their own confusions, to avoid reliance on others for the "right" reading. As one teacher puts it, "The less criticism undergraduates read on Beckett, the better their experience of the works will be." Another teacher, of upper-division and graduate students, even removes Ruby Cohn's *Casebook on Waiting for Godot* from the library shelves "so that students may not be unduly influenced by any point of view but their own."

Surely *Waiting for Godot* offers a special dramatic experience for students at any level who approach the play for the first time. For this reason, many teachers feel the need to prescribe background materials. The work to which teachers most frequently send their students (with some caution regarding terminology) is Martin Esslin's *Theatre of the Absurd*, a study that provides both a theatrical and a philosophical context for the play. In fact, every respondent who recommended secondary works mentioned Esslin, and several who resisted secondary materials conceded that if they did require ancillary reading, it would be Esslin. The book provides an introduction on "the absurdity of the absurd," chapters on several playwrights whom Esslin includes under the rubric "absurd" (Beckett, Adamov, Ionesco, Genet, and Pinter), a discussion of parallels and proselytes, and an extended analysis of the tradition and the significance of the absurd. Also appearing repeatedly on the secondary reading list is *Samuel Beckett: A Collection of Critical Essays*, edited by Martin Esslin; *Casebook on* Waiting for Godot, edited by Ruby Cohn; and *A Student's Guide to the Plays of Samuel Beckett*, edited by Beryl S. Fletcher et al.

Teachers interested in providing background on the philosophical implications of the play refer students to Camus's *Myth of Sisyphus* or Sartre's

Being and Nothingness or *Philosophy of Existentialism*, with one or two preferring readings in Descartes, Hegel, Kierkegaard, Schopenhauer, Tillich, or Dante.

A number of teachers recommend that their students read other Beckett works. *Proust* is most often cited, either the entire monograph or specific excerpts. Other suggestions include "Dante . . . Bruno. Vico . . Joyce," *Endgame, Act without Words, Play, Malone Dies, Molloy,* and *Murphy.* Several teachers have also found judicious selections from Deirdre Bair's biography of Beckett helpful.

Critical studies most often recommended are John Fletcher and John Spurling, *Beckett: A Study of His Plays,* and Hugh Kenner, *Samuel Beckett: A Critical Study.* Other studies mentioned include *Beckett at 80/Beckett in Context,* edited by Enoch Brater; *Samuel Beckett: The Comic Gamut,* by Ruby Cohn; *The Long Sonata of the Dead,* by Michael Robinson; and (in French) *Configuration critique de Samuel Beckett,* edited by Melvin J. Friedman. Respondents recommended other critical studies for use by both teachers and students, and these are included among the works noted in "The Instructor's Library" that follows.

The Instructor's Library

Approaching the ample criticism on Beckett's *Godot* can be a daunting experience for the novice instructor of the play. No other work in post–World War II drama has produced as much commentary as this play has, giving rise to what has been aptly called "the Beckett industry." *Waiting for Godot,* according to Alan Schneider, the playwright's most famous director in America, "is no longer a play, but a condition of life" (qtd. in Cohn, in Brater, *Beckett at 80* 13). That play and that condition of life have been the focus of a continuing inquiry from an international community of scholars, Beckett's "all humanity." Such a fertile situation seems right for a work about being, remaining, and un-ending. That this play was, to paraphrase the author's words, striving "all the time to avoid definition" (Reid, *All I Can Manage* 34) has proved to be anything but a critical deterrent. Quite the contrary—or to quote Beckett himself when taken for British and not the Irishman he was—*"au contraire,"* naughty bilingual pun intended.

This essay attempts to provide selective guidance on those sources most appropriate to the classroom, with the emphasis on material available in English. The essay also updates the flourishing school of Beckett criticism. Although many books about the play are available, the reader should keep in mind that some of the most suggestive interpretations of *Waiting for Godot* appear in essay form. Indeed, one of the first sustained evaluations of the play, Edith Kern's "Drama Stripped for Inaction: Beckett's *Godot*," was printed in *Yale French Studies* more than thirty-five years ago.

Of particular interest here is the *Journal of Beckett Studies*, which, although appearing erratically in London under John Calder's imprint, offers its subscribers a steady encounter with new studies in the field. Appearing more regularly is the *Beckett Circle/Le Cercle de Beckett*, the official publication of the Samuel Beckett Society of America (an Allied Organization of MLA). The twice-yearly newsletter is a minefield of current information on all areas relating to Beckett's work, including forthcoming publications and reviews of plays in production. *Modern Drama, Theatre Journal*, and *Comparative Drama* are well known in North America for their extensive history of publication on Beckett. Several major periodicals have devoted special issues to Samuel Beckett; those with information pertinent to *Godot* include *Perspective* (Autumn 1959) and *Modern Drama* (Dec. 1966), both edited by Ruby Cohn; the *James Joyce Quarterly*, edited by David Hayman (Summer 1971); the *Journal of Modern Literature*, edited by Enoch Brater (Feb. 1977); and the *Review of Contemporary Fiction*, edited by Nicholas Zurbrugg (Summer 1987).

Reference Materials

Foremost among published reference books is *Samuel Beckett: His Works and His Critics*, a key essay in bibliography edited by Raymond Federman and John Fletcher. The book documents Beckett's published work and the criticism of that work through the mid-1960s. Another, less comprehensive, bibliography of the same period is J. F. Tanner and J. D. Vann, *Samuel Beckett: A Checklist*. More recent material has been collated in the following sources: Jackson R. Bryer, "Samuel Beckett: A Checklist of Criticism"; Frederick J. Marker, "Beckett Criticism in *Modern Drama*: A Checklist"; Joseph Browne, "The 'Crritic' and Samuel Beckett: A Bibliographic Essay" in the Beckett issue of *College Literature* (ed. Oldsey); and Cathleen Culotta Andonian, *Samuel Beckett: A Reference Guide*. The Beckett issue of *Modern Fiction Studies*, edited by S. E. Gontarski, includes a brief but useful survey of other journals with special issues devoted to the author. In addition to checking the annual *MLA International Bibliography* index on new scholarship, where Beckett is listed under twentieth-century French literature, instructors may also consult Charles A. Carpenter, *Modern Drama Scholarship and Criticism, 1966–1980*. For listings of studies on the play written since 1980, they may see the annual bibliography published each June in *Modern Drama*. The computer-generated two volumes of *A Kwic Concor-*

dance to Samuel Beckett's Trilogy: Molloy, Malone Dies, *and* The Unnamable, by Michèle Aina Barale and Rubin Rabinovitz, are an invaluable resource for instances of intertextuality.

Richard L. Admussen's *Samuel Beckett Manuscripts: A Study* is especially helpful on the particulars of the original. *Samuel Beckett: The Critical Heritage*, edited by Lawrence Graver and Raymond Federman, collects original responses to the play, as does Ruby Cohn's *Casebook on* Waiting for Godot, which dates from 1967. Another Cohn *Casebook*, printed in the United Kingdom in 1987, now includes Hersh Zeifman's study of variations in the published texts for the English-language *Godot*. Two other books by Ruby Cohn help to address additional reference questions: *Disjecta*, a Beckett miscellany that sheds considerable light on *Godot*, and the 1987 *From* Desire *to* Godot: *Pocket Theater of Postwar Paris*, which provides an accurate history of the play's original production, dispelling several myths along the way. Alan Schneider's autobiography, *Entrances: An American Director's Journey*, brings the history of the play into a specifically American context, as does John Lahr's partisan biography of his famous father, *Notes on a Cowardly Lion*. (For the French experience, see Odette Aslan, *Roger Blin and Twentieth-Century Playwrights*.) *Beckett on File*, compiled by Virginia Cooke, can be counted on for spot-checking dates of productions, though the information can be found elsewhere. *A Student's Guide to the Plays of Samuel Beckett*, edited by Beryl S. Fletcher et al. (2nd ed.), is much more comprehensive in its treatment of the play. Colin Duckworth's edition of *En attendant Godot* contains essential prefatory information in English for the reader of the French text.

Dougald McMillan and Martha Fehsenfeld's influential *Beckett in the Theatre* contains revealing information about various stagings of *Godot* as well as the author's revisions of the text based on his own direction of the play at the Schiller Theater in West Berlin (1975). Two additional reference works are currently under way: a "production notebook" from Beckett's staging of *Waiting for Godot*, compiled by James Knowlson, and a selection of Samuel Beckett's letters, edited by Martha D. Fehsenfeld and Lois M. Overbeck. Any student of the play will also profit from the various catalogs available at the central repositories of manuscripts and other primary source material: the Beckett Archive at the University of Reading, England; the Humanities Research Center at the University of Texas, Austin; and the Library of Washington University in St. Louis.

Background Studies

Several teachers of the play have found that a general introduction to modernist and postmodernist theories goes a long way in setting Beckett in a proper historical perspective. *The Modern Tradition: Backgrounds of Modern Literature*, edited by Richard Ellmann and Charles Feidelson, Jr., and *Modernism 1890–1930*, edited by Malcolm Bradbury and James McFarlane, have been recommended by respondents to our survey, as have the following books: William Barrett, *Irrational Man* and *Time of Need*; Christopher Butler, *After the Wake*; Karl Jaspers, *Man in the Modern Age*; Miguel de Unamuno, *The Tragic Sense of Life*; Irving Howe, *The Idea of the Modern*; Michael Levenson, *A Genealogy of Modernism*; John Ciardi, *How Does a Poem Mean?*; Stanley Cavell, *Must We Mean What We Say?*; and Roger Shattuck, *The Innocent Eye*. Camus's *Myth of Sisyphus* provides a stunning parallel to the zeitgeist surrounding *Waiting for Godot*, as does a general familiarity with the work of Jean-Paul Sartre and Maurice Merleau-Ponty (see in particular Merleau-Ponty's *Phenomenology of Perception*).

Of more direct bearing on Beckett's play are a number of biographical and related sources. Deirdre Bair's controversial biography contains several inaccuracies, but it can be useful, especially on the playwright's correspondence with Thomas McGreevy. James Knowlson's authorized biography of Beckett is slated for publication by Simon and Schuster in 1994. The playwright's Irish background has been scrupulously traced, this time pictorially, by Eoin O'Brien in *The Beckett Country*. The Irish context of Beckett's work as a whole has been covered by Katharine Worth in *The Irish Drama of Europe: From Yeats to Beckett*. Richard Ellmann pinpoints the Joyce-Beckett connection in his biography *James Joyce*, and Stuart Gilbert includes part of their correspondence in *The Letters of James Joyce*. Lawrence E. Harvey, in *Samuel Beckett: Poet and Critic*, quotes from several revealing letters that reflect crucial aesthetic presuppositions. For other biographical notes, see Enoch Brater's *Why Beckett*; Peggy Guggenheim's anecdotal *Out of This Century*; Vivian Mercier's *Beckett/Beckett*; John Calder's *Beckett at Sixty* and *As No Other Dare Fail*; Tom F. Driver's "Beckett by the Madeleine"; and Israel Shenker's "Moody Man of Letters."

Though no book on *Godot*'s place in the modern theater has proved as enduring as Martin Esslin's *Theatre of the Absurd*, several other studies situate the play in appropriate dramatic contexts: Andrew Kennedy, *Six Dramatists in Search of a Language*; David Bradby, *Modern French Drama 1940–1980*; David I. Grossvogel, *Four Playwrights and a Postscript: Brecht, Ionesco, Beckett, and Genet*; Enoch Brater and Ruby Cohn (eds.), *Around the Absurd: Essays on Modern and Postmodern Drama*; Jacques Guicharnaud, *Modern French Theatre: From Giraudoux to Beckett*; Leonard Pronko, *Avant-Garde: The Experimental Theater in France*; Richard Gilman, *The Making of Modern Drama*; and several essays in *Beckett at 80/Beckett in Context*, edited by Enoch Brater. For a general discussion of *Godot*'s place in relation to Beckett's work as a whole, see Hugh Kenner, *A Reader's Guide* to *Samuel Beckett*; Michael Robinson, *The Long Sonata of the Dead*; John Fletcher, *Samuel Beckett's Art*; Linda Ben-Zvi, *Samuel Beckett*; Enoch Brater's richly illustrated *Why Beckett*, which contains 122 photographs; and Andrew Kennedy's *Samuel Beckett*. Martin Esslin's *Samuel Beckett: A Collection of Critical Essays* contains several seminal studies of *Godot* as well as two much-quoted pieces: the playwright's "Three Dialogues" with the art critic Georges Duthuit and Alain Robbe-Grillet's "Samuel Beckett; Or, 'Presence' in the Theatre." Lawrence Graver's *Samuel Beckett*: Waiting for Godot and Thomas Cousineau's Waiting for Godot: *Form in Movement* are helpful to students encountering the play for the first time.

Lionel Abel's *Metatheatre*, Peter Brook's *Empty Space*, Herbert Blau's *Impossible Theater*, Patrice Pavis's *Languages of the Stage*, and Anne Ubersfeld's *Lire le théâtre* shed light, however indirectly, on Beckett's play in the larger context of drama in performance. Other more general studies of the formal elements of drama that have proved useful in teaching Beckett's play include Keir Elam, *The Semiotics of Theatre and Drama*; Bernard Beckerman, *Dynamics of Drama: Theory and Method of Analysis*; Bert O. States, *Irony and Drama: A Poetics*; Albert Bermel, *Contradictory Characters*; John Russell Brown, *Theatre Language*; Thomas R. Whitaker, *Fields of Play in Modern Drama*; Normand Berlin, *The Secret Cause: A Discussion of Tragedy*; June Schlueter, *Metafictional Characters in Modern Drama*; Leslie Kane, *The Language of Silence: On the Unspoken and the Unspeakable in Modern Drama*; Richard Hornby, *Script into Performance: A Structuralist View of Play Performance*; and Michael Goldman, *The Actor's Freedom: Toward a Theory of Drama*. Jan Kott's *Shakespeare Our Contemporary* discusses *King Lear* with specific reference to *Endgame* and to Beckett in general. For an anthropological perspective on teaching the play, see Victor Turner, *From Ritual to Theatre: The Human Seriousness of Play*; more direct applications to Beckett can be found in Katherine H. Burkman, *Myth and Ritual in the Plays of Samuel Beckett*, and Mary A. Doll, *Beckett and Myth: An Archetypal Approach*. The playwright has also been discussed in the wider context of modern art in Marjorie Perloff's *Poetics of Indeterminacy: Rimbaud to Cage* and Daniel Albright's *Representation and the Imagination: Beckett, Kafka, Nabokov, and Schoenberg*. For additional studies of Beckett in the context of other modern artists, see in particular Dougald McMillan, *Transition: The History of a Literary Era, 1927–38*, and Matti Megged, *Dialogue in the Void: Beckett and Giacometti*.

Critical Studies

In general, books dealing with *Waiting for Godot* focus on the thematic and philosophical or on the play as a play, as a practical work for the theater. In the first category there exists a rich and varied selection of sophisticated material, beginning with Hugh Kenner's "Cartesian Centaur" (*Critical Study* 117–32). Because critics have found, in addition to Descartes, echoes of Kant, Nietzsche, Heidegger, Schopenhauer, Mauthner, and Wittgenstein (and, more recently, Lacan, Derrida, Barthes, Foucault, and Bakhtin), Kenner's initial instinct has been followed by a spate of incisive studies: David Hesla, *The Shape of Chaos*; Steven Rosen, *Samuel Beckett and the Pessimistic Tradition*; Lance St. John Butler, *Samuel Beckett and the Meaning of Being*; L. A. C. Dobrez, *The Existential and Its Exits* (on Beckett, Ionesco, Genet, and Pinter); John Peter, *Vladimir's Carrot: Modern Drama and the Modern Imagination*; and Sylvie Debevec Henning, *Beckett's Critical Complicity: Carnival, Contestation, and Tradition*. Steven Connor's *Samuel Beckett: Repetition, Theory and Text* provides an extremely useful application of poststructuralist perspectives that illuminates the playwright's work. Bert O. States in *The Shape of Paradox: An Essay on* Waiting for Godot is, nevertheless, one of the few critics who has bridged the crucial gap between the purely philosophical and its manifestation in dramatic form. Readers might also consult his *Great Reckonings in Little Rooms: On the Phenomenology of Theater*. Several feminist essays on Beckett are included in Linda Ben-Zvi's collection entitled *Women in Beckett: Performance and Critical Perspectives*.

Godot as a work for the stage has been the subject of an equally fruitful series of books, starting with Ruby Cohn's *Samuel Beckett: The Comic Gamut*. Two subsequent studies by the same author have paid closer attention to the specific theatrical qualities of the play and the later Beckett work it nourished: *Back to Beckett* and, in particular, *Just Play: Beckett's Theater*. Additional commentary on *Godot* can be found in John Fletcher and John Spurling, *Beckett: A Study of His Plays*; Frederick Busi, *The Transformations of Godot*; Robert Brustein, *The Theatre of Revolt*; and Alec Reid, *All I Can Manage, More Than I Could: An Approach to the Plays of Samuel Beckett*. Sidney Homan's *Beckett's Theaters: Interpretations for Performance* discusses the play's potential for enactment, and Kristin Morrison's *Canters and Chronicles: The Use of Narrative in the Plays of Samuel Beckett and Harold Pinter* evokes the heroic need for storytelling. Other studies that focus on the theatricality of *Godot* include James Knowlson, *Light and Darkness in the Theatre of Samuel Beckett*; Colin Duckworth, *Angels of Darkness: Dramatic Effect in Samuel Beckett with Special Reference to Eugène Ionesco*; Peter Gidal, *Understanding Beckett: A Study of Monologue and Gesture in the Works of Samuel Beckett*; Charles R. Lyons, *Samuel Beckett*; and Jonathan Kalb, *Beckett in Performance*. Additional material in this connection can be found in the following anthologies: *Beckett the Shape Changer*, edited by Katharine Worth; *Samuel Beckett: A Collection of Criticism*, edited by Ruby Cohn; *Beckett Translating/Translating Beckett*, edited by Alan W. Friedman, Charles Rossman, and Dina Sherzer; and *Samuel Beckett: Humanistic Perspectives*, edited by Morris Beja, S. E. Gontarski, and Pierre Astier. In *On Beckett: Essays and Criticism*, Gontarski reprints some of the more influential studies in the field.

In tracing Beckett's dramatic development from *Godot* to his later plays, critics have become sensitive to the need for periodization in his work. Such an assumption lies behind *Frescoes of the Skull: The Later Prose and Drama of Samuel Beckett* by James Knowlson and John Pilling. Enoch Brater's *Beyond Minimalism: Beckett's Late Style in the Theater* deals briefly with *Godot* to demonstrate how the playwright's work of the 1970s and 1980s builds on his earlier achievement. Jane Alison Hale's *Broken Window* and Rosemary Pountney's *Theatre of Shadows: Samuel Beckett's Drama 1956– 76* are similarly analytical in outlining the playwright's maturing sense of dramatic perspective.

Much good work on Beckett has a firm sense of *Waiting for Godot*, even when attention falls on his other works. The playwright's compositional technique has, for example, been carefully noted by S. E. Gontarski in *The Intent of Undoing in Samuel Beckett's Dramatic Texts*. Several studies of Beckett's fiction offer us a telling guide to the interconnectedness of his imaginative world: Edith Kern, *Existential Thought and Fictional Technique: Kierkegaard, Sartre, Beckett*; H. Porter Abbott, *The Fiction of Samuel Beckett: Form and Effect*; J. E. Dearlove, *Accommodating the Chaos: Samuel Beckett's Nonrelational Art*; Rubin Rabinovitz, *The Development of Samuel Beckett's Fiction*; Susan D. Brienza, *Samuel Beckett's New Worlds: Style in Metafiction*; Nicholas Zurbrugg, *Beckett and Proust*; Enoch Brater, *The Drama in the Text: Beckett's Late Fiction*; and two early studies, Raymond Federman's *Journey to Chaos* and John Fletcher's *The Novels of Samuel Beckett*. In *The Implied Reader: Patterns of Communication in Prose Fiction from Bunyan to Beckett*, Wolfgang Iser pursues what the playwright once called this "stiff interexclusiveness" in a much wider framework. Beckett's scripts for the mechanical media provide other food for thought. Two particularly prominent books are Martin Esslin's *Mediations: Essays on Brecht, Beckett, and the Media* and Clas Zilliacus's *Beckett and Broadcasting*.

Two miscellaneous items published in French deserve citation, however brief: *Cahiers de l'Herne: Samuel Beckett*, edited by Tom Bishop and Raymond Federman, and the *Revue d'esthétique: Samuel Beckett*, edited by Pierre Chabert and published on the playwright's eightieth birthday in 1986. And one must mention, at the very least, the names of some key critics working in French and other languages, among them Alfred Simon, Olga Bernal, Ludovic Janvier, Jean-Jacques Mayoux, Gabriel d'Aubarède, Aldo Tagliaferri, Brian T. Fitch, Antoni Libera, and Yasunari Takahashi.

Let the browser beware.

Audiovisual Library

"I don't want any film of *Godot*," Beckett wrote to the actor Jack MacGowran on 13 December 1967. "As it stands it is simply not cinema material. And adaptation would destroy it. Please forgive me . . . and don't think of me as a purist bastard" (Young 120). The playwright had, however, already allowed Alan Schneider to bring the work to television in 1961 in a version based on the director's original Miami production. The 16mm black-and-white film (102 min.) features Zero Mostel and Burgess Meredith. Several instructors show the film to demonstrate the play's life in performance. A supplement to the screening, particularly helpful to beginning college students, is Grove Press's *Discussion Guide to the Play* Waiting for Godot. The play is also available on record (110 min.), on which Bert Lahr and E. G. Marshall re-create their original Broadway roles. Mike Nichols's much publicized staging of the play in New York at Lincoln Center in 1988, starring Robin Williams as Gogo, Steve Martin as Didi, F. Murray Abraham as Pozzo, and a memorable Bill Irwin as Lucky, has been scheduled for video presentation.

Waiting for Godot has had an unusual relation with the San Quentin penitentiary in California. In 1957, the San Francisco Actor's Workshop staged Herbert Blau's production there before an audience of fourteen hundred male convicts. *Godot* was chosen largely because there were no women in the cast. The last time a play had been seen at San Quentin was in 1913, when Sarah Bernhardt performed (Esslin, *Theatre* 1). In Blau's audience was an impressionable young prisoner named Rick Cluchey, who later founded the San Quentin Drama Workshop (he was in prison for eleven years before winning a pardon). Working with the approval of the playwright, Cluchey's company has mounted a number of Beckett plays, including *Endgame* and *Krapp's Last Tape*. His San Quentin Players' production of *Waiting for Godot* is based on Beckett's specifications for the 1975 version as the playwright directed it for the Schiller Theater in Berlin. Under the auspices of the Beckett Directs Beckett program, funded by NEH, this *Godot* is available on video from the Visual Press of the University of Maryland. This English-language *Godot* features Cluchey in the role of Pozzo, with Bud Thorpe as Vladimir, Lawrence Held as Estragon, and Alan Mandell as Lucky. Beckett Directs Beckett (the title an obvious misnomer) has also produced a French version of the play on film. Directed by Walter Asmus and also based on Beckett's Berlin mise-en-scène, the lively French cast includes Rufus as Didi, Jean-François Balmer as Gogo, Jean-Pierre Jorris as Pozzo, and Roman Polanski as Lucky.

Global Village of New York, well known for its documentary filmmaking and also funded by NEH, completed *"Waiting for Godot* in San Quentin" as part of its work on the Beckett Project. Jan Jonson, the Swedish actor, directed a prison inmate cast in a production of the play in Kumla, Sweden, in 1985. Three years later he turned to *Godot* again, this time with an inmate cast at San Quentin. Designed for broadcast on PBS, John Reilly's highly praised documentary *"Waiting for Godot* at San Quentin" is also available on video.

Beginning to End (16mm, 58 min.), an anthology of works adapted and performed by Jack MacGowran, has been successful in introducing students to the Beckett world. Several instructors recommend *Film*, Beckett's "comic and unreal" screenplay for Evergreen Films (Grove Press), starring Buster Keaton (16mm, black-and-white, 22 min.). *Silence to Silence*, an 80-minute documentary produced and directed by Sean O Mórdha for Radio Telefis Eireann, offers students a concise overview of Beckett's life and work. The Beckett Project has also produced *Waiting for Beckett*, a cultural documentary including excerpts from his letters, archival footage of early productions, and interviews with friends, associates, and scholars.

Though not directly applicable to *Godot*, the film of *Rockaby* by D. A. Pennebaker and Chris Hegedus, produced by Daniel Labeille for the State University of New York, Programs in the Arts, offers students a view of rehearsals, discussions, and a screening of the play itself (with Billie Whitelaw as directed by Alan Schneider). The Beckett Festival of Radio Plays, distributed by Pacifica Tape Library, has produced new versions of *All That Fall, Embers, Words and Music, Cascando*, and *Rough for Radio 2*. Cassettes are available from Voices International in New York and may be used to introduce a class to the sound of Beckett's language. The Spoken Arts recording of *Krapp's Last Tape*, starring the Canadian actor Donald Davis, has been similarly effective. A television version of the same play, featuring Jack MacGowran, was directed by Alan Schneider for WNET in 1970.

For the instructor willing to travel, still other audiovisual materials are available for class preparation. The Performing Arts Research Center of the New York Public Library has a number of interesting items in its Theater on Film and Tape Collection. For a recent listing, see *The Beckett Circle/ Le Cercle de Beckett* 7.2 (Spring 1986). The audiovisual archive of the Bobst Library, New York University, has a complete holding of Beckett's television plays for the BBC and Süddeutscher Rundfunk, Stuttgart. The BBC in London houses tapes of Beckett's work specifically designed for radio as well as recordings of many readings of his prose pieces. For audiovisual material available in France, England, Ireland, Germany, and Australia, instructors should consult the listing in *Revue d'esthétique: Samuel Beckett*, edited by Pierre Chabert, pages 457–59.

Part Two

APPROACHES

INTRODUCTION

In the more than thirty-five years since its Paris premiere, *Waiting for Godot* has become a staple of both world theater and the academic curriculum. Yet the play offers as much of a challenge in the classroom today as it did to its early audiences: in Paris, at the Coconut Grove in Miami, and in California, at the San Quentin prison. The diversity of responses to those first productions suggests the plurality of readings implicit in this deceptively simple work that keeps two characters waiting for a third who never appears. Probably the most resonant play in the modern canon, *Waiting for Godot* has become the centerpiece of a range of college and university courses. Whatever the context and approach, the play continues to yield readings that richly contribute to the study of both drama and culture. It is—as Vladimir describes himself and Estragon—"inexhaustible."

In this volume, we suggest some of the possibilities for entering into a dialogue with students about Beckett's play. As seasoned teachers of the play ourselves—who still find teaching it a daunting responsibility—we were delighted to find in each of our contributors a sense of discovery that not only informs their teaching of *Godot* but energizes their writing about it. While we do not contest Vladimir's judgment, we do believe that the essays in this volume contribute significantly to an understanding of the play and offer provocative pedagogical approaches to making it accessible. As Toby Silverman Zinman points out in her essay, there is a risk involved in sharing *Godot* with students—and, we would add, with colleagues—but it is a risk that brings us closer to Beckett, an artist who says a writer, in the act of writing, "fails . . . as no other dare fail."

Ruby Cohn is first to speak in this part, situating *Godot* in the Beckett canon. The rest of the essays are arranged under five headings, designed to organize pedagogical connections. William Hutchings, Michael J. Collins, and Linda Ben-Zvi provide introductory essays: Hutchings speaks of how *Godot* confounds conventional expectations, insisting on the uncertainty of meaning; Collins explores what the play does rather than what it means; and Ben-Zvi establishes associations with the play that college-age students might make—associations she calls "life materialized."

Five essays compose the "Influences and Backgrounds" section. Martin Esslin, whose *Theatre of the Absurd* has proved seminal in teaching *Godot*, opens with his current reflections on Beckett and absurdity. Lance St. John Butler argues for the usefulness of insisting that *Godot* is not a philosophical play. Kristin Morrison examines the Christian allusions in the play. Fred Miller Robinson explores its connections with the music hall, and Claudia Clausius looks at its relation to Charlie Chaplin and the comic film gag.

Under "Course Contexts," we have included four essays that address the place of *Godot* in classroom situations. Mary Scott Simpson discusses her teaching of the play in a course on tragedy, from the Greeks through Peter Shaffer's *Equus*. Katherine H. Burkman presents *Godot* as a touchstone for a course on modern and contemporary drama. Dina Sherzer discusses *Godot* in a French drama course. And Charles Lyons offers his approach to teaching *Godot* in an advanced undergraduate course on Beckett.

The experienced teacher of *Godot* may profit most from the section "Critical Approaches," which suggests methods linked to contemporary theory. Kevin J. H. Dettmar teaches *Godot* in a course on critical theory, asking students to interpret the play from different critical perspectives. Stephen Barker's interest is in lecture and *lecture*, recitation and reading in *Godot*. J. Terence McQueeny provides a comparison of the French and English texts, noting patterns suggested by the many changes in Beckett's self-translation. Una Chaudhuri offers a semiotic approach to how meaning is produced in *Godot*, looking particularly at the tree as part of the play's signifying system.

The volume ends with a group of performance-oriented essays. Stanton B. Garner, Jr., identifies the pedagogical opportunities of teaching a play that is both dependent on the stage and antagonistic to dramatic conventions. Toby Silverman Zinman shares set- and poster-design projects that help students visualize the play and discover meanings. Sidney Homan speaks about directing the play in a Florida prison, then transferring his prison experience to the classroom. And S. E. Gontarski describes the director's task of sustaining as many of the play's dialectical tensions as possible.

Collectively, these essays invite teachers and students of *Waiting for*

Godot into an experience that is both familiar and strange. The diversity of approaches and the variety of their yield can only urge us "on."

NOTE ABOUT EDITIONS

Unless otherwise indicated, all page references to the play are from the 1954 Grove Press edition (English) or the 1952 Editions de Minuit edition (French).

PROLOGUE

Beckett and His *Godot*

Ruby Cohn

On 9 October 1948, a forty-two-year-old Irishman opened a fresh graph-paper notebook on the only table in his two-room sixth-story Paris apartment. With his fine-pointed fountain pen, Samuel Beckett began a play in French: "Route à la campagne, avec arbre."—horizontal and vertical coordinates translated from graph to words. During four months of a damp, cold Paris winter, Beckett kept scribbling in that notebook, until the final word *Rideau* of the tragicomedy that he later translated as *Waiting for Godot*. Far from feeling triumphant at the conclusion, Beckett later wrote to his American director, Alan Schneider, that he had breathed deeply of failure's vivifying air for all of his writing life.

That life began on Good Friday, 13 April 1906, in Dublin. Beckett grew into a rare combination of brilliant student and brilliant athlete. At Trinity College, he was groomed for an academic career, but he also composed arcane fiction and poetry; he enjoyed the Abbey Theatre, silent film comedies, and local pubs. In October 1928, two decades before beginning *Godot*, Beckett went to Paris on a two-year exchange fellowship at the prestigious Ecole Normale Supérieure; he soon strayed from academe to Left Bank bohemia. Gradually, his poems, stories, and criticism saw the light of publication, but Beckett nevertheless returned to Trinity to take up the pedagogical burden. If only for a short time.

Barely collecting his master's degree, Beckett sped to the Continent and, from a safe distance, resigned his Trinity post. (He returned to his alma mater in 1959 to receive an honorary degree.) In the 1930s Beckett vaguely realized that he wanted not so much to be a writer as to write; he vaguely realized that his literary fumbling would not support even his minimal needs for food and lodging. For a miserable year, he reviewed books in London. Frustrated though he was by both the city and the activity, Beckett was nevertheless spurred by them to write his first novel, *Murphy*.

Even before the 1938 publication of that novel (after forty-two rejections), Beckett returned to Paris to live. Although he usually mingled with painters rather than writers, he renewed his friendship with James Joyce. And that dean of expatriate Irish writers was horrified when a stranger stabbed Beckett, narrowly missing his heart. Life proved an appalling imitation of art: Beckett's Murphy was killed in one accident, and Beckett himself was almost killed in another. While in the hospital, however, Beckett was visited by the pianist Suzanne Dumesnil, whom he later married.

Beckett risked death more deliberately after the outbreak of World War II. When the Germans invaded Poland, Beckett was visiting his mother in Dublin. He hurried back to Paris. There, persuaded by his friend Alfred Péron (who did not survive the war), Beckett joined the French Resistance, even though he was an Irish national. When Péron was captured by the Gestapo, Beckett fled from Paris. With other refugees, Beckett spent the remainder of the war in the "unoccupied" Vaucluse, working as an agricultural laborer during the day, working at his novel *Watt* at night—always in danger. Thirty of the eighty members of his Resistance group survived the war.

Repatriated to Ireland after V-E Day, Beckett could reenter France only by joining the Irish Red Cross in war-ravaged Normandy. After six months of relief activity among the wounded and diseased, he returned to his Paris apartment—there to begin the most creative period of his life. Between 1945 and 1950 he wrote four long stories, four novels, and two plays—all in French. One play, "Eleuthéria," was soon withdrawn from circulation, and the other, *En attendant Godot*, was soon acclaimed throughout the world.

After his mother died in 1950 and his brother in 1954, Beckett rarely visited Ireland. Generous with his time and his funds, he lived simply in Paris, refusing interviews and avoiding critical commentary. Although he was never again to experience the exhilaration of those five fluid years at midcentury, Beckett continued painstakingly (and sometimes painfully) to chisel new forms in fiction and drama. He wrote in English and French, then translated each work. Not only did he write and translate but, in the mid-1960s, he began directing his plays—in German, French, and English. During 1986, the year of Beckett's eightieth birthday, celebrations were held in several cities on several continents—none of which he attended.

It may seem paradoxical to celebrate an oeuvre that articulates an anatomy of suffering, but the Nobel award committee discerned that "his writing, which—in new forms for the novel and drama—in the destitution of modern man acquires its elevation."

Although Beckett's fame rests largely on his drama, he considered his fiction a lesser failure. It begins with mannered short stories and an aborted novel ("Dream of Fair to Middling Women") from which he salvaged the protagonist, Belacqua Shuah, for a series of short stories, subsequently published as *More Pricks Than Kicks* (1934). After propelling this indolent Dantean hero through discontinuities, Beckett in 1936 composed his most traditional novel, *Murphy*. Inspired by a Mr. Endon, the eponymous hero renounces the outside world, including the fair Celia. He is oblivious of the Irish posse who hunt him down, only to discover his charred corpse. *Murphy* is at once Beckett's first complete English novel and his first French novel, since he translated it before his flight from Paris during World War II.

While waiting in the Vaucluse for the war to end, Beckett wrote *Watt*, whose hero seeks to use his senses ("his most noble faculties") and his mind ("whatever that may be") to penetrate Mr. Knott's establishment. Watt's quest is narrated by Sam, surname unknown; Sam and Watt, narrator and narrated, are the first of what Beckett would later designate as a "pseudocouple." Didi and Gogo of *Waiting for Godot* are their descendants.

Watt, a would-be Cartesian, thinks in order to try to be, but his nameless successor in Beckett's fiction, adopting the language of Descartes, deliberately does not think in order to be. This character lets the stream of sentences carry him along—up to "The End," which gives Beckett's first French story its name. Four such stories by physically feeble but linguistically febrile tellers are interrupted by the novel *Mercier et Camier*, whose titular pseudocouple prefigure the paired friends of *Godot*. And not only the couple, but also the landscape, the soulscape, and a dialogue of extensible significance.

In 1946 Beckett embarked on what is often considered his major work. Published individually in French, *Molloy* (1947), *Malone meurt* (1948), and *L'innommable* (1949) are a trilogy of fictions in their progressive concentration and obsessive repetition. In the first part of *Molloy* a grotesque old cripple, hat laced to his buttonhole, has somehow arrived in his mother's room, where he writes a choppy tale of his choppy voyage toward his mother. In the second part, Jacques Moran, a respectable but fatuous father who has just returned from his search for Molloy, writes a report for his employer, Youdi. In *Malone meurt*, a paralyzed hero, confined to his bed, tries to order his dying hours by recording an inventory of his possessions and his symptoms while composing stories. The titular speaker-protagonist of *L'innommable* probes behind fictional and linguistic formulae in quest of himself.

After the trilogy, Beckett gathered thirteen lyrics of fiction into *Texts for Nothing*. Almost a decade later, he wrote *Comment c'est*, which may be described as a fragmented novel or a prose epic poem about singular characters who meet and part, naked in a primeval slime. The grammatical first person dissolves into unpunctuated phrases in irregular verses, permuted and repeated into a melody made meaning.

Like the three French novels completed by midcentury, Beckett's later three (shorter) novels may also be viewed as a trilogy. *Company* (1979) dramatizes the wavering voice; *Mal vu mal dit* (1980) tries to focus on the hovering image; *Worstward Ho* (1984) is Beckett's boldest foray into uncharted prose, at once summoning and shrinking from human trace. In an incantation of contradictions, qualifications, and monosyllables, scene precipitates to image, being to saying, while "no" reverses to a polyvalent "on." And that monosyllable *on* may serve as the watchword of Beckett's own quest "wordward ho."

In the theater, however, Beckett lets the eye reign over the ear. Moreover, his formal invention has enriched the several media of drama—stage, radio, film, and television. With his own love of numbers in mind, we may tally his one actorless play, one aborted scene, one film, two mime plays, six radio plays, five television scripts, and sixteen plays for speaking actors in the theater. Only the fragmentary scene *Human Wishes* and the repressed play "Eleuthéria" precede *Waiting for Godot*.

The master-servant couple of *Godot* are moved to stage center in *Fin de partie* (1957), but they are also father and son, artist and audience. With parents in ashbins, they form a nuclear family. More relentless than *Godot*, stripped down to one ambulatory character, *Fin de partie* rests more gravely on an economy of purposeless play. Only the racecourse background suggests play in the radio drama *All That Fall*, where Beckett lapses into the lyricism of his native language. Radio and mime nurtured Beckett's first English stage play, *Krapp's Last Tape* (1958). As on radio, so on tape a voice emerges from the dark; but the lone actor can be as still or as lavish as a mime.

Beckett's subsequent drama dissolves the familiar world into the context of an eternal void. *Happy Days* (1961) shows Winnie sinking into her grave, and yet she prattles on under a blazing sun. *Play* (1968) views a lovers' triangle from the perspective of eternity, but it also introduces "theater-eality," the technique of almost merging stage fact and fiction. In *Play* the inquisitorial light is a theater spotlight, which ignites speech as it shifts among the three urns; but fictionally it is a mysterious force that elicits confession.

Beckett's plays of the 1970s dazzle the senses with this device. Thus, a light beam and the buzzing within the discourse of Mouth in *Not I* (1972) are also a theater spotlight and the words of that discourse. In *That Time*

(1974), we see the head of a white-haired old man, and we hear *about* a white-haired old man in two of the three voice strands that finally dissolve "that time" into no time. The very title *Footfalls* (1975) describes what we hear and hear about in the theater. *A Piece of Monologue* (1977) is a monologue about a man standing still, a lamp of the same height, and the corner of a bed, which is more or less what we see on stage. *Rockaby* (1980) imposes the titular rocking action on the eyes of the audience, while we hear about a woman who retraces the way of her mother from an external world into a cradling rocker that is also a coffin. *Ohio Impromptu* (1981) confronts us with two identical white-haired, black-coated men, a Listener and a Reader who reads aloud about a listener and a reader. Yet "theatereality" is never an exact equation of theater and reality.

By contrast with these late subtle stage images, the prolixity of *Waiting for Godot* has fertilized other arts. That tragicomedy has inspired not only the painter Avigdor Arikha and the sculptor Alberto Giacometti but even cartoonists from Charles Addams to Garry Trudeau. Beckett's old friend Kay Boyle, in the poem "For Samuel Beckett," writes, "Consider the carrots and turnips Vladimir and Estragon have to offer." Dramatists in particular have been considering that offering. From *The Road* by Wole Soyinka (1965) to Jim Cartwright's *Road* (1986), the *Godot* setting is emblematic of human life. In the coda of Tom Stoppard's *Jumpers*, his sinister academic jubilates, "Wham, bam, thank you Sam!" in homage to Sam Beckett (89), from whom Stoppard borrowed phrase and form for his *Rosencrantz and Guildenstern Are Dead*. Harold Pinter is grateful to Beckett for freeing the stage for his own enigmatic couples, like Goldberg and McCann in *The Birthday Party*, or Hirst and Spooner in *No Man's Land*. David Storey's *Home* is peopled, like *Godot*, with two couples and a loner. Tennessee Williams's *Out-Cry* is set in an entropic theater in an unnamed country, which recalls the stage of *Godot*, bared for performance. Sam Shepard cites *Godot* as the first play he remembers reading, and his *Cowboys Number Two* is imbued with similar playfulness. Plays as tonally different as Edward Albee's *Zoo Story* and David Mamet's *Duck Variations* echo the volleys of Didi and Gogo.

Beckett himself has quarried his most famous work—"That mine." After *Godot*, precise word and gesture (sometimes in contradiction) in an unlocalized but incisive setting become Beckett's theatrical hallmark. In almost all Beckett's post-*Godot* dramas, twinned contrasts determine the dramatic structure. In *Godot* Didi prevents Gogo from recounting his dreams, but later Beckett characters are compulsive storytellers—Hamm, Krapp, Henry, Winnie—each in his or her own rhythm. When they are mobile, post-*Godot* characters walk as distinctively as Didi and Gogo. Although Pozzo is the only *Godot* name found in a later Beckett work—in "Text 5" of *Stories and*

Texts for Nothing—the play's dialogue supplies titles for later works, such as *Happy Days, Enough.*

Beckett's last masterpiece of fiction, *Worstward Ho*, mines *Godot* most deeply, even to "Profounds of mind." The four adults of the tragicomedy cheer themselves on with the word *On. Worstward Ho* opens and closes on *On*, although "there's no lack of void" in either setting. Residual pipe, boots, and hat (though not a bowler) figure in the later work. Repetitions of "true" and "enough" spatter both *Godot* and *Worstward Ho.*

Beckett translates *charnier* of the original French *Godot* as "charnel-house," after the bone and graveyard imagery has conveyed the climate and even the susurrus of a moribund cultural tradition. Lucky, whose monologue encapsulates that tradition, repeats the word *skull* eight times, four in merciless sequence. In *Worstward Ho*, the head that holds and is held in the fiction is stripped down to a skull, after bones and mind have been cited as loci of pain. Toward the end of Lucky's speech, "skull"s and "stone"s thud pell-mell, but by the end of *Worstward Ho* the stones are tempered to stooping humanized gravestones, and the skull with its single pinhole for three pins barely sustains the waning words: "What left of skull not go. Into it still the hole. Into what left of soft."

In act 2 of *Godot* Estragon observes, "Everything oozes," and a few minutes later he explodes, "All my lousy life I've crawled about in the mud!" (correcting the original French *sables*). By the time of *Worstward Ho*, the ooze—repeated some dozen times—is that of plaintive words. Estragon intuits his world as a primeval slime from which he has never evolved: "Look at this muckheap! I've never stirred from it!" By the time of *Worstward Ho*, all stirring fuses into the sense and senses of the soft within the skull. In *Godot* the opening announcement breaks silence: "Nothing to be done"— that is, to be given a time, place, or form through a dramatic action. In *Worstward Ho*, "Nothing ever unseen. Of the nothing to be seen," because seeing is a concentrated, iterative, re-visionary process on the part of the seer who is Samuel Beckett.

INTRODUCING *GODOT*

Waiting for Godot and the Principle of Uncertainty
William Hutchings

In the classroom, no less than in the theater, *Waiting for Godot* deliberately confounds the conventional expectations of its audience. Long conditioned to expect a plot wherein traditional conflict leads to a resolution with few ambiguities, students and theatergoers who initially approach Beckett's work unawares are typically frustrated by its plotlessness and the obliquity of its themes. In expressing their initial response to the play, students often sound like the Cookers (or Showers) in Beckett's *Happy Days*: "What's the idea? . . . What does it mean? . . . What's it meant to mean?—and so on—lot more stuff like that—usual drivel" (42–43). Such perplexity provides an effective opening for classroom discussion, echoing as it does the characters in *Godot* who remark that "[n]othing happens, nobody comes, nobody goes, it's awful!" (27b) and complain angrily that "[n]othing is certain" (10b). These comments not only illustrate the work's radical departure from traditional literary forms but also introduce such concepts as the theater of the absurd and the minimalist aesthetic underlying Beckett's removal of a conventional plot.

Before introducing these ideas, however, teachers should define what the play is not—to dispel the expectations that traditional, familiar types of explication beget. *Waiting for Godot* is not a traditional allegory; its allusions and apparent symbols—like Kafka's—do not yield a single coherent explicable meaning, though their resonance has evoked intriguing interpretations. Like Eliot's "fragments shored against my ruins" (*Waste Land* 50), Beckett's allusions, including the play's many overt Christian references (e.g., the crucified thieves, the sheep and goats), are shards of a culture, used in the play for their suggestiveness but *without exact allegorical equation*. Among readers and audience members, as among the characters whom Beckett described as "non-knowers and non-can-ers" (Shenker 148), a disconcerting uncertainty about the meaning of the play is a crucial part of the experience of *Waiting for Godot* and any discussion of it.

Apart from the fact of the characters' waiting and the occurrence of certain events during that time (the duration of which is itself uncertain), the only certainty is that any certainty about their plight is wrong. Accordingly, any interpretation that purports to know who Godot is (or is not), whether he exists, whether he will ever come, whether he has ever come, or even whether he may have come without being recognized (or possibly in disguise) is, if not demonstrably wrong, at least not demonstrably right. This principle of literary uncertainty, which *Waiting for Godot* brought to the theater for the first time, is no less revolutionary than its counterpart in physics, discovered by Werner Heisenberg in 1927: The accuracy of a measurement (i.e., an assessment of the play) is given by the uncertainty in the result (i.e., in the interpretation), and the product of the combined uncertainties of simultaneous measurements of (critical) positions and momentum accounts for the seemingly endless variety of interpretations (those of Beckett's play are second in volume and diversity only to those of Shakespeare's *Hamlet*).

In reviewing the first London production of Beckett's play in 1955, Kenneth Tynan noted how the work affected him and described the process that it would subsequently demand of every student, teacher, critic, audience member, and reader: *Godot*, he said, "forced me to re-examine the rules that have hitherto governed the drama; and, having done so, to pronounce them not elastic enough" (70). Accordingly, an explanation of the minimalist aesthetic provides a useful context for Beckett's play; to appreciate it we must, in Guy Davenport's phrase, "reeducate our eyes" (5). In the classroom, we begin the undertaking by paying particular attention to the absence of what we are accustomed to expect. Instead of seeing only how little there is in the minimalist work that satisfies conventional expectations, students should consider how many familiar devices the artist can do *without* while still retaining meaningful and expressive communication.

The importance of this way of seeing becomes clear within the context of Beckett's subsequent dramatic works, some of which can be briefly characterized in class. *Waiting for Godot*, with its excision of traditional plot, can then be seen as the first in a series of plays that strip away inessential elements of drama but keep the essentials of theatrical form. Thus *Play* (1968) removes all gesture and, with the exception of the actors' mouths, all movement; *Not I* (1972) further reduces the essential components of the genre to a seemingly disembodied mouth and a separate, mute, rarely gesturing, cowled body. Beckett's most extreme excisions, however, occur in *Breath* (1969). This thirty-five-second "dramaticule" not only lacks a conventional plot but also has no characters, no language, no movement, and no actor in the theater at the time of the performance. In many ways, however, its austere, wordless, minimalist metaphor for human existence provides the most readily accessible introduction to the Beckettian worldview (see Hutchings).

Once students are familiar with Beckettian minimalism, the teacher can turn to a related concept, the theater of the absurd, one of the most commonly misunderstood terms in modern dramatic parlance. Again, class discussion might begin with a clarification of what the concept is not: improvisational randomness, an absence of meaning, a literary Rorschach test that allows any interpretation, however ludicrous, outrageous, unconventional, or idiosyncratic. Although works of the theater of the absurd, particularly Beckett's, are often comical, their underlying premises are wholly serious: the epistemological principle of uncertainty and our inability in this modern age to find a coherent system of meaning, order, or purpose by which to understand our existence and by which to live (see Esslin, *Theatre* 1–65, 350–77). As the actor Jack MacGowran explains in an incisive comment:

> The key word in all Beckett's writings [is] "perhaps." He is sure of only two things: he was born and he will die. Perhaps the world will be better—perhaps God will be there—this may happen and Beckett will be pleased. There is more hope than despair in Beckett. . . .
>
> (Qtd. in Bair 555)

MacGowran also contends:

> Despair is the wrong word here. Generally it is human distress. No one ever despairs for long in Beckett. Their predicaments are so much worse than life but they have to be to make them apparent.
>
> (Qtd. in Bair 555)

In the absence of the certainty for which we nevertheless yearn, in the silence of the void that cares not at all what systematic meaning we try to impose on it, we wait and hope for a coherent explanation of our plight, for a meaning in our existence, for understanding, for deliverance, for Godot. As Vladimir remarks in the second act, "[A]t this place, at this moment of time, all mankind is us, whether we like it or not" (51a). Appropriately, therefore, the play that embodies this predicament occurs anywhere, anytime—on any road, beside any tree, among characters whose nationality is as indeterminable as it is irrelevant. The world of Godot is devoid of topical references, far away from the clamor of ideologues, both secular and sacred, who offer single-minded systems of explanation and belief as they vie for attention and allegiance— whether to a preacher or politician, a teacher or prophet, or even a playwright or poet (gurus all, insofar as they purport to have discovered the key to a systematic understanding of existence, a way of finding the "meaning" of experience, a means of knowing how to live).

Although the plotlessness and epistemological uncertainty of *Waiting for Godot* account for much of its revolutionary impact, its worldview and its eloquent imagery can profitably be discussed within the context of earlier literary works, including those typically taught in sophomore survey courses and in upper-level classes as well. Thus, for example, Pozzo's famous speech—about giving "birth astride of a grave, the light gleams an instant, then it's night once more" (57b)—exactly recapitulates the earliest such image for human life in English literature, the Venerable Bede's description of the sparrow flitting from darkness through the lighted mead hall and back into the darkness of the unknown. Yet, in Bede's work this image is part of an argument in favor of accepting the new religious faith, Christianity; for Beckett, only the silence of the vast unknown can with certainty be avowed.

Within the context of more recent literary works Beckett's emphasis on an absurdist, epistemologically uncertain world may be contrasted with Wordsworth's contentions about the presence of certain "intimations of immortality": if (unknowably) there is a preexistent soul and if (as reported, though unreliably) it is immortal, it may indeed have had its beginning "elsewhere" and have come "from afar" as Wordsworth claimed (Abrams et al. 211; lines 60, 61). But was it then, for reasons unknown (a punishment, perhaps?), sent into the world at a particular place and time as a test (on which how and where one spends eternity may depend) or for no particular reason at all? While here, like Beckett's tramps beside the tree, we wait, hoping for deliverance, for understanding, for relief from suffering, but forbidden to leave (although, as shown by the hanging that Didi and Gogo consider, leaving is not impossible either). Ad interim, we pass the time in whatever way we can—in conversation and companionship, despite pain and suffering inflicted for unknown reasons or none, amid whatever diversions (like the encounter with Lucky and Pozzo) happen to come along. In the absence of clear and universally accepted instructions (no two religions being able to agree on what constitutes the truth), amid warnings to avoid both the sins of commission and those of omission (action and inaction apparently being equally damnable), "in this immense confusion one thing alone is clear," as Vladimir claims: "We are waiting for Godot to come. . . . Or for night to fall. . . . We have kept our appointment and that's an end to that" (51b). Such a plight, however tragic and bleak, is also literally absurd and therefore, in its way, comic as well; it is a predicament that is, like the ways of God, beyond our understanding and past our finding out (Rom. 11.33), however intense our longing—and however desperate our need— to know. "How better can one magnify the Almighty," Winnie asks in *Happy Days*, in a quintessentially Beckettian line, "than by sniggering with him at his little jokes, particularly the poorer ones" (31) like human existence?

Other familiar literary parallels and precedents for the seemingly unprecedented aspects of *Waiting for Godot* can be introduced into the classroom discussion. The play's sere, evening landscape, which obviously resembles that of Eliot's "Waste Land," is fundamentally similar to Matthew Arnold's "darkling plain" in "Dover Beach" (Abrams et al. 1384; line 35). Though Beckett's plain is peopled by an unknown "they" that administers beatings for unknown reasons (7a) rather than "ignorant armies [that] clash by night," it is also a world that "[h]ath really neither joy, nor love, nor light / Nor certitude, nor peace, nor help for pain" (Abrams et al. 1384; lines 37, 33– 34). Furthermore, Beckett's emphasis on our inability to find a single coherent meaning in experience is anticipated in *The Rubáiyát of Omar Khayyám*, whose speaker seeks meaning and wisdom in life from "all the Saints and Sages who discussed / Of the Two Worlds so wisely" but to no avail, as the speaker nevertheless "came out the same door where in [he] went" (Abrams et al. 1219; lines 101–02, 108).

Ultimately, like Tolstoy's Ivan Ilych, Beckett's characters confront "helplessness, . . . terrible loneliness, the cruelty of man, the cruelty of God, and the absence of God"—arguably the five most profound and recurrent themes of modern literature. The questions that Ivan Ilych asks resonate throughout Beckett's works as well: " 'Why hast Thou done all this? Why hast Thou brought me here? Why, why dost Thou torment me so terribly?' " Yet, invariably, Beckett's characters do not weep, as Ivan Ilych does, "because there was no answer and could be none" (1060). Instead, they persevere and endure, going on even when they seem least able to, waiting and hoping, refusing to give in to the temptation of despair. This perseverance remains constant throughout a body of work that, in the words of the citation awarding Beckett the Nobel Prize for literature in 1969, has "transmuted the destitution of modern man into his exaltation" (qtd. in Bair 606). The resonance of the characters' experiences, the eloquence of an understated metaphor, the uncertainty of waiting, and the apparent absence of (the perhaps nonexistent) Godot provide teachers with a particularly challenging classroom experience: that of introducing students to a play that is both meaning-full and minimalist, as provocative as it is profound.

"Let's Contradict Each Other": Responding to *Godot*

Michael J. Collins

As William Hutchings points out in the preceding essay, students, like critics, teachers, and audiences in general, come to plays with well-earned expectations: plays tell stories through dialogue and the actions and configurations that accompany it on the stage; they progress through a sequence of words, acts, and events that is, at the end, brought to completion. *Waiting for Godot*, however, disappoints these conventional and by no means naive expectations: no story is told, events seem random and disjointed, progress from beginning to end is replaced by a puzzling circularity. At the same time, the play seems, through the metaphor of the waiting tramps and the two travelers they meet on the road, to dramatize elemental human experience, to embody fundamental truths of the human condition. As a result, it often disarms students, for not only does it fail to behave in the way they expect plays to behave, it also seems at once to invite interpretation (those tramps, that road with its pair of travelers, the new leaves on the tree in act 2 must mean something) and to resist all efforts to interpret it.

Because years of studying literature lead students to assume that they must in some way have failed to understand the play, they ordinarily expect the teacher to show them how it works or, as they would more likely say, what it means. But as the students wait for their teacher to unlock the secrets of *Godot*, the teacher may also feel disarmed, for the usual ways of analyzing a play in the classroom do not seem helpful here. Whatever one might say about it often sounds trite, ingenious, or simply gratuitous and can, no doubt, be discredited by a few lines or an action somewhere in it. (What comment can one make, for example, on the function and meaning of the hat routine in act 2?) The play does not, as it progresses, create a context in which one can risk an interpretation; its words and action do not grow "to something of great constancy"; and when pressed to tell what the play finally means, a teacher may want to say with Bert Lahr, who played Estragon in the first American production, "Damned if I know" (Levy 76).

One way to help students understand that they have not necessarily failed to read the play carefully or sensitively enough (and to prepare them to discover something about the ultimate uncertainty of all interpretation) is to have them read or hear several of the responses to the first productions of *Godot*. Ruby Cohn's *Casebook* offers representative examples of the perplexity *Godot* can cause, sufficient to comfort and reassure even the most perplexed reader of the play. Mark Barron, a critic for the Associated Press, went to the first New York production looking for a plot: the play, he wrote, is "about a group of people waiting for Godot, apparently a secret agent, to come and free them to cross a forbidden border. But Godot, their one chance of escape, never arrives" (Levy 77). Brooks Atkinson, of the *New York Times*, responded more favorably than Barron did, but he too was in the end disarmed by the play: "*Waiting for Godot* is all feeling. Perhaps that is why it is puzzling and convincing at the same time" (Levy 77). Norman Mailer, apologizing for an earlier attack on *Godot*, suggested that Lucky's speech "is the one strangled cry of active meaning in the whole play, . . . a cry across the abyss from impotence to Apollo"; he added in parentheses, "I am not altogether unconvinced that Lucky himself may be Godot—it is, at the least, a possibility" (73). For critics, too, then, *Godot* is a puzzling play. Even so thoughtful and theatrically sensitive a critic as John Russell Brown wrote, "[W]hen I read *Waiting for Godot* for the first time, in 1955, I was nonplussed" ("Beckett" 25).

Once students have heard some of the responses the play has evoked, teachers might remind them that *Godot* offers an unusually intense example of the uncertainty one feels in responding to any play (or to any other work of literature). While many students expect all the individual pieces of a play to fit together in a meaningful whole in the end, *Godot* offers teachers the opportunity to make clear that every work of literature, to the extent it reflects the existential complications of human experience, leaves us uncertain. The play asks for and then (if we are honest) resists our best efforts to interpret it—to reduce its metaphorical complexity to a neatly articulated meaning. A good interpretation recognizes and faces the uncertainty any script inevitably evokes in its readers.

The example of a play that seems more conventional and more coherent than *Godot* does can often be helpful here. Tom's long speech at the end of *The Glass Menagerie*, Piet's final movements in the backyard in *A Lesson from Aloes*, Hamlet's encounter with Ophelia while her father and the king observe them, Lear's final words, "look there, look there"—all are crucial to an understanding of the plays, and yet their meanings remain uncertain. Although not a play, Mark's Gospel (because it is, for some students at least, a privileged text) offers one of the best examples: the young man in the linen cloth who appears for a moment just after Jesus is arrested (14.51–52) and then disappears forever. Like much of the action in *Godot*, the incident seems inescapably symbolic, crying out for interpretation, and yet nothing in the text suggests how it is to be interpreted. The responses of biblical critics (it is Mark's signature, an allusion to Amos 2.16, a realistic detail to suggest authenticity) seem at once as plausible and as unconvincing as those of the critics of *Godot*.

One way around the uncertainty that both students and teachers feel is to talk less about *Godot* as a play to be performed and more about its ideas, about what Michael Goldman calls its "supertext," its "overarching intel-

lectual position" ("Vitality" 74). Students who have read *Godot* in a humanities course in high school or taken the relevant course in philosophy can
easily relate the play to existentialism (and particularly to Sartre's essay
"Existentialism Is a Humanism"): God is dead, life is absurd, existence
precedes essence, ennui is endemic to the human condition, in the modern
world we live solely in the existential flow of phenomena. And while one
might admit the value of such familiar statements to understanding *Godot*,
they seem too often detached from what one sees and hears on the stage,
an evasion of the play's complexity, a way of putting to rest the uncertainty
of one's response to it. At the same time, talk about its ideas tends to forget
that *Godot* is not a treatise in philosophy but a play to be brought to life for
an audience by actors on a stage. A discussion in the classroom of the play's
ideas will lead once again to the apparently inevitable acknowledgment that
with *Godot* all we can ever be truly certain of is our own uncertainty.

Having now discovered that the familiar questions (what does it mean and
what ideas does it embody?) are the wrong questions for *Godot*, students
are ready to ask the right ones—what does it do? what effect does it have
on them? what responses does it evoke?—questions that will take them to
the heart of the play. As we come to *Godot* (either in performance or in the
script) with conventional expectations of what awaits us, we at once encounter
something strange, something that refuses to be organized by or accom-
modated to our ordinary ways of responding to plays. Brecht's description
of the alienation effect in Chinese acting helps explain the way *Godot* works:

> [T]he audience was hindered from simply identifying itself with the
> characters in the play. Acceptance or rejection of their actions and
> utterances was meant to take place on a conscious plane, instead of,
> as hitherto, in the audience's subconscious.
>
> (492)

While certainly not a piece of epic theater, *Godot* holds members of the
audience at a distance, insists throughout that they are watching a performance, and keeps them continually struggling, "on a conscious plane," to
make sense of what is happening on the stage, of what is seen and heard.

Toward the end of act 2, for example, just before he leaves the stage for
the last time, Pozzo speaks a single sentence that, for some at least, seems
(if one can judge from the number of times it has been cited) to sum up or
even illuminate what the audience has witnessed: "They give birth astride
of a grave, the light gleams an instant, then it's night once more" (57b).
While Pozzo's words plausibly articulate the play's vision of the human
condition and therefore merit prominence in performance, they are undercut

a few lines later by Didi, whose words reflect more nearly than Pozzo's do the felt rhythms of the play and seem as reasonable a summation as his: "Astride of a grave and a difficult birth. Down in the hole, lingeringly, the grave-digger puts on the forceps. We have time to grow old" (58a). As words and actions pass before us on the stage, they evoke in us a complex of responses, all of which seem plausible enough but none of which ever feels compelling or finally confirmed by the words and actions that precede or follow them.

At the same time, *Godot* often seems, both to audiences and to readers, tedious and slow moving. While the play has great comic possibilities and is sometimes in performance superbly entertaining, it nonetheless always frustrates the desire of an audience to witness a good story, to be drawn into an illusion of reality and to find pleasure in the play of recognizable human events. (Beckett, of course, is using a set of conventions with which some students may be unfamiliar, for as Robin Williams demonstrates, today's comedians work differently from the ones to whom Gogo and Didi are most closely related. Since the film version, with Zero Mostel and Burgess Meredith, does little to suggest the vaudeville and music-hall routines behind the play, a teacher might use clips from Chaplin, Laurel and Hardy, or Abbott and Costello.) While some productions may indeed provide, as Normand Berlin describes it, an "exhilarating evening . . . in the theater" ("Tragic Pleasure" 46), *Godot* does not play very well for audiences that come to it expecting conventional theater, for, like the two tramps on the stage, they are always waiting for something "significant" to happen. John Russell Brown suggests the rhythm and effect of the various incidents and routines in *Godot* when he describes Beckett's "art of the nonplus" as (in part) the "ability to stay with chosen elements until each has been tested to the point of destruction" ("Beckett" 31). Like a record on an old manual phonograph, a routine runs down and stops before a new one starts up.

By describing the responses the play evokes, students recognize that the importance and distinction of *Waiting for Godot* come from its power to evoke in its audiences the precise experience of its two main characters. For its hundred or so minutes on the stage, the play compels the audience to feel uncertainty and tedium as the abiding conditions of life. For many students, such a recognition validates their own responses to the play: "I didn't understand it"; "I thought it was boring." From this point of view, then, *Godot* is indeed an existential play with an existential vision of the world. At its end, having felt the uncertainty and ennui with which the tramps continually live, students and teachers can say with certainty only that they have seen (or read) a play. As Didi remarks toward the end of the evening:

> To-morrow, when I wake, or think I do, what shall I say of to-day?
> That with Estragon my friend, at this place, until the fall of night, I
> waited for Godot? That Pozzo passed, with his carrier, and that he
> spoke to us? Probably. But in all that what truth will there be?
>
> (58a)

Or, as we might put it in the classroom, what meaning will there be? The
"symbolism," said Jacques Audiberti in a review of the first Paris production,
"is optional" and, one might add, too easily detachable from the words and
action of the play, "but applause is obligatory" (14).

By working from familiar responses to the play in performance, students
may gain two important insights. First, as I have already suggested, they
learn to trust their responses to a play and to use those responses honestly
in the process of interpretation. As *Godot* makes clearer than most plays do,
whatever closure we find must be earned through a tenacious, even cou-
rageous submission to the script as we read it or see it performed on a stage.
If all we have at the end of the play is our uncertainty, we at least have
earned the right to speak about it. Students see that all understandings are
uncertain, dependent on our responses to the complexity of any serious play.
As Denis Donoghue comments in *The Arts without Mystery*, "[I]f you feel
anxious, well and good, keep on feeling so, don't indulge yourself in the
opportunism of clarity. . . . Nothing is worse than premature lucidity, unless
it is the satisfaction of enjoying it" (110).

Second, in the struggle to understand and interpret *Godot*, students and
teachers confront, in the safety of the theater, the abiding human problem
Kant described at the beginning of his *Critique of Pure Reason*:

> [H]uman reason has this particular fate that in one species of its knowl-
> edge it is burdened by questions which, . . . by the very nature of
> reason itself, it is not able to ignore, but which . . . it is also not able
> to answer.
>
> (A vii)

Godot simultaneously demands that we interpret it and eludes all our efforts
to do so. The play leaves us with another uncertainty as well, as Beckett
suggested in one of his best-known comments on *Godot*: "There is a wonderful sentence in Augustine. . . . 'Do not despair: one of the thieves was
saved. Do not presume: one of the thieves was damned' " (Esslin, *Theatre*
53). Like *King Lear*, *Waiting for Godot* ends in a question. It asks not
whether Godot will ever come but, more profound and troubling, whether
we live in a sane or a lunatic universe. The question can never be answered,
and yet, as *Godot* insists, it must always remain a question lest we give way

to the arrogant presumption of certitude or the debilitating despair of skepticism.

Godot remains true to the existential conditions, to the uncertainty, with which all of us must live. Its tough-minded refusal to give an answer, its very uncertainty, is the source of its power and its painful wisdom. In working with *Godot*, teachers may be able to help students temper their lust for facts and final answers. Like Gogo and Didi, we all—in the theater and in the world outside it—live in uncertainty, poised, by the conditions of our humanity and of the world in which we live, between certitude and skepticism, between presumption and despair.

Teaching *Godot* from Life

Linda Ben-Zvi

To begin, a premise: Samuel Beckett's *Waiting for Godot* is a play particularly accessible to students because it depicts the world in which they live and expresses an attitude toward that world to which they can immediately relate. Having said that, I would argue, the teacher of *Godot* has nearly said it all. There remains the doing—to indicate the ways in which the experiences of the play's characters parallel experiences students know only too well.

Whether the course is for undergraduates with little background in literature or drama or for graduate students trailing clouds of theory behind them, the first step for teachers is the same: demystifying the text, centering it in the terrain of the familiar. While Beckett posits a metaphysical condition, "Astride of a grave and a difficult birth" (58a), he also describes a common situation recognizable to all students—waiting, and what one does while waiting.

The play takes its point of departure from its title, better seen in the French version, *En attendant Godot* 'While waiting for Godot.' Waiting, doing while waiting—these are the two poles of the play. Unlike a theater audience, but like the convicts at San Quentin who immediately apprehended the meaning of *Godot*, students are a population in specific, shared circumstances. They are waiting, by and large, for the same things: for the end of class, for the end of the week or semester, for graduation, for life. I generalize, I know, but for many this period is a staging area, an antelife before *it*, whatever *it* is, begins. Theirs is a state of becoming. Yet while waiting, they do things. They take courses, like Drama 145 or seminars in Samuel Beckett; they participate in sports similar to those listed in Lucky's monologue; they meet people—listen to them, help them, ignore them, love them; and they perform the habitual tasks that living requires—changing clothes and shoes, washing, eating, sleeping, waking. All of these activities are done "while waiting."

A good starting point for teaching *Godot* is to indicate the central experiences the dramatic characters and the class have in common. Students will understand; interminableness is not a new or foreign idea—especially at twenty. What is harder—and more painful—for both teacher and student is the awareness that the short-term waiting, whether on the stage or in daily life, is only practice, a getting into shape, as it were, for the "big wait": the wait for death. On a sunny Friday afternoon, facing a group of young people only two decades into that story, teachers may be loath to push this idea too far; they also may not be believed. Beckett meliorates the situation by focusing the action of his play not on the metaphysical but on the temporal plane, on those short bursts of activity that usually last no longer than the few minutes it takes to complete some stage business, tell a story, discuss the weather, sing a song, admire a tree. Time becomes domesticated; tedium familiar.

Having indicated that the waiting in the play is exactly what students know and do, the instructor can stress that their identification with the characters can also be extrapolated from their own experiences. I find that the best essay on *Godot* for this purpose is the one published in 1963 by the French critic and novelist Alain Robbe-Grillet. Speaking of Estragon and Vladimir, he observed that "their situation can be summed up in one simple statement, beyond which it is impossible to go: they are there, they are on the stage" (110). Students don't need histories, details, or biographies. They confront Beckett's fictive figures much as they confront people in daily life—within the fixed parameters of a classroom, for example, where all they know is what they see and hear; where individuals talk, exchange ideas, and spend time, certain only that they share the same time and place.

Similarly, when *Godot* begins, the audience knows almost nothing about the characters; and when it ends, the audience knows little more—at least of those facts that traditionally constitute biography. When students accept this situation in *Godot*, as they accept it daily in their lives, they feel less threatened by what they see as the traps of the play.

In confronting modern texts for the first time, students are often troubled by a sense of uncertainty. "What is going on?" they wonder, unaware that the writer is often asking the same question. In his 1961 play *Happy Days* Beckett embeds within the text the question "What's it meant to mean?" (43), asked by two characters witnessing the spectacle of a woman slowly sinking into the earth. They are choral figures, surrogates for an audience that also observes but does not understand. If students who think they are not getting it realize that "it" is difficult—if not impossible—to "get" and that the failure is not their own but the failure of human perception in an impossible situation, then they relax and find the play less intimidating. The threat of the inexplicable should be fixed where it resides: not with Beckett or his works but with the situation he too must face and fail to comprehend—that is, with life. Students understand uncertainty; they experience it daily. But in the classroom, they have been conditioned to look for the bottom line and underline it in red for return on an examination. It is up to the teacher to emphasize that *Waiting for Godot* is a great play precisely because it re-creates life and its unfixity.

Toward this end, I find it helpful to read aloud the exchange between an irate theatergoer and the playwright Harold Pinter. The patron, who had seen Pinter's *Birthday Party*, wrote the following:

Dear Sir:
I would be obliged if you would kindly explain to me the meaning of your play *The Birthday Party*. These are the points which I do not

understand: 1. Who are the two men? 2. Where did Stanley come from? 3. Were they all supposed to be normal? You will appreciate that without the answers to my questions, I cannot fully understand your play.

Pinter "is said to have replied" in the following way:

> Dear Madam:
> I would be obliged if you would kindly explain to me the meaning of your letter. These are the points which I do not understand: 1. Who are you? 2. Where do you come from? 3. Are you supposed to be normal? You will appreciate that without the answers to my questions, I cannot fully understand your letter.
>
> (Qtd. in Esslin, *Pinter* 41–42)

The exchange always produces a laugh in class, but it also produces recognition, I believe. It is impossible to expect drama to offer what life withholds: surety and clarity. We take one another on faith all the time; we have no choice. If students learn to react to characters in Beckett as they react to their peers—not paralyzed by mysteries that cannot be answered but focused on the moment, on the physicality of place and person, on "being there"—then the works of Beckett should speak directly to them.

This connection between the way students observe people in life and the way they must confront characters in a play by Beckett, Pinter, or most contemporary writers leads to the next point: the power of the theater to approximate scenes that are played out in students' lives all the time. To make this connection, I use a passage from the poet Ted Hughes:

> A short time ago, a tramp came to our door and asked for money. I gave him something and watched him walk away. That would seem to be a simple enough experience, watching a tramp walk away. But how could I begin to describe what I saw? Words seem suddenly a bit thin. It is not enough to say, "The tramp walked away" or even "The tramp went away with a slinking sort of shuffle, as if he wished he were running full speed for the nearest corner." In ordinary descriptive writing such phrases have to suffice, simply because the writer has to economize on time, and if he sets down everything that is to be seen in a man's walk, he would never get on to the next thing, there would be no room, he would have written a whole biography, that would be a book. And even then . . . he would have missed the most important factor: that what he saw, he saw and understood in one flash, a single 1,000 volt shock, that lit up everything and drove it into his bones,

whereas in such words and phrases he is dribbling it out over pages
in tinglings that can only just be felt.

(7–8)

Beckett recognized this problem at the beginning of his career. In his
unpublished novel "Dream of Fair to Middling Women," he bemoaned the
fact that his characters could not be portrayed as musical sounds—a collection
of sounds played at one time: "[H]ow nice that would be, linear, a lovely
Phythagorean chain-chant solo of cause and effect" (8). Instead, Beckett's
characters, he knew, would always "bulge" because of their "trine" nature:
"centripetal, centrifugal, and . . . not" (107). The theater, which Beckett
turned to fifteen years later, allowed him to do what fiction did not, to
present the "single 1,000 volt shock," the "chain-chant," directly to audience
members who are free to react without the necessity of explanation, who
can apprehend life being presented, much as they do in their daily activities.
Just as it is impossible to say what Hughes's tramp meant, it is impossible
finally to say what Estragon and Vladimir mean. They are there; they can
be seen with all their bulges. The stage allows for such verisimilitude and
transference from life without the obligatory words that never quite say it
right.

A scene in act 1 illustrates how Beckett builds into his plays the impossibility of satisfactory explanation of actions and the reliance on visual images
instead of words (Ben-Zvi, *Beckett* 143–44). Estragon repeatedly tries to ask
about the pair's connection with Godot, about whether they are "[t]ied to
Godot" (14b). The questioning is interrupted by the appearance of Lucky,
who enters with a rope around his neck. He covers half the distance of the
stage before the audience and the pair see who is holding the rope. A man
held by an invisible power, tied to an unseen element, is a visual concretization of the very question Estragon has been trying to ask. "Tied" in the
person of Lucky becomes palpable: Estragon tied to Vladimir, the pair tied
to Godot, Lucky tied to Pozzo, and this second pair tied to the force that
keeps them walking. Here Beckett uses physical presence to circumvent
words and to offer up whatever meaning is possible. Like Hughes's tramp,
Lucky tied to an unseen wielder of the rope provides a visual image that
cannot finally be reduced to simple declaratory statements.

When students realize that they are confronting the stuff of life, with no
bottom line, they usually relate to the play with the same curiosity and
observation with which they relate to one another and to life. Having shown
how *Waiting for Godot* is life materialized, the teacher can then discuss
other "matter" of literature and drama: literary allusions, the nuances of
language, rhetorical techniques, philosophical parallels, religious symbolism,

lighting, staging devices. Without first grounding the play in the reader's experience, however, all these interesting avenues into the text generally lead only to some regurgitating of half-remembered answers on a final examination—in other words, to Lucky's monologue.

INFLUENCES AND BACKGROUNDS

Beckett and the "Theater of the Absurd"

Martin Esslin

[*Editors' Note: As noted in the "Materials" section of this volume, Martin Esslin's* Theatre of the Absurd *was the most frequently cited source recommended for both students and teachers of* Waiting for Godot. *We asked Esslin whether—and how—he felt the term was still appropriate, more than twenty years after the publication of that original study. His response should be useful to those who wish to use the concept in their teaching.*]

Concepts like the "Theater of the Absurd" are precarious, even problematic: if one had asked any of the writers dealt with, and hence labeled, in the book of that title whether they "belong" to the "Theater of the Absurd," one would have been certain to receive an indignant denial.

Unlike some terms used in literary history and dramatic criticism, like Romanticism, expressionism, and naturalism (which were all coined and used by well-defined groups or "movements" of artists), other such defining appellations are, as it were, applied to artistic phenomena from the outside and often ex post facto: the builders of Gothic cathedrals did not call themselves "Gothic," nor were they called "Gothic" by their contemporaries; Rubens, Bernini, or the Galli-Bibienas did not belong to a "baroque" movement.

There never was a conscious "movement" of the Gothic or baroque: it was the general atmosphere of the times, arising out of the religious, philosophical, economic, social, and technological conditions of those epochs which resulted in a certain sensibility that expressed itself in certain forms, which, to later periods had so much in common that they could be defined and described by those terms. That, of course, does not mean that those artists were not very different, as individuals, or that they did not use a wide variety of individual techniques and forms. They have certain basics in common; that is all. Both an elephant and a mouse are "mammals," which means that they are warm-blooded viviparous vertebrates. These are some essentials they have in common; apart from that, they could not be more different. Nor do they have to *know* that they belong to the category of mammals, let alone to have consciously joined it. The term *mammals* is merely a convenient shorthand for describing certain—essential—features they share.

The playwrights that can be grouped, very tentatively and without the definite inclusion or exclusion of any particular writer, under the general descriptive label "Theater of the Absurd" also, like those of the Gothic and baroque styles, clearly express a certain sensibility, a certain attitude to the world which arose from the times in which they lived: a period—after the Second World War—of deep disillusionment, even despair, over the collapse of so many certainties about the world: Marxism, religious belief, faith in the inevitable upward progress of humankind, and the consequent questioning of the very bases of human existence: human identity, language, the "Meaning of Life" itself.

In art, content and form are inseparable: the way an idea is expressed is an essential element in the nature of the idea itself. Thus similar content tends toward expression in similar forms. That is why the playwrights concerned also share certain formal similarities, however diverse their individual techniques and procedures otherwise might be.

And thirdly and inevitably, the artists of a given period, a given place, share a tradition: they look back at the preceding epoch and both derive ideas and techniques from it and react—more or less violently—against it.

The playwrights of the "Theater of the Absurd" violently reacted against the shallow, verbal, psychological "realistic" drawing-room play of the Parisian boulevards or the London West End, while absorbing the polemic against these forms of such predecessors as Alfred Jarry (the author of *Ubu Roi*); the dream-drama of Strindberg; the irreverence of dada; the experimental techniques for tapping the subconscious mind of the surrealists; the discovery of the subtext by Chekhov; and the pleas for a magical, visual dramatic art, which would relegate words to a secondary position and directly speak to the emotions, the "theater of cruelty" of Antonin Artaud.

Nor is it a coincidence that the "Theater of the Absurd" started in Paris, a place that had suffered the deepest distress and humiliation in the war, and had, being a focus of intense intellectual creativity, produced the philosophy to deal with the ethical and practical problems of humiliation, loss of identity, alienation, and resistance—existentialism.

And it is surely equally significant that the first practitioners of the "Theater of the Absurd" came from among a category of people particularly intensely exposed to these problems of loss and alienation—exiles: Adamov, a Russian-Armenian; Ionesco, a Romanian; Beckett, a Parisian Irishman; and Genet, an outcast of society everywhere as a criminal and ex-male-prostitute.

What then are some of the main features that are common to the work of the playwrights of the "Theater of the Absurd"?

Above all, there is their shared basic attitude to the world and life: a recognition that any certainties, any valid insights into the essential nature of the universe or the purpose of human life on earth are beyond our reach, humankind being too short-lived, too limited in its perceptual apparatus and in its intellect ever to penetrate these ultimate mysteries. Camus and Sartre, the creators of French postwar existentialism, coined the phrase that summed up this recognition: what is beyond explanation, inaccessible to any rational explanation or understanding must remain "senseless" and—in that special meaning of the word—"absurd." Like the protagonists of *Waiting for Godot*, all of us are uncertain about who we are and how we got here. Being rational creatures, we think there must be a purpose in our being here: we are all tending to wait for it to become clear to us, but that is an illusion. We might as well make the best of our situation as it is and learn to live within the limits of our understanding.

The recognition of the limitations of the range of our possible understanding of the world is linked with an awareness of our isolation as individuals: communication is difficult, if not impossible. We can never really know what other people feel, what it is like to be another human being. All we have is our own sensual apparatus, and that is limited, fallible, and subject to our individual moods. "Reality" is simply what we experience, and we can never be quite sure whether what we experience is dream, hallucination, wishful fantasy, or hard "reality," however that may be defined. The plays of the "Theater of the Absurd" thus tend to hover in a borderland between dream and reality: Ionesco sometimes refers to his plays as a "théâtre onirique," a theater of dream. This is a quality that his plays share with those of Adamov, Beckett, Genet, or Pinter.

Hence the "Theater of the Absurd" cannot be a "realistic" theater. It makes no pretense to realism or to theatrical illusion, the mainstay of the traditional theater of the nineteenth and twentieth centuries. There are no missing fourth walls here, no pretense that the characters on the stage are unaware of the presence of an audience. This is a theatrical theater that presents itself as a self-conscious "performance," with the actors knowing that they are being watched by an audience. (In this respect the "Theater of the Absurd" parallels the Brechtian "epic theater," which also insists on being non- or anti-illusionistic.)

In a world so short of certainties, anything that smacks of too rational or logical structures is suspect: plots with rigid motivational chains of cause and effect ("he is so cruel today *because* he was beaten as a child") appear oversimplified and simple-minded to such a worldview. And so does too firm a definition of character. If one believes, as Christians do, that each human soul was specially created by God and will retain its unique identity for all eternity (whether in heaven or hell), character is a rigidly defined entity. To the playwrights of the "Theater of the Absurd," there are no such definitions. The self itself is a mystery. We often experience ourselves as bundles of contradictory tendencies, and we know that we change through time: are we the same character now that we were as children or teenagers; shall we be the same when old and decrepit? With plot and character thus made more problematic, these plays tend to be less easily "decoded" at first sight. We do never quite clearly know who the characters really are or where they come from, and endings tend to be inconclusive.

Moreover, language itself, in the light of so much uncertainty, will be perceived as being far from so unproblematic a medium of exchange and communication as it appears in traditional realistic theater. The characters talk to each other, but are they really communicating? Or is language merely a form of reassurance that they are still there, that some sort of contact is still in being? Hence the presence of clichés in the discourse of the characters points toward the fact that in "real" life most verbal exchanges are equally devoid of real communication, that the daily dose of prepackaged phrases merely serves as noise to fill the void created by the absence of meaningful human contact.

But if there can be no highly structured plot, no well-defined characters, no deeply meaningful dialogue, what have these plays to offer? What makes them work in defiance of all the established rules of dramatic technique?

The "Theater of the Absurd" is essentially a theater of *images*, of metaphors: images in the widest sense—a landscape, the first impression we get of another individual (love or hate at first sight)—always precede our rational analysis of what we have experienced. They are immediate, emotionally charged, multivalent, and rich in their impact. Poetry has always used images of this kind. If a lover calls his beloved "a rose," the image hints at her beauty, her fragrance, her softness, but also at her capability to wound (with her "thorns"), the evanescence of her beauty, the certainty of her withering away, and a multitude of other possible implications and associations. It is in the form of "images" of this kind that we experience the world, "real," dreamt, or hallucinatory: the confrontation of an audience with such images, richly textured and structured in space and time, is the main concern of a theater like the "Theater of the Absurd." This is not to say that the traditional theater does not rely on such richly charged images: Lear naked on the storm-tossed heath, Romeo under the balcony are just such images. The difference is that in these cases the images arise as secondary elements out of a strong narrative plot, whereas in the "Theater of the Absurd" they are the primary element, around which a narrative plot, if any, is formed as a secondary element.

The difference between the way images work in painting or sculpture, or in lyrical poetry, and the way those in the "Theater of the Absurd" work arises from the fact that the theater imports an element of time to the construction of these images. We are watching the image, or the dense texture of images that constitute the play, unfold, as we watch the unfolding of a flower in accelerated motion on film.

This is also the source of that indispensable element for any theatrical performance—suspense, expectation—in a theater devoid of intricate char- acterization and plotting. In the traditional theater which arises from a nar- rative, a story being told, we are constantly asking ourselves, "What is going to happen next?" In a theater of images, we are asking ourselves, "What is happening? What will the image be when it has fully unfolded itself?" In a play like Ionesco's *The Chairs*, that finally unfolded image is that of rows of empty chairs being addressed by a deaf-mute orator. In *Waiting for Godot*, the image completes itself when we realize that the structure of the second act corresponds to that of the first act, that we are seeing an image of a senselessly repetitious existence: "one day just like any other day!" which adds up to a powerful experience of the very nature of time and its relentless flow.

The "Theater of the Absurd" therefore is essentially a theater of three- dimensional metaphoric images unfolding in time and space. If Brecht's theater is "epic," the "Theater of the Absurd" is essentially "lyrical."

It is also, necessarily, a "comic" theater, although it deals with subject matter that is "pessimistic," even "despairing," in the perspective of tradi- tional consolatory worldviews like Marxism or Christian faith. In stressing the "absurdity" of human existence, its evanescence and nugatory nature in the face of eternal mystery and the absence of a discernible purpose of our lives, even the saddest events cannot be taken too seriously, must—in the face of eternal darkness and the inevitability of death—appear as comic. The highest form of laughter (the "risus purus" Beckett calls it in his early novel *Watt*) is the laughter about human unhappiness.

Yet, ultimately, this tragicomic theater is life-enhancing: for it tries to remind the audience of the need to face human existence "knowing the worst," which ultimately is a liberation, with the courage and the humility of not taking oneself and one's own pains too seriously, and to bear all life's mysteries and uncertainties, and thus to make the best of what we have rather than to hanker after illusory certainties and rewards.

And in presenting existence as deeply mysterious, in stressing the inanity of worldly pursuits, the "Theater of the Absurd," dealing as it does with the ultimate truths, is—in the highest sense—also a religious theater even if its approach is that of the "via negativa," the negative theology which reaches out toward the divine by exploring all the qualities that God does *not* and *cannot* possess in order to establish that area of darkness beyond our ken, which God, who is eternally beyond the reach of our imagination and knowledge, occupies in the vast darkness that is ever closed to us and which we can only experience in our awe in the face of something so utterly different from our puny selves.

Waiting for Godot and Philosophy

Lance St. John Butler

Waiting for Godot is not a philosophical play in any direct sense of the term. It does not set out to demonstrate or examine a particular philosophy. Plays by Beckett's contemporary Jean-Paul Sartre, for example *Les mouches (The Flies,* 1942) or *Huis clos (No Exit,* 1944), are philosophical in a way that *Godot* is not. Sartre's plays contain characters who have clearly defined philosophical roles, and they explicitly discuss questions, such as the nature of human freedom and responsibility, that are also discussed in his philosophical works of the period such as *L'être et le néant (Being and Nothingness,* 1942). Beckett, of course, wrote no philosophy. His plays try to avoid simple identifications of all sorts, including philosophical ones, and they do not offer any coherent discussion of the issues they raise. They are, we may say, the opposite of Sartre's.

When I teach *Waiting for Godot,* I make it clear that the play does not need philosophical explanations. As this volume illustrates, there are plenty of valid approaches to the work that do not employ philosophy. Because *Godot* is in some senses a difficult play, more than one critic has been misled into thinking that it requires some loose general philosophizing to help with the difficulties. Certainly the issues raised in the play, the materials out of which it is built, involve the quasi-philosophical concepts of time, death, identity, freedom, and suicide, but I always remind my students that Beckett's own approach to such matters is inclined to be comic and satiric.

Whereas Albert Camus proposes that suicide is "the only serious philosophical question" (*Myth,* my translation), Vladimir and Estragon turn the business of hanging themselves into a comic routine:

> VLADIMIR: What do we do now?
> ESTRAGON: Wait.
> VLADIMIR: Yes, but while waiting.
> ESTRAGON: What about hanging ourselves?
> VLADIMIR: Hmm. It'd give us an erection.
> ESTRAGON: *(highly excited).* An erection!
> VLADIMIR: With all that follows. . . .
> ESTRAGON: Let's hang ourselves immediately!
>
> (12a)

Similarly, Beckett's use of time in the play—one of its most obviously "philosophical" issues—is often comic, as in the treatment of nightfall (which has to be seen in the theater for its full effect). At the end of act 1, the boy runs away from the tramps' questions:

He steps back, hesitates, turns and exit running. The light suddenly fails. In a moment it is night. The moon rises at back, mounts in the sky, stands still, shedding a pale light on the scene.
VLADIMIR: At last!

(34a–34b)

Time and suicide are presented with no exposition or explanation, from no particular point of view; we are not invited into a serious discussion of them. Philosophical analogies may prove useful, but they are certainly not direct —that is, clearly discussed in the text. They must instead be taken with great caution as dramatic entities that should only be approached indirectly. Beckett may bring in philosophical references to create a particular tone or mood, to reap the dramatic advantages they might give him. But any truly philosophical conclusions must be drawn at another level.

Even the issue of freedom, a topic of great concern to Sartre and to the whole generation in France, including Beckett, that suffered the German occupation, is treated in *Godot* ironically and bathetically. In act 1, it appears in a way that seems to promise enlightenment but that soon runs into the sands. Estragon tries to pursue it:

ESTRAGON: Charming spot. . . . Let's go.
VLADIMIR: We can't.
ESTRAGON: Why not?
VLADIMIR: We're waiting for Godot.
ESTRAGON: *(despairingly)*. Ah!

(10a)

Estragon returns to the matter a little later:

ESTRAGON: *(anxious)*. And we?
VLADIMIR: I beg your pardon?
ESTRAGON: I said, And we?
VLADIMIR: I don't understand.
ESTRAGON: Where do we come in?
VLADIMIR: Come in?
ESTRAGON: Take your time.
VLADIMIR: Come in? On our hands and knees.

(13a–13b)

Estragon is not to be put off, however:

ESTRAGON: We've lost our rights?

VLADIMIR: *(distinctly).* We got rid of them.
Silence. They remain motionless, arms dangling, heads sunk, sagging at the knees.
ESTRAGON: *(feebly).* We're not tied? *(Pause.)* We're not—

(13b)

After their exchange has been interrupted and Estragon has been given a carrot, he pursues his topic with surprising perseverance:

ESTRAGON: *(chewing).* I asked you a question.
VLADIMIR: Ah.
ESTRAGON: Did you reply?
VLADIMIR: How's the carrot?

(14a)

Estragon then claims to have forgotten what his question was, but, amazingly, he remembers it:

ESTRAGON: . . . Ah yes, now I remember.
VLADIMIR: Well?
ESTRAGON: *(his mouth full, vacuously).* We're not tied?
VLADIMIR: I don't hear a word you're saying.
ESTRAGON: *(chews, swallows).* I'm asking you if we're tied.
VLADIMIR: Tied?
ESTRAGON: Ti-ed.
VLADIMIR: How do you mean tied?
ESTRAGON: Down.
VLADIMIR: But to whom? By whom?
ESTRAGON: To your man.
VLADIMIR: To Godot? Tied to Godot! What an idea! No question of it. *(Pause.)* For the moment.

(14a–14b)

And that seems to be as far as Estragon (or Vladimir) gets. Beckett very carefully uses his stage directions to control these deliberately labored exchanges. Estragon is despairing, anxious, feeble, and his speech is impeded by a mouthful of carrot. He poses the philosophical problem of necessity and free will—Are we free?—but in the end he gives this up, becomes absorbed in his (necessary?) carrot, and allows Vladimir to terminate the exchange with bathos. He doesn't challenge Vladimir's "For the moment" but instead loses interest:

ESTRAGON: His name is Godot?
VLADIMIR: I think so.

ESTRAGON: Fancy that. *(He raises what remains of the carrot by the stub of leaf, twirls it before his eyes.)* Funny, the more you eat the worse it gets.

(14b)

Beckett hasn't forgotten the question, however, and he too pursues it, but his treatment of the subject is as dubious as Vladimir's. After the tramps have discussed whether food tends to get worse as you go along, Vladimir is allowed to bring that topic, too, back to his favored level of cliché:

VLADIMIR: Question of temperament.
ESTRAGON: Of character.

(14b)

Vladimir takes up the incantation and leads it straight back to the question of necessity and free will:

VLADIMIR: Nothing you can do about it.
ESTRAGON: No use struggling.
VLADIMIR: One is what one is.
ESTRAGON: No use wriggling.
VLADIMIR: The essential doesn't change.

(14b)

Then Estragon, immediately before the entrance of Pozzo and Lucky, concludes this section and the opening movement of the play with the words he used at the beginning: "Nothing to be done" (7a). In another play, this statement might represent a firm commitment to necessity—to the notion that it's "[n]o use wriggling"—and a return to the play's opening position. But how seriously can we take this implication? "Nothing to be done" rounds off one of those litanies that the tramps use to pass the time. They don't mean what they are saying. As Vladimir asks concerning a few simple sentences, "But in all that what truth will there be?" (58a). The philosophical topic of necessity has been raised but not discussed, and no conclusions have been offered. Even if we could somehow demonstrate that the tramps do mean what they are saying about the essential not changing, we would have to take into account their ignorance, the tone of their exchanges, their present situation, and the misunderstanding with which the phrase "Nothing to be done" was greeted in the first lines of the play. The whole dramatic structure of the play works against our taking the tramps' philosophical conclusions at face value.

Philosophical issues such as freedom form part of *Godot*, but they are discussed too comically and inconclusively for us to be able to say that any philosophy has been done. Even in Lucky's speech (28b–29a), philosophy is *used* and not *done*. What he delivers is a pastiche of an academic lecture, with its references to learned authorities ("Puncher and Wattmann," "Fartov and Belcher") and its absurdly calm "I resumes." The subject of the lecture is the diminution of the human species in physical size. Not only is the delivery of this lecture hopelessly garbled, but the audience's attention is diverted by the actions of the other three characters onstage, who groan, protest, and finally attack Lucky to silence him. Most audience members cannot get more than a few shreds of the speech, but the impression of complete senselessness is slightly modified by its philosophical scraps. The God mentioned at the outset is "without extension," as in Descartes, for whom the mental-spiritual world of God (and *res cogitans*) is not "extended" in space (as opposed to the material world, which is *res extensa*). From Descartes, too, comes the method of systematic doubt in philosophical in- quiry: "all other doubt than that which clings to the labors of men" (28b). "Essy" and "Possy" are English pronunciations of *esse* and *posse*—"being" and "being able." Taken from the Scholastic philosophy of the Middle Ages, the words appear courtesy of "Testew and Cunard." Bishop Berkeley, for whom the existence of things was a philosophical question (for whom "essy" was "being perceived"), also makes a brief and enigmatic appearance.

These ill-heard and unconnected scraps do not mean that Lucky's speech is a farrago of nonsensical elements. His inability to "think" properly reflects a desperation that is not merely satiric. He balances the labors of scholars and the hope that they offer ("God," "beyond all doubt," "penicilline") with the despair of ignorance and uncertainty ("quaquaquaqua," "the labors un- finished," "for reasons unknown"), and he places particular emphasis on "man," about whom it is hard to say anything at all: "it is established what many deny that man in Possy of Testew and Cunard that man in Essy that man in short that man in brief in spite of the strides of alimentation and defecation . . ." (29a). We are left with King Lear's "unaccommodated man," to whom philosophy seems hopelessly irrelevant or even threatening in that it asks unanswerable questions and leaves us to the "labor unfinished" of waiting for Godot.

If, however, we stand back from the play and try to see it whole, we can read it as a parable that points into the philosophical domain. It is the parable of the Two Tramps Waiting, in which waiting is the ontological position of humankind. Like a New Testament parable, *Godot* reveals the situation of the human being sub specie aeternitatis.

That the tramps represent all humanity is clear not so much from what they say ("all mankind is us" [51a], which might only be a convenient apho- rism and must anyway be unreliable) as from their unexplained, provisional, and vulnerable status. They are human beings in a classic allegorical position, on a road. Unlike Bunyan's Christian, however, they are not on a journey; instead they have nowhere to go. They are not traveling, but waiting— *Godot* has achieved almost mythic status as the *waiting* play. Sartre best expresses the meaningful side of the parable when he deals with waiting in *Being and Nothingness*.

Everything in the play is subsumed under the heading of waiting. Lucky's speech, for instance, is at first waited for as if it might reveal something important: when he is ordered to speak, Vladimir and Estragon are at once "*all attention*." But when nothing is revealed, Vladimir and Estragon "*protest violently*" (28a) and then fall on Lucky, punishing him, surely, for his failure to deliver what they have been waiting for. Pozzo waits to sell Lucky but is unable to do so. He waits for illumination, but he goes blind. Pozzo falls and waits for help to get up; the tramps assist him only because it is dramatically necessary that they are alone onstage at the end of the play. As soon as they get him off the stage, he collapses again.

Pozzo's great outburst on the subject of time starts with references to the past ("one day he went dumb" [57b]), but, typically, it moves to the future, to that which awaits us ("one day we'll go deaf . . . one day we shall die" [57b]). As Pozzo says, "[T]he light gleams an instant, then it's night once more" (57b); indeed, the thing that can be successfully waited for in this play is night, which is only to say that time passes, that darkness follows light. Vladimir catches the significance in his juxtaposition of night and Godot:

> VLADIMIR: Yes, in this immense confusion one thing alone is clear.
> We are waiting for Godot to come—
> ESTRAGON: Ah!
> POZZO: Help!
> VLADIMIR: Or for night to fall.
>
> (51b)

In *Being and Nothingness*, Sartre describes the limitations that freedom imposes on freedom: we freely choose to do something in the present, but the meaning of this choice will only become apparent in the future when, by another free choice, we confirm or deny what we thought we were about. Adolescents going through a religious phase may grow into adults who look back at the time when they were "passing through a crisis of puberty"; alternatively, they may "engage . . . in earnest in the way of devotion," in which case they will see their adolescent faith as the first step on the ladder of perfection. Only the future, then, allows us to know what the present is, but by the time we reach the future, the present will, of course, be the past (537). This predicament, says Sartre, creates the "necessity for us to *wait for ourselves.* Our life is only a long waiting: first a waiting for the realization of our ends . . . and especially a waiting for ourselves" (538–39). According to Sartre, people are human to the extent that they "temporalize" or tell stories about themselves. "Thus it is necessary to consider our life as being made up not only of waitings but of waitings which themselves wait for waitings" (538). For Sartre, human beings can never catch up with themselves or *be* in any final or satisfying way. They are forever engaged in playing provisional roles, in expectation of becoming fulfilled.

Such a chain of thought inevitably pushes us forward to the end of life:

> These waitings evidently all include a reference to a final term which would be *waited for* without waiting for anything more. A repose which would be *being* and no longer a waiting for being. The whole series is suspended from this final term which on principle is never *given* and which is the value of our being.
>
> (*Being* 538)

This "final term," for Sartre, if it ever came, would be God.

Or Godot. Vladimir and Estragon (and all humankind) wait for a final term from which they are quite obviously suspended (they are "hanging around," as we say). Were Godot to come, they would know the meaning of their lives, but he is ("on principle") never given. Godot does not come in the play not because he has better things to do but because by not coming he forces the tramps into the Sartrean position of waiting, that is, into an allegorical version of human life itself. The pretense that Godot can come is analogous to the creation by human beings of an imaginary telos, a god who will at the end of time explain, adjust, and fulfill all. It is not just a question of the simple equation Godot = God, there is no God so there is no Godot; such an emptiness could perhaps be filled by a robust atheist humanism. Beckett clearly wants to avoid that path. Why? It can only be that his system of mathematics is different. For Beckett, as for Sartre, human beings are condemned to a life of waiting for a telos that, by definition, would be God if it came but that, also by definition, could not come without turning human beings into something that was not human. To be human is to wait for what cannot come.

Suicide, then, is beside the point. It assumes that the problems in the play are problems within the world. Beckett's concern, rather, is with the nature of the world itself, its condition of existence, which is Sartrean in the sense that there can be no world at all, no question of suicide, for instance, except on the basis of a human reality that exists only in a state of expectation, never in a state of fulfillment. Vladimir and Estragon would solve nothing by hanging themselves because, paradoxically, the only meaning they can have is the provisional Sartrean meaning that lies in the ever-deferred hope of present expectation (although "[h]ope deferred maketh the something sick" [8a], we remember). Death is not God or Godot; death finally removes the possibility of even provisional meaning from life: "If I am a waiting for waitings for waiting and if suddenly the object of my final waiting and the one who awaits it are suppressed, the waiting takes on retrospectively the character of *absurdity*" (Sartre, *Being* 539). There lies the trap, Sartre's and Beckett's: there is an absurdity in life, which is waiting for that which never comes, and an absurdity in death, which cancels even the possibility of waiting for what never comes.

In many of his works, Beckett creates, whether consciously or not, a series of philosophical parables. In his novels and stories, especially those written after 1945, complex parabolic elements often call for reference not only to Descartes and Berkeley but also to Hegel, Heidegger, Bergson, and others. His plays are simpler; as relatively univocal creations, they have the strong, immediate effect of parables and do not require philosophical explication. They generally use philosophical references for comic or derogatory purposes, but their overall fit with certain existentialist ideas encourages us to perceive their parabolic relation especially with the work of Sartre. *Waiting for Godot* is the parable of Humankind Waiting. It so happens that the best expression of the meaning of this can be found in Sartre. Beyond this, philosophical explanation should not seek to go.

Biblical Allusions in *Waiting for Godot*

Kristin Morrison

The chief difficulty in teaching students about the biblical material in *Waiting for Godot* is to achieve an appropriate balance between explanation and emphasis. Since most students do not know the Bible well, they require detailed explanation of the allusions present in the play. These references, however, do not dominate the play and must not be allowed to seem, through sheer length of discussion, overly important. Two hazards threaten this balance: overanalyzing biblical material that in Beckett's Ireland or Beckett's France would have been taken for granted as part of an audience's intellectual-cultural world or, at the other extreme, overvaluing the religious elements in the play, making the piece seem more affirmative or more "religious" than it really is.

The first passage dealing with biblical material, Vladimir's discussion of the two thieves (8b–9b), is one of the most extensive. Very early in the play, in what appears (but is not) a non sequitur after remarks about anonymous beatings and painful boots, Vladimir suddenly announces, "One of the thieves was saved" (8b), and insists on telling the story to an unwilling Estragon. Here are three important issues: the nature of the story itself; the historical fact that biblical versions differ; and the dramatic fact that Vladimir chooses to tell this particular story at this particular time. Although I begin by trying to elicit amplification of this biblical reference, students tend to be vague, if not altogether uninformed. To avoid giving the impression that identifying the passage is the most important task, I move on quickly and read the appropriate biblical verses to establish basic correct information:

> And one of the malefactors which were hanged railed on him, saying, if thou be Christ, save thyself and us. But the other answering rebuked him, saying, Dost not thou fear God, seeing thou art in the same condemnation? And we indeed justly; for we receive the due reward of our deeds: but this man hath done nothing amiss. And he said unto Jesus, Lord, remember me when thou comest into thy kingdom. And Jesus said unto him, Verily I say unto thee, To day shalt thou be with me in paradise.
>
> (Luke 23.39–43; King James Version)

The conflicting version that Vladimir mentions—which I do not read at this point but have ready if students seem interested later—is Matthew 27.44, "The thieves also, which were crucified with him, cast the same [mockery] in his teeth." Although Vladimir is technically correct that "[o]f the other three [evangelists] two don't mention any thieves at all" (9b), Mark 15.32 refers to others not *called* thieves but executed at the same time: "And they that were crucified with him reviled him." After we read the relevant passage, we move on to examine a much more interesting issue: the way Beckett uses this allusion dramatically.

Line-by-line examination is essential here to show the pattern of affirmation and negation, the juxtaposition of opposites, that constitutes part of the comedy of this sequence and that ultimately determines the overall tenor of the play. The assertion "One of the thieves was saved" (a thoughtful reference to a serious story) is followed by what could be either a flippant or a serious judgment: "It's a reasonable percentage" (8b). Whether or not the comedy of that line is maximized by the mode of delivery, the line itself introduces considerations of a different order: the secular world of economics, mathematics, sociology; the world of cost-benefit analysis rather than the divine order of the soul's salvation. The irreverence implied by this quick shift from the divine to the secular shocks and surprises an informed audience, and from this experience of shock and surprise comes a response of uneasy humor. And so the sequence continues throughout. The serious issue of repentance is undercut by the comic evasiveness of not going into details. The best-selling book of the Judeo-Christian tradition is trivialized to some pretty colored maps (8b). The central figure in Christianity becomes a vaudeville double take: "Our Saviour" . . . "Our what?" (9a). A significant theological term, a word used daily by ordinary people, is momentarily forgotten as if it were abstruse: Vladimir searches for the opposite of *saved* and finally remembers *damned*. Students seem best able to catch these humorous shifts when I combine this kind of explanation (kept minimal) with reading through the passage using voice and gestures to convey those shifts. It is essential not to overintellectualize the passage or to lose the brisk rhythm of its juxtapositions: the juxtapositions and the rapidity of their presentation, not the subject, provide the humor.

Since the sequence dealing with the "disharmony" of the Gospels is self-explanatory (those variant versions that so exercise Vladimir) and since brisk rhythms continue to the end ("Who?" "What?" "hell," "death"), teachers should read through to the climax:

ESTRAGON: Who believes him?
VLADIMIR: Everybody. It's the only version they know.
ESTRAGON: People are bloody ignorant apes.

(9b)

Having ridden the comedy to this terminus, the students are now ready to double back and reflect on how this climax functions and to consider the question of why Beckett devoted so much stage time to this particular biblical allusion.

As he does in many other points in the play, Beckett bounces his humor off the audience as well as off the characters. Estragon is bored with a story he does not want to hear (does the audience laugh at his sarcastic "I find this really most extraordinarily interesting" [9a] because its thoughts have been voiced?). Yanked unwillingly through a tired old problem from the nineteenth-century Higher Criticism and forced to face the critical question of which evangelist to believe, Estragon quips, "Who believes him?" While some audience members may accept the Bible as truth, others may not believe "the old stories": thus Estragon's annoyed irreverence can produce a gasp of shocked surprise and a laugh of recognition. The next pair of lines similarly engages the audience: "Everybody [believes him]. It's the only version they know" is met by the judgment "People are bloody ignorant apes" (9b). Once again, the audience can be shocked and amused—but this time caught as well. For they realize that they, too, may have only a vague knowledge of the crucifixion story and the two thieves: having been lured into laughing at other people as "bloody ignorant apes," they then find themselves included.

The biblical material has thus been used to achieve two ends: It introduces a theme central to the play as a whole and sounds a note of cynical humor that is heard throughout. The theme, of course, is that suffering permeates human life, makes it a kind of hell; the cynical humor depends on seeing the major story of the Christian tradition, meant to be good news, as really bad news, garbled and ineffective. The joke is on those who have believed it. "Hope deferred maketh the something sick," Vladimir says (8a), groping for Proverbs 13.12: "Hope deferred maketh the heart sick: but when the desire cometh, it is a tree of life." Waiting for what does not come indeed makes the heart (and feet and other body appendages) sick. And yet, by a withered tree, he and Estragon continue to wait.

Individual teaching styles and preferred critical positions determine where a class goes next with this kind of text and this kind of information. Readers schooled in the literature of mysticism might see the play as expressing a "dark night of the soul," in which absence is really a presence. Others might find the play a picture or an indictment of a world in which God (or some important value) is dead: Didi and Gogo wait for a nonexistent hope and thus miss the "real thing" (the possibility of such a real thing being suggested by the leaves appearing on the tree in act 2). Students often find the play depressing and want, somehow, to make it more comfortable for themselves.

My own view is that such affirmations distort the play, which seems to me both splendidly comic and unmitigatedly pessimistic. The piece is, after all, a tragicomedy, and it deals with that "mysterious situation before which, horrified, we laugh" (Sastre 103). Vladimir's emphasis on the story of the two thieves, dwelling on its textual uncertainties, betrays his own conflicting hope and despair. Beckett's placement of this story early in the play indicates his authorial concern with establishing immediately the theme of blighted hope, the tone of grieving despair. The comic mode of delivery underscores the tragicomic nature of the play.

Notes sounded in this early section on the two thieves continue to be heard in briefer biblical allusions. The Crucifixion is kept before the audience by references such as Vladimir's use of the cliché "To every man his little cross" (40a) and by Estragon's Crucifixion posture when he does the yoga exercise "the tree," asking, "Do you think God sees me?" (49b); the implied answer seems to be no since he cries out for pity. Estragon's comparison of himself with Christ emphasizes the protracted suffering of human life: If the terrible slow torture of Christ's Crucifixion is considered "quick," then the pain and despair of Vladimir and Estragon's lingering life is even further accentuated (34b). Vladimir's false alarm concerning Godot's arrival is met with a line suggesting a messianic herald: "The wind in the reeds" (13b) echoes Jesus's remarks about John the Baptist:

> What went ye out into the wilderness to see? A reed shaken with the wind? . . . But what went ye out for to see? A prophet? yea, I say unto you, and more than a prophet. For this is *he*, of whom it is written, Behold, I send my messenger before thy face, which shall prepare thy way before thee.
>
> (Matt. 11.7–10)

This reference to hope and salvation, along with the others, ironically indicates the extent to which Vladimir and Estragon have been misled by their culture, conned into desiring, awaiting the impossible or the nonexistent.

Other biblical or theological and religious references in the play serve similar ironic functions: the well-known biblical injunction "Seek and ye shall find" is garbled to "When you seek you hear. . . . That prevents you from finding" (41a); Pozzo, condescending and punitive, seems at times a parody of God the Father, though "not particularly human" (19b), happy to meet "the meanest creature" (20a), "[o]f the same species as Pozzo! Made in God's image" (15b), "even when the likeness is an imperfect one" (16b); Vladimir and Estragon seem parodies of humankind, Estragon giving his name as Adam (25a) and Vladimir sententiously concluding that "all mankind is us" (51a); Godot seems a parody of popular images of God, having a significant white beard (59a), little boys for messengers (angels), and a nasty tendency to punish those who refuse to wait on him (59b). The irony of these references keeps alive in the play what the story of the two thieves had suggested, that there is no happy salvation for Vladimir and Estragon.

Lucky's monologue (28a–29b) also sounds the note of blighted hope. Although this passage is intellectually complex, it has always seemed to me one of the easiest sections to teach. Once again the students need to guard against overintellectualizing, to be reminded that *Waiting for Godot* is a play and as such offers the audience only one opportunity to catch the words, understand the meaning. For the first time through, I ask them not to look at the text, but simply to listen as I read it aloud; I ask them to relax, not to strain after meaning, but to let the welter of repetitions, puns, and pseudophilosophical jargon carry them along. After I finish Lucky's tirade (which I read quite fast), I ask them to jot down everything they remember, not worrying about being orderly, logical, or coherent, not worrying about "getting it right." As we play with these jottings, what emerges collectively is usually something like this paraphrase of Lucky's argument: Despite the supposed existence of a personal God—both popular (with white beard) and philosophical (God qua God)—who supposedly loves humankind (while at the same time having neither sensitivity to human suffering nor power to relieve that suffering and sometimes even causing torment) and despite supposed intellectual and physical progress, humankind wastes and pines: No distractions of physical activity or mental contrivance can hide the fact that humankind is only a "skull," fading, dying, only a skull that has been abandoned unfinished. A given group of students may not catch this whole statement any more than an audience does, nor do they need to. Different individuals notice different words and phrases; by the end, repetitions alone arrest everyone's attention: "the skull the skull the skull the skull" and the last word, literally the last word on the subject, "unfinished." The discourse is unfinished; humankind, that mere skull, is unfinished.

Although this monologue is largely a pastiche of philosophical and theological terms and concepts, it concludes with an emphatic echo of a significant biblical reference. In a play where the word *saved* is used frequently and desperately, in a play that virtually begins with a "sacred" but untrustworthy story about salvation, it can be unsettling to hear even chaotic denial of the main hope of Western thought concerning the relationship between God and human beings. The word *skull* climaxes that denial. Not only does *skull* obviously suggest death and disintegration, but to those who know their Bible it also suggests the name "Golgotha," that place of the skull (as the name signifies [Matt. 27.33]) where the two thieves were crucified. If, as Lucky's monologue indicates, humankind is only a skull, then special places like Golgotha and special salvations from dying Gods or delaying Godots are the mere delusion Vladimir uneasily fears they may be. Lucky's "discourse" thus becomes one more story to put beside Vladimir's story of the two thieves, both ironic commentaries on the present situation of blighted hope.

This connection between "skull" and "Golgotha" reveals a frequent characteristic of Beckett's use of biblical material. Occasionally, Beckett identifies his allusions and elaborates his use of them (as he has Vladimir do with the story of the two thieves in this text); but more often he touches on an allusion using only a few salient words: not, I think, to be obscure or even minimalist but rather because the words and myths of the Bible are so significant a part of his cultural and intellectual world that they need no elaboration. As Beckett said of himself, "Christianity is a mythology with which I am perfectly familiar, so naturally I use it" (Duckworth, *Angels* 18). Vivian Mercier has corroborated this familiarity in a description of his own and Beckett's boyhood study of Scripture and religion at Portora Royal School, founded by the same King James I whose commanded translation of the Bible frequently sounds in Beckett's work (Mercier, "Bible Reader"). Thus, when Beckett alludes to scriptural passages, a few words suggest the whole and make the point. (Advanced students interested in pursuing this issue should be referred to Beckett's manuscripts and working notes, which often specify the scriptural roots of a phrase.)

Two of these brief allusions are of particular interest. At the end of act 1, when the boy arrives to say that Mr. Godot "won't come this evening but surely to-morrow" (33b) and Vladimir proceeds to question him about his "credentials," the boy reveals that he minds the goats and his brother minds the sheep. Placing these two words together is enough to suggest one of Jesus's best-known parables, frequently used in art and sermon, the parable of the sheep and the goats:

> When the Son of man shall come in his glory, and all the holy angels with him, then shall he sit upon the throne of his glory: And before him shall be gathered all nations; and he shall separate them one from another, as a shepherd divideth *his* sheep from the goats: And he shall set the sheep on his right hand, but the goats on the left. Then shall the King say unto them on his right hand, Come, ye blessed of my Father, inherit the kingdom prepared for you from the foundation of the world. . . . Then shall he say also unto them on the left hand, Depart from me, ye cursed, into everlasting fire, prepared for the devil and his angels. . . . And these shall go away into everlasting punishment: but the righteous into life eternal.
>
> (Matt. 25.31–46)

This parable is, of course, a narrative about salvation and damnation; the sheep are the saved, the goats the damned. It is significant that the messenger who attends Vladimir and Estragon is the goatherd. Previous ironies about the nature of the God parodied in this play are intensified by his perverse beating of the boy who tends the sheep, not the one who tends the goats (the damned are damned and the saved get beaten). Act 2 ends after the appearance of a similar messenger (apparently not the same one, but not necessarily his shepherd brother either). This boy, in response to questions, provides the information that Godot has a white beard, frightening Vladimir into pleas for mercy and expectations of punishment (59a–59b).

The sense that Vladimir and Estragon will not be saved is reinforced by a second parable, the well-known story of the wise and foolish virgins:

> Then shall the kingdom of heaven be likened unto ten virgins, which took their lamps, and went forth to meet the bridegroom. And five of them were wise, and five were foolish. They that *were* foolish took their lamps, and took no oil with them: But the wise took oil in their vessels with their lamps. While the bridegroom tarried, they all slumbered and slept. And at midnight there was a cry made, Behold, the bridegroom cometh; go ye out to meet him. . . . and they that were ready went in with him to the marriage: and the door was shut. Afterward came also the other virgins [who had gone to buy oil for their lamps], saying, Lord, Lord, open to us. But he answered and said, Verily I say unto you, I know you not. Watch, therefore, for ye know neither the day nor the hour wherein the Son of man cometh.
>
> (Matt. 25.1–13)

Although in *Waiting for Godot* this parable is alluded to only briefly, Beckett has used it more fully elsewhere in his work (most notably in *Endgame*: "When old Mother Pegg asked you for oil for her lamp and you told her to get out to hell, you knew what was happening. . . . You know what she died of, Mother Pegg? Of darkness" [75]; see Morrison, "Neglected Biblical Allusions"). The biblical words "Behold, the bridegroom cometh; go ye out to meet him" are echoed in Vladimir's triumphant announcement, "It's Godot! We're saved! Let's go and meet him!" (47b). Like attendant virgins of ancient ceremony, these two derelicts have awaited one who they are sure has a special claim on them and in waiting have proved themselves worthy: "What are we doing here, *that* is the question. And we are blessed in this, that we happen to know the answer. Yes, in this immense confusion one thing alone is clear. We are waiting for Godot to come—" (51b). In the parable, the bridegroom does finally arrive and takes those who are ready into the wedding feast (an image for the kingdom of heaven or salvation; see Matthew 22.1–14 for a similar parable associating darkness and damnation). But in this play, Vladimir is wrong, they are not saved (or blessed), and Estragon is right, they are "in hell" (47b). Once again, a biblical parable serves as ironic contrast to the dramatic scene: the received wisdom of Vladimir's world is untrue; Vladimir may regulate his behavior and set his expectations according to the old stories, but in fact these stories are not reliable: he may keep his appointment, but the bridegroom does not. In the parable, of course, the bridegroom tarries, arriving finally at midnight; it is precisely this detail of the story that traps Vladimir, who never knows whether he has waited long enough: perhaps Godot will come tomorrow, "[w]ithout fail" (58b).

Vladimir is not, of course, consciously referring to this parable; but its ethic resides in him, as his echo of its words suggests. Thus the audience senses one more grimly comic moment of blighted hope: "Your only hope left is to disappear" (47b). But Didi and Gogo continue to wait, hoping for a salvation, a deliverance, even though all their biblical stories of salvation —the two thieves, the sheep and goats, the ten virgins—mock those hopes.

In class discussion of such material, certain questions are inevitable: "Did Beckett really think of all this?" and "Are we supposed to know all this?" Here I try to redress any imbalance that may have occurred about the relative importance of the biblical references. These verbal allusions really are in the text; they are not questionable "symbols" to be interpreted (like the leaves on the tree). And there are many of them, some placed quite strategically (at the beginning of the play, toward the ends of the two acts, at the climax of Lucky's monologue). Their theme usually has to do with salvation and damnation (or psychological equivalents, hope and despair), and their use is consistently ironic. All that seems to me unassailable.

But is the play then chiefly "about" God, belief, and religious experience? Each instructor has his or her own way of dealing with that pesky word *about*, and I will not belabor my own approach here. But I do argue that the biblical references are very important and that the play is enhanced for the reader or spectator who recognizes them or at least senses their import. While not the controlling element, they skillfully reinforce the many other elements that make up the play. No, at the moment of dramatic experience, the audience does not think about all this, but if the play is successfully performed, the audience should certainly feel all this. Later, when we search to understand what makes this play so powerful and unsettling, we find as part of our answer the subtlety with which Beckett, using biblical allusions, has invoked and questioned that central human experience of time— waiting—and the emotion that makes it bearable: hope.

Tray Bong! *Godot* and Music Hall

Fred Miller Robinson

> The Elizabethan drama was aimed at a public which
> wanted *entertainment* of a crude sort, but would *stand*
> a good deal of poetry; our problem should be to take a
> form of entertainment, and subject it to the process
> which would leave it a form of art. Perhaps the music-
> hall comedian is the best material.
>
> T. S. Eliot, "The Possibility of a Poetic Drama"

> This is a comedy scene. These are music hall bits.
>
> Bert Lahr

As Bert Lahr learned in Miami, if *Waiting for Godot* is played as symbolic
and existential, the work will die on the stage. So it is in the classroom.
Most students dread reading the play, just as students of previous generations
dreaded T. S. Eliot's poetry. To them it is the philosophical pill we must
take: modern, difficult, ambiguous, long-faced, God-haunted, bitter to the
taste. When these students attend even mildly successful productions of
Godot and discover how much they and the rest of the audience are amused,
how often they laugh outright, they are more likely to be confused than
enlightened by the experience. Or, worse—so powerful is the cultural con-
ditioning that identifies gravity with seriousness, the modern with the
despairing—they deny the experience: Charming evening we're having. Yes,
it's awful.

This denial and confusion can be overcome or alleviated in the classroom
by a consideration of the comic ways in which Beckett is being serious—in
particular, the forms of popular entertainment he employs. After all, Beckett,
uncharacteristically and hence emphatically, tips his bowler hat in this direction when Didi and Gogo, bored with Pozzo's having lost his expensive
pipe, have this exchange in act 1:

> VLADIMIR: Charming evening we're having.
> ESTRAGON: Unforgettable.
> VLADIMIR: And it's not over.
> ESTRAGON: Apparently not.
> VLADIMIR: It's only beginning.
> ESTRAGON: It's awful.
> VLADIMIR: Worse than the pantomime.
> ESTRAGON: The circus.
> VLADIMIR: The music-hall.
> ESTRAGON: The circus.

(23a–23b)

The pantomime, circus, and music hall are related entertainments. "Panto" acts were part of the music hall and still are integral to the circus; music halls often had acrobatics and animal and trapeze acts; and when circuses were in decline they incorporated music-hall comics and singers. All have in common a structure of variety acts or numbers or "turns." In this passage, Pozzo is regarded as one such act. Gogo, in the manner of music-hall audiences, laughs at the poor quality of the act, and Didi, whose prostate gland reacts painfully to laughter, exits to urinate, saying, "Keep my seat" (23b). A bit later, when Pozzo has performed his speech explaining the twilight and asks his small audience to appraise it, Gogo says, "Oh tray bong, tray tray tray bong" (25b)—a comically dandyish signature phrase from the music-hall act of Charles Chaplin, Sr. (see fig. 1).

Music-hall elements in *Godot* have been noted by many. My concern here is with the form and spirit of the play as a whole. In the absence of acts peculiar to the circus and in the presence of only a little pantomime, I propose that music hall, mutatis mutandis, is the fundamental structure and ambience of *Godot*, the source of its dramaturgical life. English music hall is the dramatic tradition that informs Beckett's play. We are offered a series of turns in a spirit of fun (*Spass*, Brecht often said, is what the modern theater needs). Of course these turns are seldom discrete and vary in length from a gag to a full-blown routine. Consider the following, chosen at random: comic business with boots and hats (staples of the music hall); cross talk about the Bible; joking about the audience ("that bog" [10b]); an exchange about Godot as *haut bourgeois*; Pozzo's turn as arrogant landowner and master; Lucky's dance and speech, a *coup de théâtre*; a hilariously polite exchange of adieux; imitations of Pozzo and Lucky; Didi's and Gogo's considering how to hang themselves from a prop tree that usually is, or should be, shorter than they—and so on, not to mention the classic pants-dropping that concludes the play. Every prop is the subject of humor. As Didi says, they can't let

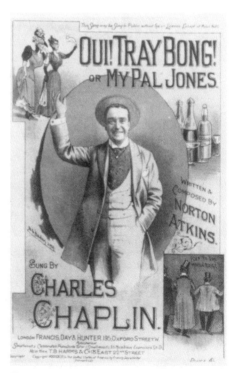

Fig. 1.

diversions go to waste: "Come, let's get to work!" Without these diversions they'll be "in the midst of nothingness!" (52a)—just like the music-hall performer who, as Max Beerbohm noted in his obituary of Dan Leno, is all by himself on the stage, making his effects quickly "without the aid of any but the slightest 'properties' and scenery" (*Selected Prose* 376).

It is a question not of the teacher's reducing the resonance of *Godot* to the noise of popular entertainment (Brecht certainly never thought of *Spass* as trivial) but of helping students to understand the particular chambers in which Beckett's thought resonates. By recovering the structure and ambience of music hall for our students (there are, for example, tapes of radio double-act cross talk; see, in particular, Wilmut), we can tell them a great deal about the comic shape of Beckett's vision. They will understand how entertaining it is to entertain ideas. Then the play as a staged thing will become more expressive, less distant, less a problem to be solved.

The simple mise-en-scène of *Godot* suggests the scenery of variety music hall in this century, when the halls became more respectable and theatrical. Since the tree and the moon are so proplike, the country road might well, I think, be painted trompe l'oeil on a music-hall-like backcloth behind the mound and tree. Everything in the play points to its taking place on a stage—and before an audience ready to deplore the failures of its "awful" turns. Pozzo's turn is slow and faltering. Lucky's dance, though practiced (as Gogo discovers when he tries to imitate it and almost falls), is in pathetic decline, and his thinking, which Pozzo says he used to do "prettily" (26b), is worse. And Didi's and Gogo's cross talk can become "really insignificant" (44a) or not insignificant enough; it can peter out, and new routines have to be improvised to alleviate their waiting. As Gogo says, after looking at a cloud proves to be less than wonderful, "Let's pass on now to something else, do you mind?" (54a). Yet even the continual reminders of how badly they all are doing are part of the comic routine; like professional comedians, they recover from their failures by acknowledging them, sharing their dismay with the audience, getting another laugh. As Beckett has written them, the turns *should* be entertaining. But they can't be if they're played as though burdened with significance—in which case they deserve "the bird" (a music-hall display of audience contempt), which is just what Alan Schneider and company got in Miami: catcalls and walkouts (see, e.g., Lahr 269–72).

In the Victorian period, music-hall entertainment was designed for and patronized by working-class and lower-middle-class audiences who mingled and drank and ate and could ignore or talk back to the performers, themselves mostly from working-class backgrounds. The atmosphere was never "respectable" except in the days of the genteel decline of the halls. The vulgarity in *Godot*—the penis humor and the references to farting, garlic breath, stinking feet, and urination—is a vestige of this ambience and helps to identify the play as "popular" theater. But the costumes and dialogue recall another aspect of music hall, one that T. J. Clark discusses in reference to the French café-concerts of the same period: the combination of travesty and imitation of gentility and respectability that described both the performers and the audience. (Many commentators on music hall note the unity of the two, the audience as part of the performance atmosphere.) The proprieties of class were both affirmed and deranged. Drunken swells in top hats tottered and spoke in real and botched French, performers in middle-class bowlers and lounge suits or in evening dress did pratfalls or sang sentimental or vulgar ditties in local accents before an audience dressed up in their best clothes and enjoying their new leisure time. Gradually, artists and intellectuals, as well as the rich and fashionable, were drawn to the halls, and—for a while, say, before 1912—a truly "mixed" audience mingled.

We know from Deirdre Bair's biography that Beckett loved the music hall, certainly in Dublin in the 1920s and in Paris in the early 1950s, if not all his life (48, 417). His insistence that all four main characters wear bowlers reflects this taste as well as his love of silent film comedy. The characters are not so respectable as they once were. They still have their genteel bowlers and the remnants of intellectual thought these hats seem to contain. Didi's and Gogo's cast-out existence has left them with pants baggy enough to contain food and rubbish and old boots that, in Gogo's case, no longer fit. Their Chaplinesque appearance signals a blurring or ambiguity of class. They are vulgar knockabout bums who remember better days and still comically, ineffectually aspire to a thinking or reasoning that is allied to their aspiration to be "saved" by Godot. This aspiration is mirrored in Lucky's parody of academic discourse (containing the vulgar names and the comically stuttering pronunciation often used in music-hall routines) on the mysteries of God and human mortality. Lucky's bowler, which triggers this discourse, is worn by Didi after the hat exchange.

Like Chaplin, Beckett uses this music-hall tradition to transform the democratic into the universal. Chaplin's "little man" (a Victorian phrase for the lower classes) becomes "Everyman." Beckett's tramps become humankind. If the play works, the audience sees itself in the performers, acting out human life as a series of variety turns, with inevitably mixed results: funny and awful.

The question to be posed to students is, How does Beckett convey his vision of human life and consciousness in the form of popular entertainment? A good example is the "little canter" (42a) that Didi and Gogo divert themselves with in act 2. It takes the form of cross talk on "thinking." In music hall (and in American vaudeville), to cross-talk the idea, through swift exchanges, is to derange and parody communication. It's the combination of mutual and failed understanding, based on wordplay, that keeps the talk going—nowhere.

Didi and Gogo have already mentioned that they talk incessantly so they "won't think" and "won't hear" (40a–40b)—presumably the silence of the nothingness in which they are entrapped. Afraid of this silence, they self-consciously start up some cross talk ("You can start from anything"):

VLADIMIR:	When you seek you hear.
ESTRAGON:	You do.
VLADIMIR:	That prevents you from finding.
ESTRAGON:	It does.
VLADIMIR:	That prevents you from thinking.
ESTRAGON:	You think all the same.
VLADIMIR:	No no, impossible.
ESTRAGON:	That's the idea, let's contradict each other.
VLADIMIR:	Impossible.

(41a)

The contradiction implied is between thinking as something distinct from talk (words) and thinking as the object of talking. The first helps you find what you seek, the second prevents you from finding. But when Didi says it's impossible for them to contradict each other, he implies that, since they've both been thinking this subject through, they are both seeking and not finding because they are seeking. (In Arsene's logic, in *Watt*, "it is useless not to seek . . . for when you cease to seek you start to find," and if you find what you seek you lose it because then you realize "what it is"—that is, not the mysterious and desired thing you sought [44].) Gogo confirms the inevitability of the process when he responds to Didi's "Impossible" with "You think so?": even the idea that thinking is impossible involves thinking. Hence the cross talk can continue:

VLADIMIR:	We're in no danger of ever thinking any more.
ESTRAGON:	Then what are we complaining about?
VLADIMIR:	Thinking is not the worst.
ESTRAGON:	Perhaps not. But at least there's that.
VLADIMIR:	That what?
ESTRAGON:	That's the idea, let's ask each other questions.
VLADIMIR:	What do you mean, at least there's that?
ESTRAGON:	That much less misery.
VLADIMIR:	True.
ESTRAGON:	Well? If we gave thanks for our mercies?
VLADIMIR:	What is terrible is to *have* thought.
ESTRAGON:	But did that ever happen to us?

(41b)

Amid the comic miscues and interruptions, Didi makes a distinction between "thinking" and "to *have* thought." "Thinking," they agree, is "not the worst" because it lessens the misery of silence, but it is terrible to have thought in the past (and had it come to nothing) as well as to possess thought. The terror of thought-as-possession has been demonstrated for them in Lucky's speech, a sort of cassette tape he carries around inside him that only reminds him of the futility of having thought about what must remain "unfinished."

How to distinguish between thought and thinking, between that which makes and that which alleviates misery? Gogo confuses the issue by wondering if they ever had any thought, and Didi's responses about the corpses, skeletons, and tombs seem to refer to the very words they're using, the nature of their talk ("All the dead voices" [40b]), which so easily can become hardened into futile, past ideas like "We should turn resolutely towards Nature" (41b). Thought comes to naught, but you can't stop thinking:

> VLADIMIR: Oh it's not the worst, I know.
> ESTRAGON: What?
> VLADIMIR: To have thought.
> ESTRAGON: Obviously.
> VLADIMIR: But we could have done without it.
>   (41b–42a)

Their cross talk results in their thinking that even having thought is not the worst. Thinking is the balm for its own poison. Nothing has been found, and now, after this "little canter. . . . we'll have to find something else" (42a).

To analyze the passage in this way is to realize how the unstabilizing quality of comic patter is the perfect medium for expressing the conceptual heart of Didi's and Gogo's condition. Routines like these constitute, after all, their waiting. They seek Godot, whom they cannot find. They seek to be "saved" but are condemned to wait and think, infinitely. And thinking is playing with words, which can only elaborate themselves. Words, in their finite variety, comprise the acts that take place on a stage that Godot cannot enter because to be Godot he must remain offstage, the headliner act that never happens. Beckett makes music-hall turns out of his profoundest concerns. The very awfulness of the routines is funny, an occasion for surrendering to the "communal emotion" that W. R. Titterton considers the essence of music hall (206). The futility of the tramps' waiting can be celebrated because, if properly understood, it's everyone's condition; that's what the audience's laughter expresses.

As many have said, Max Beerbohm and T. S. Eliot (in his obituary of Marie Lloyd) prominent among them, music hall is a "popular art." Beerbohm called the music hall a "temple of modernity" precisely because it put spectators in touch with "modern life," the life of the masses of people ("At the Tivoli" 16–17). If he declared himself superior to its garish vulgarity, he was—like so many others—impressed by its art. *Waiting for Godot* is a popular play because it is a work of popular art; it is quintessentially modern because it is addressed to everyone. All of us are drawn to its comedy, squalor, and charm. That's how students will be drawn to it as well. Treating the play as a series of music-hall acts is the best way to help students overcome their resistance to it and comprehend its vision of life, a vision full of life.

Waiting for Godot and the Chaplinesque Comic Film Gag

Claudia Clausius

Charlie Chaplin's classic silent film gags can effectively introduce students to the comedy in Samuel Beckett's *Waiting for Godot*. In *The Immigrant* (1917), a violently seasick Charlie leans over the balustrade of a swaying ship. We smile at his comical misfortune. He then turns toward us, holding a fishing rod at the end of which hangs a fighting fish. Now we suddenly laugh at ourselves. In *The Idle Class* (1921), a wealthy Charlie learns that his wife has just left him. He turns away from us and shakes with melodramatic grief. Despite our laughter, we empathize. Next we see him pivot toward us, this time with a cocktail mixer in his hand. In *Monsieur Verdoux* (1947), a jaunty gentleman strolls in his garden with an armful of freshly picked flowers. He spies a caterpillar on the path, stoops, and gently moves it to the safety of the grass. In the background, a smokestack emits dark clouds. We later learn that this smoke is the last remains of the man's murdered wife.

The comic machinery of these classic film gags is as complex as it is effective. In "The Anatomy of the Gag," the Czech dramatist Václav Havel explains that a gag always concerns an action with which the audience is comfortably, indeed complacently, familiar. Students can identify with seasickness, grief, and compassion. The action is thus a habit, an automatism by virtue of its function and our recognition of it. The comic absurdity of the gag occurs when this familiar action is suddenly put in a surprising and ingenious context, one that disrupts or defamiliarizes both the automatism itself and the automatic recognition it first evoked. Although defamiliarization may involve the fictional characters (Didi and Gogo for instance), its primary effect is on the audience. Charlie Chaplin knows exactly what he is doing; we make the mistake of misinterpreting the familiar gesture. The gag's play on convention or habit wakes us from our lethargy, from our acceptance and continuation of mechanical behavior or thought. In "unprogramming" behavior and thought, Havel argues, the comic gag makes us more human.

Havel broadly defines the classic silent film gag as consisting "minimally of two basic phases which in themselves need not be either comical or absurd, but which begin to evoke the sense of absurdity and laughter at the moment of their encounter" (13–14). To our surprise and delight, mal de mer becomes a fishing expedition, a separation turns into a martini, and an animal lover reveals himself as a modern Bluebeard. Thus, the essence of the silent film gag is collision, whether physical (slapstick, pratfall, knockabout) or metaphoric (a clash of ideas). Havel notes that the first phase of the gag (the seasickness) is "the exposition of the situation," which is defamiliarized by the second phase (the struggling fish), which reveals the inherent absurdity

(15). However, the characterizing feature of this absurdity is, paradoxically, its essential reality. As a starved immigrant, Charlie seeks a meal; as an intoxicated fop, Charlie craves another drink. Havel, therefore, concludes that the prime purpose of defamiliarization is to extract reality from the automatism (16).

In witnessing the gag process, we simultaneously participate in a crucial inversion. Since we originally endowed the automatism with meaning (we recognize the symptoms of discomfort, grief, and consideration), only our perception can clarify, unmask, and expose that same convention or habit. We mistakenly conclude that Charlie regrets his wife's departure while in reality he is more concerned with mixing himself another drink. Havel claims that to peel away this human interpretation of the automatism is to lose the human context initially responsible for the meaning, and "[t]hat which loses its human context becomes absurd" (16). Hence our laughter. In Beckett, the exfoliation of the surface human context reveals the pitiful, vulnerable human absurdity, which remains the only authentic reality. In Havel's words, "defamiliarization occurs when accepted notions are replaced by descriptions of reality as it really is" (17).

Havel warns that although the gag's two phases work with two distinct automatisms, they are not interchangeable. The difference separating them even while connecting them in a strict chronology is that the first phase, reflecting an ostensible and superficial reality, is deceptively in harmony with the humanity of the subject performing the convention. By attributing suffering and gentleness to Charlie in *The Idle Class* and *Monsieur Verdoux*, we deny him his own character, make him less of himself and more of an artificial ideal or convention. The second phase returns Charlie to himself by exposing his authentic reality. The second phase denies us the emotional scope to sympathize or empathize with the character and to see ourselves thereby as compassionate human beings. Indeed, the second phase actively mocks our desire to feel compassion and companionship. Simultaneously, as the second phase defamiliarizes the first, the subject who was previously dehumanized by convention is suddenly humanized and returned to himself or herself through the process of defamiliarization. In part this process succeeds because the human subject can "recognize when the automatism ceases to serve him, and when he begins to serve the automatism" (Havel 23). It is good to feel compassion but not at the expense of forfeiting the reality of the situation or of the character (Charlie or ourselves). In Chaplin, those automatisms of daily life through which Charlie travels away from himself are the focus of the humor, while in Beckett the tramps' deliberate use of such automatisms renders them comic even as their recognition of these same automatisms burdens them with a sense of futility.

Havel acknowledges the tension between the authentic reality surrounding us (hunger, cruelty) and the ostensible reality (regret, kindness) that we actively create and endow with meaning (23). He argues that our personal development is "realized in and through" the automatisms to which we resort and which are capable of "enslaving . . . deceiving . . . [and] automating [us]" (23). In *Waiting for Godot,* Beckett characterizes his tramps through their various manipulations of habit. Didi's and Gogo's self-consciousness demonstrates that, in defamiliarizing such parasitic automatisms, "man is able to defend himself against self-alienation, recapturing always anew his own identity, returning to himself, to his nature and principal" (Havel 24). Havel believes that this process of defamiliarization offers a new experience of catharsis—a purification and redemption. Neither the purging of pity and fear of Aristotelian tragedy nor the dance and marriage of the conventional comic resolution can suffice in contemporary reality, because the structures that carefully order and illustrate the contrived problems alienate human beings from themselves; such philosophical and aesthetic pacifiers perpetuate obsolete patterns of perception.

The extent to which an instructor uses the Havelian material largely depends on the type and level of the class itself. (For further discussion of Havel, see Clausius, "Bad Habits.") I have found it best to go through this definition and function of the gag after the class views a Charlie Chaplin film. In some ways, Havel's observations appear more apt in reference to *Waiting for Godot,* and students often fail to appreciate or even understand his analysis until they discuss the play using the Chaplin tradition as source material and comic illustration. The choice of a particular Chaplin film depends on the personal emphasis of the instructor and the specific class.[1] The film I investigate with reference to parody and satire and their subsequent defamiliarization is *Easy Street* (1917), an early Chaplin film that is readily available.[2]

Near the beginning of *Easy Street,* Charlie the Tramp huddles outside in the corner of a house porch. He suddenly hears singing and follows it into the Hope Mission. Finding a seat in a pew, he tries to participate in the service. When the collection box comes around, he is understandably embarrassed at not having a contribution, and he lightly shakes the box to give the impression of coins dropping into it. After the service, the minister and the beautiful organist (Edna Purviance, who later plays the social worker) try to convert him and succeed so well that, as Charlie tries to leave the mission, his conscience overcomes him and he brings the stolen box out from under his clothes. We laugh not only at Charlie's guilt and shame but also at his revealed reasons for shaking the box: to camouflage his poverty and, simultaneously, to make sure that the contents would be worth stealing. The gag consists of the collision of the two conflicting automatisms of almsgiving and theft in which the second phase, more accurately reflecting Charlie's true position and character, defamiliarizes the first dehumanizing phase, his pride-motivated pretense at charity.

Later in the film, after Charlie has got a job as a police officer, we see him walking his beat on Easy Street, where he witnesses a woman stealing from a sleeping greengrocer. Charlie begins to reprimand her but soon becomes so moved by her tale of poverty that he surreptitiously adds to the fresh produce already in her apron. He then escorts her home, where they encounter the beautiful social worker, who expresses delight at what she thinks is Charlie's generosity. He modestly gestures that it is nothing and refers to her own selfless work among the poor of Easy Street. Meanwhile, the woman beside them faints under the strain of her heavy apron and her weakness and hunger. Although Charlie and Edna feel genuine compassion for the woman, their conventional humanitarian feelings are briefly defamiliarized by their more authentic, mutual romantic interest. The second phase of the gag characteristically reveals the authentic reality of the human context. Shortly after this episode, the social worker and Charlie visit a large family. Inside, there are children everywhere—in boxes, crates, laundry tubs. Given a box of cereal to distribute, Charlie decides that the best way to feed all these hungry mouths is to scatter the cereal by the handful to the children on the floor. Chicken noises from the soundtrack accompany his actions. The absurd intersection at which the two conventional phases (feeding children and chickens) collide is the implicit metaphor comparing impoverished people to farm animals. The action inaugurating the defamiliarization is Charlie's familiar scattering gesture, which reveals the shameful reality of urban life.

Chaplin's gags are strictly visual, as are many routines in Beckett. But in Beckett, we also find verbal correlatives to this comic silent-film principle. *Waiting for Godot* demonstrates two automatisms in collision. Half of the gag is represented by the miniature plays within a play that the characters enact. The other half of the gag is the timeless automatism subtly implied in the ambiguous gerund or participle of the title—waiting. Inevitably, this second phase overpowers the dehumanizing first phase, the merely ostensible reality of the deadening habits that Didi and Gogo adopt to try to escape at least momentarily from the suffocating stasis of the authentic reality through which they must live.

In the play, three levels of defamiliarization work interdependently to expose the former, now impotent significance of the conventions parodied in the plays within a play, in the drama written by Beckett and presented aesthetically on stage for the audience's benefit, and in the performance of life in which we as human beings participate. I discuss each of these theatrical arenas separately with the class, asking the students to point out instances from the play. We move slowly from the most basic parodic-satiric level, through the second level with its self-conscious allusions to roles, and finally to the third more indirect level, which implicates not only the audience but also the class analyzing the text and the instructor orchestrating the analysis.

On the first level, Havel's defamiliarization is effected when the tramps, bored with and frightened by empty space and time, attempt to fill up this vacancy with games and skits; their absurdity announces itself when they momentarily slip up in some way, intentionally or not; the instant the mask or role is dropped, their real desperation is exposed. The extended puns, for instance, that function schizophrenically in a literal and a metaphoric sense represent only one Beckettian adaptation of the Chaplin gag. While trying to say goodbye to Pozzo, the tramps suddenly find themselves in a net of social niceties and clichés. Pozzo finally declares his inability to depart, and Gogo sums up the ritual with a ridiculous and painful truism: "Such is life" (31a; equally conventional in the French version's "C'est la vie" [79]). The words strike the audience as a supercilious response, but the remark immediately undergoes defamiliarization as Didi's and Gogo's dilemma is mercilessly exposed to the tramps and to us.

The sly, scarcely noticeable change of a crucial word in a linguistic formula is another way in which Beckett defamiliarizes accepted beliefs, forcing us to recognize their conventionality and our mechanistic adoption of them as a panacea. Didi's comment "Well? If we gave thanks for our mercies?" (41b) instead of the catechistic "thanks for His mercies" inverts religion so that human beings must now be merciful and forgiving to a formerly omnipotent God. In this example, Havel's two phases are still intact if less explicit. Beckett demonstrates the irony of religious automatism by omitting the first phase since he expects the audience to share a religious education and background, a heritage that in itself constitutes the first phase, the absurd automatism that awaits exposure as the reality is unmasked.

The technique of defamiliarizing the automatism or convention works also in the play's imagery. Beckett's extended canine imagery, for instance, equates a human being to a dog "chained to his vomit" (Beckett, *Proust* 8), an analogy that belies Gogo's insistence that they are "not tied" (14a). Despite their awareness, even Didi and Gogo illustrate doglike features in waiting for Godot. The subtle orthographic difference between god and dog depends entirely on perspective and brings up the embarrassing question of human origin. Are humans made in God's image, sharing in certain divine characteristics, or do they bear a greater resemblance to the domestic pet so lauded for its patience and loyalty? Lucky, however, is the character most closely associated with the dog imagery, and he also suffers most obviously from automation. Pozzo commands him with a whip, and everything Lucky does is a performance of some sort. Pozzo asks the tramps, "Shall we have him dance, or sing, or recite, or think, or—" (26a). Lucky's actual performance is the closest Beckett's play ever comes to a machine analogy (28a–30b). Not only do the heaps of academic verbal formulas point to intellectual automatism but Lucky's working parts also stutter and cough: "quaquaquaqua" and "Acacacacademy" equate the ostensibly learned text with duck nonsense and excrement (28b). The audience of three becomes alarmed at Lucky's machine behavior, which is now clearly out of control, and they try to stop him; only by seizing his hat does Didi render Lucky silent.

In Chaplin, the deflation or defamiliarization of performance occurs when we recognize the *real* reason for a gag. Charlie's collisions with the social and economic machinery of society expose the essential absurdity beneath this pretense at civilization and its alienating effect on the participants. However, Charlie is Chaplin's unconscious victim; his hilarious struggles represent our instructive entertainment because they mirror and, therefore, implicate our own difficulties. Beckett's tramps function similarly but with the crucial difference that they are acutely aware of their performances. The purpose of this second level of defamiliarization is to demonstrate the subhumanity of human beings' imprisonment in convention and alienation from themselves. To return to themselves, to regain their souls, human beings must play spectator to their own acting, their own theatricality. The displacement or deflation of performance is thus at the center of Beckett's play.

Didi and Gogo feel their performance defamiliarized when they arrive at the end of a skit to face renewed boredom and stasis. The long inventory of idioms and clichés beginning with "Don't let's do anything. It's safer" (12b) ends abruptly with the conventional verbal formula "I think it is," "I think so too" (13a), the unnerving ambiguity of which fails to continue the previous linguistic anesthetic by bringing the two tramps face-to-face with the consciousness implicit in the verb "think." In other words, thoughtless or automatic dialogue is still the safest means of communication. Although the tramps jump in and out of roles, they are never far from an awareness of the larger performance that is life. Didi moans, "Come on, Gogo, return the ball, can't you, once in a way?" (9a). I encourage the class to discuss the play's several self-references to performance: "Off we go again" (32a, 58b); "Here we go" (24b); "But it is not for nothing I have lived through this long day and I can assure you it is very near the end of its repertory" (55a). All these quotations indicate the extent of the tramps' recognition of their theatrical roles, a recognition that brings with it the suspicion that the performance must be on someone's behalf. Their "waiting for . . . waiting" (50a) represents the drama they enact for us, perhaps, but also possibly for Godot, who has little reason to appear since that would effectively put an end to his personal entertainment. His repeated nonappearance makes clear his own need and desire for distraction. However, the two tramps occasionally enjoy being spectators themselves. Gogo directs his friend to the men's room: "End of the corridor, on the left," while Didi tells him, "Keep my seat" (23b). For a change, Didi and Gogo have the benefit of Pozzo and Lucky's performance. Their indulgence in watching as distraction from being watched is given comic and dramatic focus in act 2, where Didi and Gogo enjoy the spectacle of Pozzo's pitiful predicament, equating it first to a racing event and then to a boxing match: "He's off! (*Pozzo collapses.*) He's down!" (53b). Didi's heartless metaphors not only denigrate Pozzo's suffering but also reveal how the tramps view their own endless imprisonment with regard to Godot, who takes inexplicable delight in keeping them on stage for his amusement.

On the third level of defamiliarization are Beckett's references to the audience and to our necessary and correlative role as spectators in the performance of attending the theater: "Inspiring prospects" (10a); "Not a soul in sight!" (47b). Indeed, Didi claims that they are at the right place because he recognizes it from before: "All the same . . . that tree . . . (*turning towards auditorium*) that bog . . ." (10b). This ambiguous analogy implies that any audience is no better than a swampy, foul-smelling waste receptacle. The direct references to the audience are only the most obvious signs of this third level. Throughout the drama, Beckett has his characters display themselves both as actors and as spectators to bring home to us the essential "drama" of life in which we play roles and expect others to play back.

If the class is performance-oriented, group presentations of selected sections of the drama are effective in forcing the participants to confront the theatricality of Beckett's work. Even during the first rehearsals, the students realize they are acting a play within a larger play. The performance (for example, of saying goodbye to Pozzo) within a performance (as actors posing as tramps playing for us and for Godot) within a performance (as students in front of a class and a teacher) demonstrates to them the artificiality and pretense that Beckett sees as the basis of existence.

My classroom treatment of *Waiting for Godot* concludes with a discussion of the inadequacy of conventional definitions in describing the play. I reiterate the process of the defamiliarization of performance, which exposes the absurdity and reveals the authentic reality both of the self and of that self in a specific setting. What the drama demands of us is an anagnorisis, an intrinsic part of Havel's idea of contemporary catharsis. In recognizing the pretenses of the ostensible reality that we actively and passively create, we rid ourselves of our previous slavery to such automation. However, Beckett asks not that we abolish all conventions and habits, only that we recognize our need for them and our role in creating them. Whether we as a class see the drama onstage or discuss it in the classroom, we need to explore the conventions that constitute our own activity of waiting. Approaching the play through the Chaplinesque film gag can help us do so.

NOTES

[1]If an instructor wishes to focus sharply on Beckettian parody and satire through Chaplin and Havel, a film such as *The Tramp* (1915) is an excellent choice since its humor deals with the deflation of specific literary and social traditions. For a discussion of the various Chaplin films, see Clausius, *The Gentleman Is a Tramp*. Others who connect Beckett with the comic film tradition, albeit indirectly, include Pilling (69) and Cohn (*Comic Gamut* 211; *Currents* 190).

[2]A word of caution about the film *Easy Street*: Although the character Charlie is a tramp at the beginning of the film, he plays a police officer throughout; an explanation is therefore required of the derby, cane, and boots tradition (so obvious in *The Tramp*) to which Beckett alludes in the costumes and some of the properties he specifies.

COURSE CONTEXTS

Waiting for Godot and the Forms of Tragedy

Mary Scott Simpson

In the course Forms of Drama: Tragedy, my goal is to help students understand the reasons audiences have turned to that genre throughout the centuries. What needs—emotional, intellectual, and spiritual—has tragedy perennially addressed, and why does it survive? In class, we move together inductively through twelve plays in fourteen weeks, beginning with the Greeks and ending with *Equus* (my syllabus dictated in part, of course, by the anthologies available at the time), accumulating as we go an increasingly complex understanding of the boundaries of the form. By the time we reach *Waiting for Godot* in its penultimate slot on the syllabus, students have learned to accommodate, indeed appreciate, the elasticity of the outlines of tragic form. This is good, because Beckett's play pushes the boundaries not just of traditional genres but of dramatic form itself about as far as can be without leaving the form behind.

The first half of the course consists of encounters with six classic tragedies: *Agamemnon, Oedipus Rex, The Bacchae, Hamlet, King Lear,* and *Phaedra*. Students record their developing understanding of the character and career of the tragic protagonist in a five-page critical essay. In it, they test one of three theories (those of Robert Heilman, Susanne Langer, and Maud Bodkin) against their experience of three classic plays, two Greek and one Shakespearean. In the second half of the course, we extend and refine our understanding of tragic form by studying six modern plays: *Hedda Gabler, The*

Cherry Orchard, Saint Joan, Death of a Salesman, Waiting for Godot, and *Equus.* In a second five-page paper, students evaluate the prospects for tragedy as a form in the present age. They examine one of the six modern plays in the light both of our discussions and of ideas raised in perspectives by Arthur Miller, Joseph Wood Krutch, Orrin E. Klapp, and John Gassner. (The critical essays referred to here appear in the first edition of Robert W. Corrigan's anthology, *Tragedy: Vision and Form,* which I place on reserve in the library.)

In the first lecture of the course, I present a scheme that we use throughout the semester to organize our discussions of the plays. I propose that we sort the issues we'll consider into these four "bins":

1. the tragic universe (the context in which the action occurs—metaphysical, theological, social, historical, etc.)
2. the tragic protagonist (his or her attributes, virtues, vices, values; the trajectory followed by that character's fortunes in the play)
3. tragic form (plot, subplots, dialogue—e.g., prose or verse, lyrical or dramatic, structure and pacing of scenes)
4. the emotional effects of tragedy (Does it raise and expel fear and pity? Does it make us weep? How do we feel during and at the end of the play?)

Students are, quite naturally, preoccupied with the tragic hero for most of the course; it is identification (or the failure thereof) with that character that determines their feelings toward each play. I find I must emphasize fairly energetically the four-part scheme. Without it, students tend to bestow the approving label *tragedy* on the basis of whether they like or dislike a play's central character and whether they are glad or sorry to see that character suffer. To succeed in the primary goal announced in my first paragraph, I must succeed in a secondary goal: teaching students to see the interrelations between tragic universe and tragic protagonist, tragic form and its effects on us.

Students appreciate, in the second half of their semester, the colloquial dialogue of modern realism; they tend to respond to Hedda Gabler and the Loman family, for instance, as they would to next-door neighbors or troubled kinfolk. But they realize, in retrospect, that the formality of the Greeks' interest in a play's characters, together with the resonances of imagery-rich verse, lends a dignity to classic tragic characters that is lacking in the moderns. This use of informal language means that a diluted intellectual and spiritual effect accompanies the greater emotional impact of the realistic dialogue and approach to character. Similarly, having come to understand the connection between the subplot in *King Lear* and that play's assurance that its action occurs in a lawful (if harsh) universe, students can appreciate the modern playwrights' search for compensatory formal means to impose coherence—intelligibility—on the worlds they embody in their plays.

In other words, by the time we reach *Godot*, students have learned to make a fairly subtle inventory of a play before proclaiming what it is or means. They have learned that tragic "status" is conferred on a protagonist in part by the laws of the universe into which he or she is thrust; that elements of form such as repeated patterns in the action, reversals of expectation, and recognition scenes are used by playwrights to reveal what laws govern that universe, what is possible within it; that the effects of tragic drama on the audience may be as much a matter of pleasure in the apprehension of form imposed on suffering as they are a consequence of identifying with a character's inner life.

I have learned by now to allocate a few moments at the start of class discussion of *Waiting for Godot* to general grousing: "Who *are* these people?" "*Why* are you making us read this?" The moaning and groaning are all the louder since the play follows *Death of a Salesman*, with its ardent courtship of audience sympathy for its characters. Didi and Gogo make only abstract claims on the attention of today's students, who require some coaching to warm up to them. I usually begin by inviting students to make a list of the questions they ask themselves as they read the play, and I solicit their help in making sure that we get around to considering those questions—if not resolving them—by the time we finish our discussion.

Didi's perplexity over the Christian story of the two thieves, raised early in the play, helps students see the epistemology in which the play is grounded; for me, this epistemology is the key to understanding both the behavior of the characters and the form of the play. Students usually need to be reminded of the biblical material in the story to which Didi alludes. This done, I ask why Beckett would include this material so early in the play—in what sense it might serve as a springboard for all that follows. I point out (or sometimes a student points out) that the Bible has been for centuries a primary source of guidance to Western culture. Then we observe that, according to Didi, the story of the two thieves—with its implicit instruction about what one does to be damned, what one does to be saved—is of uncertain authority (9a–9b). The conclusion easily follows that Beckett is here raising questions about the reliability of the knowledge on which many people base their lives. Whether or not we are Christian, individually, we have inherited a culture dominated by the precepts of Christianity; to undermine those precepts— as do the conflicting accounts of the fates of the two thieves—is to undermine radically the basis for all action. If a Christian, for example, cannot be assured that to affirm Christ will bring salvation and that to deny Christ will bring damnation, what can he or she be sure of? (That I teach in a Catholic college is of considerable help in driving home this point.) Later in the discussion when we examine Lucky's "thinking" speech, his contradictory propositions about God, which parody both medieval theologians and modern-day pastors, neatly secure this impression of the unreliability of traditional guides to human action (28b–29b).

Having perceived the shaky epistemology with which Didi and Gogo must be content, students are quick to point out the myriad other terms of the tramps' existence that are shrouded in uncertainty: Who is Godot? What does he want? What will he give in return? Will he come? What will they do if he doesn't? The tramps are beset (the students with them) by other questions as well: Why does Gogo get beaten day after day? Who are Pozzo and Lucky? Why can't they get up when they fall down and, then, why can they get up later? Is there one boy or two? Are those Gogo's boots on stage at the start of act 2? What day is it? What year? What country? How long has this been going on? Beckett's refusal to give us firm answers to these questions is, of course, his way of putting his audience in the same universe—intellectually, emotionally, spiritually—that his characters inhabit.

By plunging headlong into the unanswered questions of the play, I encourage the students to trust their reactions to it. This seems to me the best way to get them to entertain the possibility that the universe is essentially whimsical, arbitrary in its operations, that it is not grounded in that firm (if harsh) lawfulness that we glimpsed in the classic tragedies. Why, I ask, are good intentions sometimes enough and sometimes not? Why are some people victims and others not, despite apparently identical circumstances? Why must virtue sometimes be its own, its only, reward? In other words, I encourage identification with the predicament of Didi and Gogo—the perception that their universe is our universe, stripped of diversions. It is a predicament that must be suffered if the play is to have its effect on us.

At this point, I remind students of Hamlet's perplexity, his slowness to act. Like Didi and Gogo, he is thrown into a world he did not make, called on to right wrongs he did not commit, given orders of dubious authority. The crucial difference is, of course, that Hamlet's world is saturated by clear and present evil; Didi and Gogo must contend with an indifferent wisp of a God who may, or more likely may not, approve and reward their service. Having easily forgiven Hamlet his procrastination, students are now willing to reconsider the reasonableness of Beckett's refrain, "Nothing to be done" (7a, 8a, 8b, 14b). They are also ready to consider the possibility that Beckett has produced the perfect drama, the perfect "doing," the perfect form for these characters and their world to inhabit—a form at least as suitable for Beckett's matter as was that of the Greeks or of Shakespeare for theirs.

Godot is difficult for students not only because it raises and refuses to answer so many questions but also because its characters, as one student put it, "seem to be going around in circles." (She had at that point, alas, finished only the first act!) The apparent repetition of act 1 in the events of act 2 is especially frustrating to students by now accustomed to grand actions that sweep across the stage like natural disasters—lightning bolts or floods, leaving behind them dead bodies and blasted lives. The repeated stage direction *"They do not move"* (35b, 60b) seems to mock not only the characters but the audience as well. This stasis exists on a large scale in the play but also occurs within smaller scenic units. I show students the many small starts and stops in the first act—the moving from one "routine" to the next. And I ask them what effect this repeated pattern—this rhythm—of action leading nowhere over and over again has on Didi and Gogo and, eventually, on their audience. They say it's depressing, and I agree.

Critics often argue that *Waiting for Godot* is essentially plotless, if by *plot* we mean a movement through the actions of characters from one condition or situation to another—action effecting change. (This claim is especially meaningful to students who have come to consider a change in the condition of the protagonist as a prime criterion for labeling an action as "tragic.") To evaluate this critical consensus, I ask students to reconsider the apparent changelessness of the play and to list differences between the two acts.

For one thing, act 2 is considerably shorter than act 1. Pozzo and Lucky are changed—for the worse—in the second act, gone blind and dumb, respectively. The second act begins with the round song (37a–37b), which both reasserts the pattern of pointless and inescapable repetition that governed act 1 and announces more of the same for act 2. Having spent much of act 1 wondering where all this is leading, the audience, on hearing the round song, is ushered into act 2 with lowered expectations, dimmer hopes. Further, the tone of the routines in act 2, like the tone of its opening song (about the death of a dog), is considerably gloomier than that of act 1. The elegiac mood of the "[a]ll the dead voices" routine is typical (40b).

Finally, I ask students to consider Didi's pair of conversations with the boy (or boys) at the end of acts 1 and 2. Questions that appeared in act 1 have become weary statements at the end of act 2, statements that the boy can only affirm. This shift, too, represents a significant change in mood and in tone. The exchange in act 2 follows what can be called, legitimately I believe, a "recognition speech" from Didi:

> Was I sleeping, while the others suffered? Am I sleeping now? To-morrow, when I wake, or think I do, what shall I say of to-day? That with Estragon my friend, at this place, until the fall of night, I waited for Godot? That Pozzo passed, with his carrier, and that he spoke to us? Probably. But in all that what truth will there be?
>
> (58a)

Tutored by the embittered Pozzo, Didi repeats his lesson: "Astride of a grave and a difficult birth. Down in the hole, lingeringly, the grave-digger puts on the forceps" (58a).

Students can now appreciate Beckett's skill in sending thoroughly human characters through an action, a "doing" that leaves the more reflective and articulate Didi, at least, more knowing at the end of the play than he was at the start. Didi, I argue, has learned as a result of his urgent but futile initiatives through the course of the play. Because Didi and Gogo are invested with such elemental humanity and because Beckett has teased us into whiling away with them a couple of hours, scratching our heads as they scratch theirs, bumping our noses on the inscrutable as they bump theirs, we are in a position to learn along with Didi. We are in a position to be moved by his declaration, "The air is full of our cries" (58a–58b).

I may now remind students that their response to the Greek characters was generally cooler than their response to Shakespeare's eloquent sufferers and to the realists' acutely drawn psyches. I also observe that our discussion of *Godot* has required more intellectual and aesthetic but less emotional and psychological sensitivity from them. I ask them what this pair of facts about reader or viewer response tells us about the possible effects of tragedy on an audience. Accustomed by now to such modulations in their understanding of tragedy, the students can produce, working together, a fairly sophisticated insight: that writing (or receiving) tragedy is not a matter of following a simple recipe—so many fatal flaws, so many deaths, so many soliloquies or choral odes.

The four-part scheme used throughout the course helps alert students to the widely differing components of an experience that necessarily depends on the playwright and the age, theatrical conventions, and the disposition of the audience. But the scheme merely helps us think about the plays; it cannot make judgments for us on the propriety of calling *Death of a Salesman*, for instance, or *Waiting for Godot* a tragedy. Calling *Godot* a tragedy would be particularly impertinent, since its author does not make that claim on its behalf; and, as for Miller's play, most students conclude—despite the author's essay "Tragedy and the Common Man"—that Willy Loman is not a satisfactory tragic hero.

The scheme does, however, give students a thread to hold on to as they wander in the formal labyrinth devised for them by Beckett. They see that if Didi and Gogo cannot be called tragic heroes, it is not for lack of trying to take action—it is for lack of a lawful (that is, predictable, orderly) universe in which to act. Beckett, by imposing the clarity of perfect form on the chaos of modern life, has enlightened his audience and reconciled us to our makeshift humanity.

Waiting for Godot as a Touchstone in a Modern and Contemporary Drama Course

Katherine H. Burkman

I often use *Waiting for Godot* to begin my undergraduate course on modern drama, which treats dramatists from Ibsen to Marsha Norman; I also begin with *Godot* in my graduate seminars, whether they cover several modern and contemporary playwrights or focus on Chekhov, Beckett, and Pinter. This placement allows the play to become a touchstone for both what has come before and what has come since. It helps students to see the thematic relation of *Godot* to other modern and contemporary plays and to focus on ways that Beckett's dramatic techniques have grown out of the drama of the past and have influenced today's playwrights.

Through *Waiting for Godot* teachers may introduce two major, seemingly contradictory, themes in modern drama, those of homelessness and confinement. The situation of Didi and Gogo out there in the void, with Estragon repeatedly suggesting that they depart and Vladimir always reminding him that they are bound to wait for Godot, may appear absurd. Of course, since Martin Esslin coined the term theater of the absurd, such combinations of exile and bondage have been explored in the absurdist context. But the logic of such absurdity has not escaped my students, who laughed with me when a classmate suggested that the tramps simply should go out and find a job.

The situation becomes clearer, however, when the class explores Ibsen's Hedda Gabler, entrapped in a world that offers her no "job" and so alienated from a home that cannot in any way be truly hers that she chooses suicide, an idea with which the *Godot* tramps merely flirt. The combination of exile and bondage becomes clearer still when students explore the Chekhovian landscape, which is filled with arrivals and departures that often lead to dispossession from the home (*The Three Sisters* or *The Cherry Orchard*), or when they consider characters such as Firs of *The Cherry Orchard*, who, like Lucky, deals with the void by embracing a form of bondage. If students see how the combination of exile and bondage works in the realistic plays of Ibsen or the naturalistic plays of Chekhov and O'Neill (it is no more absurd to think of Didi and Gogo looking for a job than it is to think of the bums in O'Neill's *Iceman Cometh* returning to a world of work), they can grasp the existential condition that is somewhat subtextual in those plays and that is explored in all its absurdity by Beckett.

Indeed, although teachers may pursue these themes as they are worked out under the *Godot* influence by such absurdist playwrights as Stoppard, Pinter, or Shepard, students can also see how they still linger in Norman's realistic play *'Night, Mother*, in which the nonarriving Godot is the hero herself: "I'm what was worth waiting for and I didn't make it" (76), Jessie tells her elderly mother as an explanation for her planned suicide. Suicide as a possible way out of the alienation of the modern condition has been prevalent from Ibsen's Hedda and Hedvig (*The Wild Duck*) to Strindberg's Miss Julie to Albee's Jerry (*The Zoo Story*) to Ionesco's octogenarians (*The Chairs*), and the class may better understand its possibility as an alternative to waiting in Beckett's play by looking at Norman's treatment of it in the later play. As one of my students writes, "What Didi and Gogo are bound to suffer forever in the absurd world, Jessie can bring to an end in the realistic one" (Gorjanc 5). The many comparisons this student makes between the two plays suggest to me not only that she came to understand Jessie's situation by her study of *Godot* but that she had new insight into the Beckett play because of her understanding of Norman's. Mama, she says of Jessie's mother, would not come to accept Jessie's death as she does in the play if she lived in the *Godot* world where "she still would be wondering what she could have done to change Jessie's mind, in essence what she could have done to change reality" (8). Perhaps what we can teach our students through this kind of contextualizing of the *Godot* situation is the thin line, if there even is one, between the real and the absurd.

In *The Theatre of the Absurd* Esslin helps us to see how central Beckett is to a discussion of the contemporary sense of homelessness as part of a cosmic sense of alienation that leaves people in a state of "metaphysical anguish" (5). Indeed, Jessie's way of resolving her "waiting" problem, her refusal to seek salvation from an outside force, sets her apart from many other characters in the modern canon. For the modern playwright's quest, according to Robert Brustein, is still a religious one; having given up a belief in traditional savior figures, the playwright tries "to make a new union out of his secession—to make his initial act of revolt the occasion for a new kind of grace" (11). *Waiting for Godot*, in these terms, becomes a seminal work for the discussion of the quest for salvation in modern drama; and Godot himself may become a symbol for savior figures whose arrival or expulsion is central to the action of many plays (Burkman, *Arrival* 14).

Students begin to understand the absurdity of *Waiting for Godot* as they focus on the "existential anguish" involved in the modern quest for salvation. Hedda, after all, may not have been able to get a job in her day, but the plight of women has improved somewhat since then. The denizens of Harry Hope's bar may be unable to join the outside world, but that world is still a possibility in O'Neill's drama. We can help our students get closer to the existential nature of the absurd in Beckett's drama, then, not only by inviting them to look at its themes in more realistic plays but also by introducing them to less realistic plays; for, as Ruby Cohn suggests in "Growing (Up?) with Godot," "In its own rebellion against realism *Waiting for Godot* enfolds some of its dramatic predecessors . . ." (23). Hence, when the class encounters Pirandello—whose six characters have been rejected by their creator and left to seek an author and to try to create a sense of self in a melodramatic plot that they do not understand—students may better understand why Didi and Gogo await a figure who they hope will give meaning to their lives. In Strindberg's *Ghost Sonata*, in which the realistic facade that Arkenholtz perceives at the play's opening hides those ghosts (the Mummy, the vampire servant) that Ibsen only speaks about in *Ghosts*, students come to see how Arkenholtz's initiation into the house's poisoned nothingness is akin to Vladimir's initiation into the void in *Waiting for Godot*.

The antirealistic techniques of Ionesco also do much to clarify the encounter with nothingness that is, in my view, the action of *Waiting for Godot* (Burkman, *Arrival* 33–52); similarly, Beckett's play illuminates the encounter with nothingness that makes up the dramatic action of such plays as *The Chairs* or *The Killer*. In *The Chairs* when the orator, who is to speak the Old Man's message about the meaning of life to invited guests, turns out to be a mute addressing an invisible multitude, Godot in a sense has arrived, but he is a false messiah whose silence is as much an absence as Godot's is in Beckett's play. In *The Killer* when Berenger confronts the killer, who possibly isn't even present, he confronts his own sense of nothingness in a godless world. This confrontation is closely related to the fragile sense of self that haunts Didi and Gogo and accounts for their insistence that the messenger tell Godot he saw them.

The muteness of the orator and the killer, of course, parallels the muteness that Lucky acquires in *Godot* and easily leads to a discussion of the uses of silence in modern drama. John Russell Brown, in "Beckett and the Art of Nonplus," points out that in Beckett's plays "action is constantly arrested in silence" (31). Beckett, Brown suggests, is the master of what often happens in the silence in Chekhov, a moment of "nonplus" that offers insight into the "action of the author's mind as it works toward the place where it can reach no more" (45). Brown cites similar moments in *The Woods*, by David Mamet, or in *The Caretaker* and *Old Times*, by Harold Pinter: for example, in *Old Times* "Pinter's skeptical romanticism comes to delicate life in silence" (43). Whether it be the mute children in Pirandello's *Six Characters in Search of an Author*, the mute daughter in Brecht's *Mother Courage*, the silent Matchseller in Pinter's *Slight Ache*, or Ionesco's mute orator, the question of silence both as it works symbolically in these characters and as it works in the pauses and silences that are part of the rhythms of the plays is illuminated by Lucky's silence. Similarly, the silence in these other dramas tells us something about Lucky's situation or the rhythms of Beckett's drama.

The silence in postmodern literature, Ihab Hassan suggests, although it leaves us "with uneasy intimations of outrage and apocalypse" (3), need not be wholly negative. Hassan, who is talking about Beckett but who might as well be talking specifically about Lucky, suggests that "revulsion against the self serves as a link between the destructive and visionary impulses of modern apocalypse; it prepares for rebirth" (5). When I teach *Waiting for Godot* in the context of other modern and contemporary plays, I am particularly concerned with this rebirth, which Hassan suggests may be part of the silence in postmodern literature. I have never found the play nihilistic or despairing, but I have had difficulty conveying to my students (and to several colleagues) my sense that the play is, in part, very affirmative. To place it in the context of other modern dramas, however, is helpful.

Exploring *Waiting for Godot* in relation to Tom Stoppard's *Rosencrantz and Guildenstern Are Dead* and Harold Pinter's *Slight Ache* may be of particular use here. Stoppard is deeply influenced by Beckett not only in his metatheatrics—which Beryl S. Fletcher and John Fletcher call "the one possible unifying characteristic of modernist drama" (29)—but also in his creation of a pair of disoriented fools. Lost in *Hamlet*, even as Didi and Gogo are lost in their particular void, Stoppard's duo escapes nihilism through game playing. We accept their lostness, their inability to figure out their roles in life, because this disorientation is treated tragicomically; as in much modern drama, the tragicomic allows distance from "metaphysical anguish" so that we, like Pozzo, can go "on" in the face of it. But the play also suggests that Stoppard's pair has a greater complicity in their fate than Didi and Gogo do in theirs:

> GUIL: Our names shouted in a certain dawn . . . a message . . . a summons. . . . There must have been a moment, at the beginning, where we could have said—no. But somehow we missed it.
>
> (125)

Didi and Gogo don't miss a thing. Vladimir goes beyond his intellectualizing to a true crisis of faith, which, beneath a seeming disorientation, Estragon has been undergoing all along. Fools indeed, but with that wisdom of the fool that allows their disorientation to suggest a new orientation and openness to the mystery of things, in which they never quite lose their faith. Unlike Stoppard's fools, who never manage to "be" and who hence disappear instead of dying, or Simon Gray's fools in such plays as *Butley* and *Otherwise Engaged*, who are defeated by the disintegrating society they reflect and mock, Beckett's fools endure and share the mystery with us—affirmation enough.

Of today's playwrights, however, Pinter may be the most instructive for an exploration of Beckett's play. Beckett's influence on several contemporary playwrights is pervasive, of course, as we see in Susan D. Brienza's discussion of Shepard and Beckett or in Albee's forays into the dislocations of language in a play such as *The American Dream*. But Pinter remains, in my estimation,

Beckett's most important successor (see Esslin, "Godot and His Children"), and the study of Pinter's plays is instructive for helping students understand *Waiting for Godot* in the context of modern drama.

In *A Slight Ache*, for example, the Matchseller may be examined as a figure of mystery whose silence, like the pauses or silences that are part of the rhythm of the dialogue, invites the journey of interior exploration that Edward takes as he confronts him. The Matchseller may also be discussed as a character who brings renewal to the frustrated Flora. What I am suggesting here is a tragicomic arrival of Godot (Burkman, *Dramatic World* 47–64). Pinter goes beyond Beckett in investigating the actual rhythms of renewal; Godot almost always does arrive in one form or another in his plays, but through fool characters such as the Matchseller or mythic arrivals such as that of Ruth in *The Homecoming*. Pinter's Godots could not conceivably have arrived had they not evolved in some special way from Beckett's mysterious nonarriving Godot. Pinter, in the poetry of his language, silences, and stage images, has gone further down the *Godot* road than most others who have traveled it. His mythic vision is so infused with Beckettian poetry that the journeys of the two playwrights seem entirely interdependent.

Teachers who use *Waiting for Godot* as a touchstone in the study of modern drama help students grasp how the genre has moved from Chekhovian dispossession to the Beckettian void and beyond. While the play offers insight into what has come before and after its creation, its study in the context of other dramas illuminates its complexity both as a meditation on the wasteland and as a drama fertile with endless and mysterious riches.

Teaching *Waiting for Godot* in a French Drama Course

Dina Sherzer

In *Waiting for Godot*, Beckett has invented an idiosyncratic dramatic language that for many students transforms all previously familiar modes of expression. For students in a French drama course to understand this deceptively simple and seemingly uneventful play, it is important to consider several of its textual features. Thus, after giving some brief biographical and stage-historical background information, instructors may proceed by analyzing the genre, structure, content, characters, and language of the play. Then they may discuss the possible meanings of the play as a metaphysical and existential statement, as a work that inserts itself into our postmodernity, as a contribution to the theater of the absurd, and as a landmark or launching pad in Beckett's career.

Background

La cantatrice chauve (*The Bald Soprano*), by Eugène Ionesco, was performed for the first time in Paris in 1950. Spectators watched an unusual play that had no soprano, bald or otherwise. They heard the characters engage in nonsensical dialogues and interchanges. In 1953, Beckett's *En attendant Godot* was staged in Paris, and the theater of the absurd was born. This time, the spectators saw tramps waiting on an empty stage, behaving like clowns, falling, exchanging hats and words, and making time go by. *The Bald Soprano* is still performed in Paris, and *Waiting for Godot*, perhaps the most famous play of the twentieth century, has been translated into many languages and staged in many countries.

Beckett, an Irishman with a degree from Trinity College, Dublin, where he had studied French and Italian, wrote *Godot* while living in Paris. He had decided to write in French and was already the author of *Molloy*, *Malone meurt*, *L'innommable*, a trilogy of novels. Ironically, the manuscript of *Molloy* had been rejected by several publishing houses before Jérôme Lindon, the director of a new publishing company, Editions de Minuit, accepted it. With *Molloy*, Beckett became the first of the many prestigious experimental novelists, grouped under the label *nouveau roman*, who were associated with Editions de Minuit. Two of these authors, Beckett and Claude Simon, were later awarded the Nobel Prize for literature.

Genre

When students think of French theater two genres come to mind, comedy and tragedy. Comedy is synonymous with Molière, the seventeenth-century dramatist who mocks hypocrisy, miserliness, and pedantry in such plays as *Tartuffe*, *L'avare*, and *Les femmes savantes*. Molière sees his task as making spectators laugh in order to instruct them (*faire rire pour les corriger*). After several events skirt catastrophe, his plays end with happy resolutions. Bad characters are punished or neutralized, and good ones, usually young people, have their way and get married. Comedy in France is also associated with the names of Marivaux and Beaumarchais in the eighteenth century and with Musset in the nineteenth century. Marivaux explores the nuances of love in *Le jeu de l'amour et du hasard*. His refined and polite characters exchange an elegant "badinage." Beaumarchais in *Le barbier de Séville* and *Le mariage de Figaro* deploys a biting satire against nobility. His servants dare to be insolent, to confront the nobility, and to point out injustices. Musset's *On ne badine pas avec l'amour* creates a mood both pathetic and comic in its presentation of love.

Tragedy, in the works of Corneille and Racine, evokes knots and tangles, complicated intrigues that involve issues of honor, war, politics, and passion. Characters are kings, princesses, and heroes in the grips of a dilemma. In Corneille's *Le Cid*, Rodrigue has been charged by his father to fight in a duel with the father of his beloved, Chimène. If he refuses the duel and does not avenge his family's honor, he spares Chimène's father but loses her esteem. If he kills Don Gomès, he kills his beloved's father. In *Phèdre*, Racine masterfully depicts the torments of Phèdre's passion for her stepson, Hippolyte. The young man is destroyed by the gods at the request of his own father, Thésée, who has been told that Hippolyte is attracted to Phèdre. Sorrow, violence, jealousy, cruelty, and fatality are the ingredients of tragedy familiar to students in a French drama class.

Waiting for Godot fits neither of these categories. With regard to its characters, its content, and its outcome, it is neither a classic comedy nor a classic tragedy. To find plays that are comparable to it, we must turn to the beginning of the twentieth century, to Alfred Jarry's *Ubu roi* and Roger Vitrac's *Victor ou les enfants au pouvoir*. *Ubu* is a farce full of vulgarity and grotesque happenings. Parodying Shakespeare and Racine, it contains murders, betrayals, killings, and exploitation. Vitrac's *Victor*, a surrealist play conceived in the spirit of *Ubu*, is a biting satire of the family and of adult hypocrisy. It mingles incongruous behaviors and surrealist monologues, which are meant to shock and disturb. Like these plays, *Waiting for Godot* belongs to a blurred genre that mixes tragedy and comedy and proposes an uncanny experience for the spectator. This blurred or hybrid genre is characteristic of the theater of the absurd. In France, in addition to Beckett, playwrights Arthur Adamov, Fernando Arrabal, Eugène Ionesco, and Robert Pinget have each contributed works in which the comic skirts the tragic and vice versa.

Structure and Content

Waiting for Godot is "a two-act play where nothing happens, twice," wrote Vivian Mercier in a review entitled "The Uneventful Event" (*Beckett/Beckett* 74). The same situation is repeated in both acts: Vladimir and Estragon are waiting; Pozzo and Lucky arrive, then leave; Vladimir and Estragon wait again. In addition, the same unmarked space, a road to somewhere not specified, and the same time of day, nightfall, provide the setting for the action. But the term *action* must be qualified for students since nothing happens or so it seems. While the play contains no descending movement toward an impending catastrophe or ascending movement toward a happy resolution, the succession of comic, sad, animated, and calm moments during which the characters interact moves the play along. Interestingly, this circular structure is not a static construction but a masterful orchestration of movements, face-to-face interactions, and verbal play. As Estragon says to Vladimir in the second act, "On trouve toujours quelque chose, hein, Didi, pour nous donner l'impression d'exister?" (116–17); "We always find something, eh Didi, to give us the impression we exist?" (44b).

Instead of resolving problems, clearing up a crisis, or giving answers, *Waiting for Godot* raises questions that remain unanswered. Who is Godot? Beckett said facetiously that if he knew he would have said so (qtd. by Schneider, in Esslin, *Collection* 55). Why are the characters waiting? They vaguely mention their hope of a warm place and a full stomach. Where do these characters come from? Why are they here? Why is one of them beaten during the night? How long is the interval, during which Pozzo becomes blind and Lucky deaf, between the two appearances of Pozzo and Lucky? The fact that the tree has leaves in the second act is not a precise indicator students can count on. The spectators are placed in a space outside time, history, and causality. Such lack of orientation in the content is in sharp contrast to traditional comedy or tragedy, in which dialogues or monologues inform the spectators who the characters are, why they are where they are, and what is at stake in their relationships and tangles. In addition, since Godot does not appear at the end of the two acts, the play does not really end. This open-endedness does not exist in the traditional comedy or tragedy students know, where the action is oriented toward a goal and resolutions always take place. Thus, the structure and content of *Waiting for Godot* are characterized by balance, symmetry, circularity, and indeterminacy.

Characters

Beckett's characters are not kings or princes as in the plays of Corneille and Racine; not servants, nobles, or members of the bourgeoisie as in the plays of Molière; not intellectuals or existentialists as in the plays of Sartre; and not middle- or upper-class characters as in the plays of Giraudoux. Rather, they are half tramp and half clown, that is, characters whose status in society is felt to be marginal. In that regard, the stage directions for the clothes, body positions, and activities of the characters give specific information that helps the student (and even the director who stages the play) to visualize or to create the type of character invented by Beckett. For instance, the text indicates that Estragon points to his *"haillons"* (17), *"rags"* (9a); that Vladimir searches in his pockets, *"archibondées de saletés de toutes sortes"* (22), *"bursting with miscellaneous rubbish"* (10b); and that the characters sleep outdoors in ditches. All these details are characteristics of the tramp. The stage directions specify many gestures, movements, or activities that we expect in Charlie Chaplin, the Marx Brothers, or a circus clown, such as spitting, eating a carrot or a turnip, zipping up one's fly or pulling up one's pants in public, juggling hats or words, falling down, or walking with short, stiff strides, legs wide apart. These behaviors display mechanical inelasticity, clumsiness, rigidity, stiffness, repetitiveness, and incongruity, all elements that, according to Henri Bergson, are the ingredients of the comic and provoke laughter.

The characters are grouped in two couples, with each pair forming a self-sufficient unit. The personalities of Vladimir and Estragon are complementary; like two brothers, two friends, or husband and wife, they address each other with the diminutives Didi and Gogo. Their relationship is one of dependence on each other in which friendship, hatred, tenderness, impatience, and hostility are expressed. Pozzo and Lucky also have a complementary relationship, but theirs is one of master and slave with a blend of sadism and masochism.

Language

What do the characters talk about in *Waiting for Godot?* Vladimir and Estragon talk about Godot, whom they are supposed to meet and do not know. They mention that Godot will give them food and shelter and often repeat that they have to wait for him. When Pozzo and Lucky come by, circumstantial questions are asked, and comments about the place and the weather are made. Lucky is ordered to deliver a speech just like an animal in a zoo is ordered to perform a special act. What he says is rather garbled. Indeed, the content of the play is flat, and not much meaningful information seems to be generated. But with Beckett, students need to adopt a perspective that does not focus only on the content but instead also pays attention to what characters do with language when they are speaking. In *Waiting for Godot*, the characters talk to make time pass, engaging in a series of speech activities such as asking questions, telling jokes, insulting each other, singing a song, delivering a long tirade, or clownishly bouncing words or expressions at each other as if playing Ping-Pong with them. These exchanges do not amount to an overall story that can be summed up at the end as in other plays from which students can extrapolate a narrative. An instance of this inconclusiveness and of the juggling with words appears when Estragon asks what Godot answered to the vague request that was made of him. Vladimir answers, "Qu'il verrait" (28), "That he'd see" (13a). Then the mechanism is started and words and expressions bounce back and forth, yielding no definitive answer:

ESTRAGON: Qu'il ne pouvait rien promettre.	That he couldn't promise anything.
VLADIMIR: Qu'il lui fallait réfléchir.	That he'd have to think it over.
ESTRAGON: A tête reposée.	In the quiet of his home.
VLADIMIR: Consulter sa famille.	Consult his family.
ESTRAGON: Ses amis.	His friends.
VLADIMIR: Ses agents.	His agents.
ESTRAGON: Ses correspondants.	His correspondents.
VLADIMIR: Ses registres.	His books.
ESTRAGON: Son compte en banque.	His bank account.

(28)   (13a)

Furthermore, students remember that characters in a play typically express themselves in the social register characteristic of their class. Molière, for instance, has his servants speak popular seventeenth-century French, while their masters speak a refined French. Racine is famous for the elegance and poetic quality of his dialogues. In the works of both authors, the verbal texture of the plays is characterized by linguistic unity and uniformity. Jarry is the first playwright who flouts this tradition. His scandalous *merdre* 'shittr,' which begins *Ubu*, is only the first of the semiobscene neologisms he invents. In addition, Ubu uses a mixture of slang, popular, and refined language. In *Waiting for Godot*, as well as in other longer plays, Beckett adopts the same strategy. Didi, Gogo, Pozzo, and Lucky, whose class and background are undetermined, are able to express themselves in high and low French and to use incongruous and vulgar as well as pedantic French. But they can also be refined, even poetic. They use baby talk and petit-nègre and make fun of the English. The play is truly a mosaic of linguistic registers and forms of talk. In fact, much of the pleasure that students of French derive from the play is due to these unexpected juxtapositions of style, these uncanny bouncings of words, the clownish repetitions of words and expressions, and the moments of sheer poetry, all of which happen in the most banal, uneventful situation: that of waiting (see Sherzer). To appreciate the linguistic versatility of Beckett's language, students need to compare the French and English in several passages. In the following examples, Beckett has a keen sense of French slang and popular speech:

> ESTRAGON: Assez. Aide-moi à enlever cette saloperie. (13)
> ESTRAGON: Ah stop blathering and help me off with this bloody thing. (7b)
>
> ESTRAGON: Les gens sont des cons. (19)
> ESTRAGON: People are bloody ignorant apes. (9b)
>
> VLADIMIR: Ah non, là tu te goures. (21)
> VLADIMIR: Ah no, there you're mistaken. (10b)

Students should also note the syntactic differences in the following passages:

> ESTRAGON: Possible. Je me rappelle les cartes de la Terre-Sainte. En couleur. Très jolies. La Mer-Morte était bleu pâle. J'avais soif rien qu'en la regardant. Je me disais, c'est là que nous irons passer notre lune de miel. Nous nagerons. Nous serons heureux. (16–17)
>
> ESTRAGON: I remember the maps of the Holy Land. Coloured they were. Very pretty. The Dead Sea was pale blue. The very look of it made me thirsty. That's where we'll go, I used to say, that's where we'll go for our honeymoon. We'll swim. We'll be happy. (8b)

The translation of a place name with a scatological wordplay should be emphasized by the instructor in the following example:

> ESTRAGON: Mais non, je n'ai jamais été dans le Vaucluse! J'ai coulé toute ma chaudepisse d'existence ici, je te dis! Ici! Dans la Merdecluse! (104)
>
> ESTRAGON: No I was never in the Macon country! I've puked my puke of a life away here, I tell you! Here! In the Cackon country! (40a)

Meanings and Interpretations

Our discussion then turns to possible interpretations of the play and the degree to which we can judge the power of a work by the variety of interpretations it suggests. After attending a performance of the play, the dramatist Jean Anouilh declared that he had seen "*Les pensées* de Pascal mises en sketches et jouées par les frères Fratellini" 'Pascal's *Pensées* arranged into skits and acted by the Fratellini Brothers [famous clowns]' (qtd. in Graver and Federman 92). This statement reflects the intellectual climate of the early 1950s. Pascal, the seventeenth-century Jansenist philosopher, is considered in France as a precursor of existentialism. In his pithy, powerful, and awe-inspiring texts, he emphasized the absurdity, smallness, and loneliness of the individual in the world and the impossibility of living without "divertissements." Pascal described the individual's plight in the world in order to turn people toward God. Existentialism also describes the plight of the individual in the world, but its aim is to emphasize the individual's freedom, responsibility, and necessity to act and to be committed. Beckett's play, with its two tramps waiting and talking about what to do to pass time, was read in the 1950s as a metaphysical statement about the human condition analogous to Pascal's and existentialist formulations. Beckett's new twist, which is, of course, an old tradition, is to invent characters who are clowns. This choice was a perfect one because clowns represent wisdom and are incongruous, but their incongruity is meaningful. Liminal characters, outsiders, they have their own power and knowledge, and with their seeming triviality, they speak the truth (see Willeford). Didi, Gogo, Pozzo, and Lucky are such clowns; they utter statements akin to those in Pascal's *Pensées*.

Another consideration with an existential orientation emerges if class discussions examine the genre of the play in the light of an article by René Girard in which he demonstrates (comparing Molière's *Le bourgeois gentilhomme* and Sophocles's *Oedipus Rex*) that both tragedy and comedy are organized by a principle of repetition that imprisons the individual. *Waiting for Godot*, which is both tragedy and comedy and is structured by repetition, is a metaphor representing the lack of freedom of individuals in the world.

Another subject for class consideration is the way in which, not surprisingly, *Waiting for Godot* also speaks to our postmodernity. Beckett wrote the play at the beginning of the postmodern period, after the creation of all the expressive innovations of modernism. The play is postmodern in many ways. It is an open work rather than a closed one, and it belongs to a blurred genre. Hovering between comedy and tragedy, it is a striking example of undecidability, a mode of expression privileged by the philosopher Jacques Derrida and poststructuralism in general because, instead of establishing dichotomies on the model either/or, it combines two modes considered divergent or at opposite poles. Thus, instead of the equation either/or, it posits the equation either *and* or. Undecidability is not a refusal or an impossibility to choose but the creation of a more refined, more ambiguous, and more powerful experience (Derrida, *Positions* 54–61). Also in the perspective of postmodernism, students should notice that the diminished emphasis on plot and causality does not give a teleological orientation to the play; rather, anything could happen, anything could be said, anytime. Heterogeneity, one of the traits of postmodern works, is present in the play's mosaic of linguistic registers. Most salient for classroom discussion is the fact that the play raises questions instead of providing answers.

   Waiting for Godot is also postmodern because it exists in the wake of Artaud's *Le théâtre et son double*. *Godot*, Beckett's first produced play, creates a new type of theatrical experience: spatially the clown-tramps are placed in a stark, stylized setting; they are most often seated; the dialogues unfold slowly, with many pauses, and do not focus on psychological, historical, or sociological issues. Rather, the dialogues constitute exchanges of banalities that are metaphysical statements as well. Such a theatrical experience, which is of the type that Artaud was advocating in his study, has the power to move spectators. With examples drawn from various domains, Artaud argues that theater should not be intellectual but should be emotional and should touch the nerves and the unconscious of the spectators. *Waiting for Godot*, while not spectacular and violent like Arrabal's panic theater, does affect spectators. It disturbs them, but at the same time it amuses them.

   In relation to Beckett's career, *Waiting for Godot* begins a series of explorations in the semiotic properties of theater having to do with spatial organization on stage, with groupings of and relationships between and among characters, and with language. Students might be encouraged to consider how the symmetry, balance, and interest in shapes and patternings continue with variations in Beckett's other plays. *Fin de partie (Endgame)* stages two couples, Hamm, an invalid, and Clov, who can move around, as well as Nell and Nagg in garbage cans. *Oh les beaux jours (Happy Days)* has two characters, Winnie, first buried to the waist in a mound, then buried to the neck, and Willie, who lies on the ground behind the mound. *Pas moi (Not I)* features one pair of lips hovering in darkness talking to a mute figure barely seen in the darkness of the empty stage. *Quad* (a video production) shows four silent creatures who keep walking toward a center without ever reaching it. These groupings and patternings involving variations on the number of characters, their body positions, their speaking, and the lighting, can provide students with striking visual metaphors of the human condition (see Brater, *Beyond Minimalism*; Esslin, "Poetry").

   Waiting for Godot is a powerful dramatic creation in the canon of French drama. Its power derives from its success in being both slapstick and metaphysical, in belonging to both popular and high culture with its clowns, its slang and popular language, and its implicit ties to Bergson and to Pascal. A Japanese scholar, Yasunari Takahashi, even finds striking similarities between Noh theater and *Waiting for Godot* and other plays by Beckett. The power of the play can also be measured by the diversity of appeal it has had (see Brater, *Why Beckett*). Its 1953 world-premiere performance at the Théâtre Babylone in Paris made a strong, positive impression on French intellectuals and critics such as Anouilh (Graver and Federman 92) and Robbe-Grillet. In 1957, it was performed by the San Francisco Actor's Workshop at San Quentin: the sense it made to the convicts has become legendary (Esslin, "San Quentin"). In the 1970s, the Moroccan stage director Taieb Sadikki transformed the characters of *Waiting for Godot* into unemployed men from the Third World (Duvignaud 61). And the 1980s saw a number of all-female productions (Ben-Zvi, "Women in *Godot*"). Written in French by an Irish writer, *Waiting for Godot* has proved to be the essence of universality.

Teaching *Waiting for Godot* in a Course on Beckett

Charles R. Lyons

A recent revision of our curriculum in the Department of Drama, Stanford University, has added advanced undergraduate courses devoted to the works of a single playwright. Because the course on Samuel Beckett is designed for seniors, I assume that these students have taken a three-quarter survey of dramatic literature from Greek to contemporary works, a course or two in Shakespeare, an introduction to dramatic criticism, and perhaps one course in theater history; I also assume that most of the class has had some experience in performance, either in productions or in acting classes. A few graduate students from drama and related fields may take the course as well, to remedy inadequate preparation in contemporary drama.

In teaching *En attendant Godot* and *Waiting for Godot*, I attempt to provide students with an opportunity to work with the play as an individual dramatic work; at the same time, I encourage them to think of the text as a cultural artifact, as the concretion of a moment in theatrical history, and as an important unit in the larger project of Beckett's writing. Consequently, the activities that I plan for the classes devoted to *Godot* concern themselves with the text as a self-sufficient aesthetic work and also as a reflective marker that directs our attention to cultural and theatrical contexts and to the situation of *Godot* within Beckett's work as a whole. To solve the problem created by these two needs, I move between the two strategies of lecture and discussion. The lectures on *Godot* focus on the following topics: (1) the theatrical milieu of Paris in January 1953 when the first stage performance of the play took place at the Théâtre Babylone; (2) the immediate critical reception of *Godot* and its rapid transformation into an emblem of the postwar period; (3) the relation of the play to Beckett's previous work in prose fiction and poetry. (Recommended reading includes Cohn, *From* Desire *to* Godot; Lyons, "Beckett's Major Plays.")

Because the students in this class have grown up with performances that reflect the influence of Beckett, they have difficulty perceiving the play's radicalism; the effect of its diminished reference to place, character, and history; and its independence from conventional practices of plotting. Consequently, I review conventions that the play rejects or diminishes. Here I develop a critical model that demonstrates the processes in which Henrik Ibsen represents the relation of Hjalmar Ekdal and Gregers Werle through specific references to the economic, social, political, psychological, biological, and philosophical systems with which the late nineteenth century detailed objective reality. With that model in mind, I ask the students to consider the absence in *Godot* of all but minimal reference to analogous systems and, more important, to consider the aesthetic implications of that absence in the dramatization of the interaction between Estragon and Vladimir. After a brief introduction to *Murphy, Watt,* and the trilogy, which some of the students may have read, I talk about both *Eleuthéria* and *Godot* as disjunctive interruptions of Beckett's narrative writing and as translations of similar material into another genre. I emphasize Beckett's surprising movement into the physical tangibility of dramatic performance at the very moment when his narratives seem to create and then destroy the fictional presence of their speakers (see Robbe-Grillet).

For the remainder of the time scheduled, we address issues of text, structure, conceptual paradigms, genre, dramatic conventions, and the conventions of Beckett's writing.

Text

The impossibility of dealing with the text of the play as a fixed, closed artifact. How do we perceive the relation between the "original" *En attendant Godot* and Beckett's "translation," *Waiting for Godot?* Do we endow the French text with special value as the original, or do we give priority to the English text as a more finished revision? Do the alterations that Beckett made in Elmar Tophoven's German translation, during Beckett's work on the 1974–75 production at the Schiller Theater, constitute a new text? (Beckett seems to have confirmed some of those changes in his 1984 revision for a production in English; see Cohn, *From* Desire 162–63.) This discussion illustrates the idea that the text of a major work, despite the authority of publication, is not a fixed document but, rather, because of authorial and editorial intervention and the dynamics of performance and criticism, a phenomenon that remains unstable or transitive. I also focus on the continuing demand to reify our perception of the text in new interpretations, both in performance and critical discourse.

Differences between En attendant Godot *and* Waiting for Godot. We consider the implications of the changes made in the translation, for example, the increased dependence on biblical and Shakespearean references in the English. What are the functions of quotation and verbal echo, particularly in the English text? In what sense are the texts interactive? To what degree do the French and English texts refer to separate cultures?

Structure

The substitution of a sequence of verbal and nonverbal activities for a conventional mythos.[1] To clarify students' perception of units of the text that hold discrete focus for the actor-character, I build on the students' experiences as actors. My objectives are to reveal the uses of language and action to structure immediate experience when a more inclusive sense of time and history fails; to demonstrate Beckett's exploitation of the actor's dependence on concrete objects that do not yield themselves easily to familiar or comforting use; to show the differences between Vladimir and Estragon that are revealed in their responses to specific phenomena; and to suggest that when the sense of literal narrative recedes spectators become keenly aware of the performance as a dramatic event. Without the organizing convenience of a familiar narrative, spectators need to process the immediate significance of individual dramatic acts or moments. Of course, it is interesting to consider what our response to *Waiting for Godot* would be if the sequence of behaviors enacted by Vladimir and Estragon were not enclosed within the general narrative frame of the afternoon's wait for Godot. Beckett's dramatic strategies may be radical, but he does ground this sequence of conversations and *divertissements* in a defined, consciously implemented action: to wait for Godot. While the identity of Godot remains equivocal and while each individual act or gesture performed by Vladimir and Estragon does not appear informed by that intention, the sequence is framed by this fictional explanation of the two characters' presence in this place at this time.

The use of repetition, recurrence, and doubling. I ask the students to mark recurrences in language, action, and character relationships to isolate organizational or structural schemes that influence response. Examples include the pairing of Vladimir and Estragon, Pozzo and Lucky, the shepherd and the goatherd, the Macon country and the Cackon country, and the two thieves crucified with Christ. This discussion analyzes act 2 as a variation of act 1 and focuses on the potential lack of closure at the end of act 2. The students consider the significance of the temporal unit *day* and discuss whether the day of act 2 functions as the representation of the day after act 1. Beckett's simplicity of action, in combination with the dramatic use of the time structure, day, has affinities with neoclassic unities; it is helpful to consider *Godot* in relation to these dramatic and theatrical conventions. A further objective is to identify the relation between the larger, enclosing pattern of the afternoon's wait for Godot, initiated by the tramps' reunion and closed by the postponement offered by the boy-messenger, and the apparently random sequence of smaller units that occur during the two specific periods of waiting. This discussion centers on two organizational strategies: the characters' uses of individual actions to structure their experience and the audience's use of the resulting pattern to process the aesthetic experience. Beckett's text foregrounds organizational strategies that do not relate to literal narratives or conventional dramatic plots but, in a sense, substitute for them. The looseness of the enclosure provided by the intention of waiting for Godot, in combination with the conceptual paradigms noted below, informs the spectators' perception of the performance as the embodiment of organizational principles other than narrative pattern or *mythos*.

Conceptual Paradigms

The image of Christ and the two thieves. Here I point to Beckett's earlier use of the image in the trilogy, its use as a means to conceptualize chance or fortune, and its use as a method of positioning the characters' perceptions of themselves within theological, political, and social schemes. The students discuss the relation of this image to other biblical references and consider the playwright's provocative reference to theological concepts.

The Hegelian-Marxian master and slave. This discussion considers the paradigm of lordship and bondage in both Hegel's and Marx's theories of social power. These ideas inform our examination of the interdependence of Pozzo and Lucky and, as well, Vladimir's use of the image of the author-itarian Godot in his conceptualization of himself as Godot's subservient and as a suppliant to his potential benevolence (see Lyons, *Samuel Beckett* 42–43; Cohn, *From* Desire 146–47). The students investigate the degree to which Pozzo's notion of his identity depends on his use of Lucky. While the Hegelian-Marxian paradigm does not provide a key to the drama's "mean-ing," this paradigm is very important in a course on Beckett because Beckett's next play, *Fin de partie (Endgame)*, builds on it. Beckett's dramatization of Pozzo and Lucky both implements the philosophical or political paradigm and critiques it. Students note, for example, that the slave Lucky has, ac-cording to Pozzo, acted as his tutor, providing his language, perhaps. In the later play, Hamm dominates Clov in part because he provides Clov with the language—and, hence, conceptual structures—that allows the servant to perceive his relationship to his master.

The image of the fool or lunatic. Lucky—like Shakespeare's fools, Lear in madness, and Hamlet within his "antic disposition"—voices a kind of truth in the apparent nonsense of his single speech. Students recognize the conventionality of this figure. By analyzing this extended narrative, they may also perceive the rhetorical significance within its apparently random verbiage.[2]

The image of the road. Beckett's text invokes an image, such as the one of Christ and the two thieves or the image of the fool or lunatic, and then undercuts its function with irony. The play works with the idea of the journey—temporally and spatially—in tension with the possible fixed lo-cation of one point on the road. The inaccessibility of the past and the future isolates the actor-characters and the audience in one site in a temporal and spatial continuum that remains hypothetical. Students need to perceive Beckett's ironic play with traditional dramas of journey or quest and the dependence of these narratives on the dramatization of various stations en route to the objective. That is, they need to see the isolation of this segment of the road in terms of conventional narratives that point backward to the origin of the quest and forward to its completion.

Genre

Beckett's identification of the English text as a tragicomedy. The students attempt to relate Beckett's predication with the traditional definitions of tragicomedy and their contemporary variations.

Beckett's play as an example of Northrop Frye's notion of irony as a dramatic mode. The students, most of whom have had an introduction to Frye earlier, discuss the usefulness of his category as a way of relating *Waiting for Godot* to other modes of drama.

Beckett's play as an example of William Empson's idea of pastoral. Using the political perspective described by Empson in *Some Versions of Pastoral*, students examine Beckett's use of the removed world of pastoral as an arena in which to place mixed social classes in new relationships (3–84). Analyses of *Godot* rarely discuss the structures of authority, knowledge, freedom, and autonomy, and Empson's idea of the political content of pastoral and the function of double plots helps remedy this deficiency. As students discuss the interaction between the routines enacted by Vladimir and Estragon and the two episodes in which Pozzo and Lucky appear, they can apply Empson's interpretation of the convention of the double plot. Empson's scheme of the difference between the proletarian and the heroic provides a different vocabulary for discussing the play and the function of its characters.

Dramatic Conventions

The scene of exile. Serious dramatic works, particularly those we classify as tragedies, often place their protagonists in alien environments in which they are isolated from comfort or palliation. Examples abound: Prometheus held at the extremity of the world; Oedipus at Colonus, after years of wandering in exile; Philoctetes abandoned on Lemnos; Phèdre in Troezen; Lear driven to the storm-battered heath and the blinded Gloucester led to the cliffs of Dover; and Willy Loman, whose suburban home has been made alien by the encroaching city. In each of these examples, the hero manifests an ambivalent relation to the space he or she inhabits, creating a self-image that derives from it and yet seeing it as both strange and hostile. In this discussion, students consider the barren landscape of *Godot* as a conventionally alien, hostile environment that Vladimir and Estragon use to identify themselves and their estrangement from both society and nature.

The absent or enigmatic authority. Students examine the relationship between Didi and Gogo and Godot in the light of the following: Orestes and Apollo, Prometheus and Zeus, Oedipus and Apollo, Hamlet and God.

The messenger, the prophecy. Students analyze the function of the young boy who delivers the message from Godot as the implementation of two conventions: the messenger who describes an action or place external to the immediate scene; and the statement of prophecy that enigmatically defines the subsequent action.

The characters of the music hall or cinema. Students discuss Beckett's use of the comedy-pathos of the tramps as conventionalized theatrical figures exemplified in Charlie Chaplin's characterization of the tramp. This discussion focuses on comic action that suggests the routines of vaudeville, the typical dress of the conventionalized tramps, and the characters' ironic self-characterization. Using the classical comic juxtaposition of the *alazon* and *eiron*, *Godot* presents a variant of the modern image of the tramp in relation to the pretentious authority figure of Pozzo.[3] The dialogue of Vladimir and Estragon implements this action of comic deflation.

Conventions of Beckett's Writing

The couple. Didi and Gogo use the pairing of the earlier narrative *Mercier and Camier* and anticipate Hamm and Clov, Winnie and Willie, the doubles in *Ohio Impromptu*. Students who are familiar with Beckett may recognize a number of the rhetorical and theatrical devices in *Godot* that later works use. This discussion seeks to clarify both differentiation and symbiosis in Beckett's representation of the couple.

Aged and infirm characters. Students consider Beckett's persistent use of aging characters with physical infirmities—failing powers of locomotion, hearing, sight, and mental acuity—that are aggravated by hostile environments.

Storytelling. This analysis points toward the lesser dependence in *Godot* on storytelling as well as the emphasis given to Lucky's speech, which becomes, like the stories recited by characters in other plays and fictions, a bravado rhetorical performance.

Statement and correction. The texts of Beckett's trilogy contain assertions and denials or revisions of those statements. This pattern gives the narrative discourses something of the feeling of a dialogue within a single consciousness. When Beckett shifts into actual dialogue in *Godot* and later dramas, he continues this practice of statement and correction. To demonstrate the continuity of this rhetorical pattern I ask students to read certain passages from the trilogy as dialogue—for example the last page of *The Unnamable* —and immediately afterward, a section or two of dialogue from *Godot*.

Formal self-consciousness. Vladimir's exit from the stage to seek the off-stage toilet focuses the spectator's attention on the event as a theatrical performance. While the audience has not forgotten that the figures on the stage are actors representing characters, Beckett foregrounds that awareness as part of the representation itself. Consequently, as spectators we need to attend to these figures as characters within the terms of the fiction, however equivocal, and as actors whose perception encompasses the dramatic event and the event of performance. That perception is amplified, of course, by the audience's secondary awareness that the actors playing Vladimir and Estragon at this moment expand their performance to include Beckett's representation of actors playing Vladimir and Estragon. That is, we recognize that these comments are not those of the actual actors but rather the speech of actors playing the actors playing the characters.

The preceding paragraphs suggest more points than can be encompassed in lectures and discussions on a single play within a ten-week course that deals with many plays. Some of these issues become the subjects of essays in examinations or provide material for critical papers, projects that allow the students to work independently. Since we also use *Waiting for Godot* to show how later plays develop certain conceptual paradigms and aesthetic conventions, our analyses of the succeeding dramatic works take up some of the topics I detail above. One of the pleasures of studying Beckett's plays is to realize the ways in which the later texts illuminate our understanding of the earlier.

NOTES

[1] I use *mythos* here in Northrop Frye's sense: "The narrative of a work of literature, considered as the grammar or order of words (literal narrative), plot or 'argument' (descriptive narrative), secondary imitation of action (formal narrative), imitation of generic or recurrent action or ritual (archetypal narrative) . . ." (366–67).

[2] I relate Lucky's speech to the recurrent and concise insights of the Fool in Shakespeare's *King Lear* and to the breadth of vision of Cassandra's ecstatic vision in the *Agamemnon*. I also relate the vision of Lucky and Pozzo in the second act to the image of Antigone and Oedipus in Sophocles's final tragedy or to Lear and the Fool. Ruby Cohn sees reference here to Gloucester's " 'Tis the time's plague when madmen lead the blind" (*From* Desire 146).

[3] Northrop Frye's discussion of these classic characterological conventions (40, 172–75) does not refer to Beckett, but the concepts help students of *Godot* to relate this unconventional play to traditional theatrical schemes. It is useful to think of Lucky as a variant of the clever servant that has been a familiar character since Roman comedy.

CRITICAL APPROACHES

Waiting for Godot and Critical Theory

Kevin J. H. Dettmar

In the introduction to a 1986 collection of critical essays on Samuel Beckett, Patrick McCarthy writes that *Waiting for Godot* "seems both to attract and to resist overly neat identifications" (1). Surely *Godot* stands alone among twentieth-century dramas for the wealth of critical discussion that has grown up around it; as early as 1966, Melvin J. Friedman could already say, in a special Beckett issue of *Modern Drama*, that "Beckett's play *En attendant Godot* has produced a heated and sustained colloquy, which is comparable to the critical dialogue engendered by Eliot's 'Waste Land' and Hopkins' 'Windhover' " (300). Friedman goes on to indicate some of the different directions that dialogue had taken during the first ten years of *Godot* criticism:

> While the play has not proved grist for the mills of committed schools of literary criticism, there has been an occasional essay in those directions. Thus, Bernard Dukore's "Gogo, Didi, and the Absent Godot" uses Freudian terminology, while Eva Metman's "Reflections on Samuel Beckett's Plays" uses Jungian categories. The Myth critics would find Robert Champigny's "Interprétation de *En attendant Godot*" (*PMLA*, June 1960) sympathetic, and the Marxists would enjoy interpretations of Pozzo-Lucky as capital-labor; yet they would have to dismiss the play because it is so uncompromisingly *hors de situation*. The Berg-

sonian critics—explaining literature in terms of "human" or "psychological" time—should be delighted with Ross Chambers' "Beckett's
Brinkmanship." . . .

(308)

Friedman's comments remind us of just how much the critical scene has
changed since the 1960s. But regardless of the particular theoretical alle-
giances we recognize today, we find ourselves in much the same situation
that Friedman describes: "The commentators on *Godot* have tripped over
one another's toes in their urgency to elucidate it and to find some of their
own problems solved in it" (301). Since its first production in 1953, *Godot*
has become something of a dramatic Rorschach test for critics; and to judge
by recent journal articles, the battle for *Godot* is not about to die down—
of the forty-five theory-oriented essays listed in the bibliography at the end
of this essay, fully one-quarter were published between 1983 and 1987.

I teach *Waiting for Godot* in Critical Reading and Writing, the first required class in the English major at the University of California, Los Angeles.
The course introduces students to the full spectrum of literary genres and
the various styles of writing about them; additionally, I think it important
to introduce students, however briefly, to the major schools of literary criticism. This is quite a bit to accomplish in ten weeks. The introduction of
critical theory is the most troublesome aspect of the course; students at this
level (primarily freshmen and sophomores) are much more interested in
what Robert Scholes calls *interpretation*, which asks "all texts to stand and
yield their hidden meanings," than they are in *criticism*, "moving beyond
reading and interpretation . . . discovering the codes that are invoked by a
text and exposing the means by which the text seeks to control our responses
to it" (40, 42). In response to this difficulty, I have developed a method of
teaching *Waiting for Godot* that brings critical theory and *Godot* together
in ways that have been suggestive both to my students and to me.

Introducing beginning literature students to critical theory is still somewhat controversial. The Northeastern Center for Literary Studies held a
series of three symposia on the topic Critical Theory and the Teaching of
Literature in 1984; the addresses by Christopher Ricks, Robert Scholes, and
Richard Ohmann graphically illustrate the diversity of opinion on this important topic (Peterfreund). The "importation" of critical theory into the
classroom is, of course, nothing new, nor can it be laid at the doorstep of
poststructuralism; the New Critics were nothing if not devoted and respected
teachers, and their theory was uniquely well suited to the college classroom.
But the New Critics were never as good with drama, or even with fiction,
as they were with poetry, and new texts such as *Waiting for Godot* may
have necessitated new pedagogies as well as new critical theories. I tend,

then, to agree with Susan R. Horton's assessment of the current situation in college and university literature classrooms:

> Behind the debate—and more importantly behind the *vehemence* of the debate—over whether theory should or shouldn't be imported into the classroom, for instance, is a hidden ambivalence about whether we do or don't want to lead students out of what in our secret heart of hearts we perceive as their beautiful, prelapsarian ignorance of our professional infighting, all our uncertainty about truth and beauty and un-hold-onto-able meanings, all that knowledge about how language and power create truth.
>
> (55)

The question becomes, perhaps, not whether we should be teaching theory to undergraduates but whether we will make the theory that undergirds all our teaching explicit or choose instead to let it remain implicit. The pedagogy outlined here assumes that students are better served when our interpretive "agendas" are made public.

The first step in bringing critical theory and *Godot* together is to familiarize students in at least a cursory way with the diversity of contemporary theory. Capsule discussions of the major threads of current critical theory, such as those found in M. H. Abrams's *Glossary of Literary Terms* or C. Hugh Holman and William Harmon's *Handbook to Literature*, can introduce students to the basic ideological differences among the various approaches. For classroom discussion, I divide the spectrum of critical theory into four broad areas and group specific critical methodologies under these categories:

1. Psychological: psychoanalytic, reader response
2. Sociohistorical: Marxist, feminist,[1] new historicist, Frankfurt school, reception theory, speech-act theory
3. Mythic: ritual, Christian, archetypal
4. Formal: semiotic, structuralist, New Critical, hermeneutic, Russian formalist

While this framework leaves out some schools of interpretation, it gives beginning English majors a good idea of the critical methodologies they are likely to encounter as they explore literary criticism.

Once the critical territory has been mapped out, students have a go at *Godot* on their own. Out-of-class reading of the play is followed in the next class session by a screening of a performance of the play. Neither the reading nor the viewing, however, is the subject of in-depth discussion at this point;

instead we take some time to articulate—but not to answer—the questions that the students' first encounter with *Godot* has provoked. These questions are reproduced on a handout that the students use to direct their own interrogation of the critical texts they read.

After this initial exposure to the play and collective airing of the questions it raises, students break up into four work groups, with each group looking at one of the four general categories of critical theory: psychological, sociohistorical, mythic, formal. The panoply of responses to *Godot* then becomes a teaching aid rather than a hindrance; brought into dialogue with one another in the classroom, different critical perspectives on the play can be wrested from the void in which so much contemporary critical debate takes place.

In the critical work groups, selected essays are distributed to students, who are asked to read the essays individually as an outside assignment. Each essay is read by two students, so that at the next class session students who have studied the same essay can sit together and compare notes about what they have just read. Students appreciate this collaborative approach; "It was good that we discussed the essays in pairs," one student commented, "because some of them were a little difficult to understand."

Looking over the items on *Waiting for Godot* that appear in the *MLA International Bibliography* and in Raymond Federman and John Fletcher's *Samuel Beckett: His Works and His Critics* from 1954 to 1987, I have put together a selection of critical essays for each group. Students in the group examining sociohistorical approaches, for instance, read essays such as Gábor Mihályi's "Beckett's *Godot* and the Myth of Alienation" and Eric Gans's "Beckett and the Problem of Modern Culture." I have built up a large working file of essays that treat *Godot* from various theoretical perspectives and can tailor the readings to the size of the class and the individual work groups.

A short bibliography of some of the more useful material appears in the appendix to this essay. Using even this selective list, however, requires a good bit of caution and planning on the instructor's part. The essays listed are not uniform either in length or in difficulty, and a few have been published only in French; therefore, the instructor needs to become familiar with the essays before assigning them and to think carefully about the gifts and needs of individual students in order to achieve a good fit. The essays are also not uniformly theoretical; if the class is small enough, I prefer to omit those readings that either do not hold closely to an identifiable theoretical perspective or that are not "pure types"—essays that employ more than one recognizable methodology, as for instance Norman Mailer's "Public Notice" (in the sociohistorical category).

In teaching *Godot*, I have found an additional precaution especially helpful. I do not have students work with the deconstructive essays. Essays like

Kimball Lockhart's "Figure of the Ground" give many instructors problems, and an undergraduate previously unacquainted with critical theory cannot make head or tail of it; a brief introduction to deconstruction is, I think, best left to the instructor. Some other essays in the bibliography are nearly impenetrable to most students without some assistance. A good example of this is Manuela Corfariu and Daniela Roventa-Frumuşani's "Absurd Dialogue and Speech Acts," a thoughtful speech-act discussion of *Godot* that is, unfortunately, like much speech-act theory, riddled with jargon inaccessible to the student. But by spending time with the essay myself and providing a paraphrase of some of the more difficult sections of the argument and a glossary of its specialized terminology, I have found it valuable in classroom discussion. Other essays in the bibliography that students may find difficult include those by Anne C. Murch and Eric Gans and the two essays by Dina Sherzer.

Having read essays informed by particular critical theories, the members of each work group are given two tasks. First, they come together to discuss their essays, trying to discover similarities in approach among them. Some of the similarities are fairly obvious; all the essays read by the sociohistorical-criticism group, for instance, focus on the relation of *Godot* to the play's cultural, social, economic, political, or historical context. Other, less obvious similarities also exist, and I try to encourage thorough exploration by circulating among the groups. Each group then prepares a brief (one-page) statement of the methodological principles underlying that group's perspective and distributes it to the other students and the instructor.

For the second assignment, each pair of students makes a joint, five- to ten-minute presentation to the class in which they summarize the reading in the article they have studied, discuss the theoretical presuppositions of the essay, and assess the strengths and shortcomings of this theoretical perspective in shedding new light on *Godot*. Students sometimes need to be encouraged to be critical (suspicious) of the reading material; while most of the essays present intelligent and rhetorically powerful arguments, even the cleverest critical systems seem to miss something at the very heart of *Godot*, and students should readily say so. The pairs of students take questions from the class at the close of their presentations. During the student presentations, I take notes. After all the presentations have been made, we review the blindnesses and insights of the various methodologies.

We next look as a class at Beckett's pronouncements on art—on his own writing in particular and on art in general. I hand out material from Beckett's dialogues with Georges Duthuit and early interviews with Beckett; some of Beckett's comments, such as "to be an artist is to fail, as no other dare fail" (Beckett and Duthuit 21), make the transition to deconstruction seem almost natural:

BECKETT: I speak of an art . . . weary of puny exploits, weary of pretending to be able, of being able, of doing a little better the same old thing, of going a little further along a dreary road.

DUTHUIT: And preferring what?

BECKETT: The expression that there is nothing to express, nothing with which to express, nothing from which to express, no power to express, no desire to express, together with the obligation to express.

(Beckett and Duthuit 17)

The kind of work I do is one in which I'm not master of my material. The more Joyce knew the more he could. He's tending toward omniscience and omnipotence as an artist. I'm working with impotence, ignorance. I don't think impotence has been exploited in the past.

(Qtd. in Shenker 148)

There is, however, a very real danger in presenting Beckett's views on art at the end, after all the critical essays have been discussed. Students may come away with the message that Beckett's is the authoritative final word on the subject. No contemporary school of criticism would support introducing the author's comments at the end, and yet even today recourse to Beckett's pronouncements is a mainstay of Beckett criticism. A brief summary of W. K. Wimsatt, Jr., and Monroe C. Beardsley's "intentional fallacy" may come in handy here; while New Criticism is hardly "new" any longer, its dissociation of the author from the text is surely one of their more helpful and lasting contributions to literary theory.

I close my unit on *Godot* with a very basic deconstructive reading of *Godot* presented as an informal lecture, which I put together using the essays listed in the bibliography along with my sense of what happens when one reads *Godot* "against itself." This lecture gives the students a feel for what deconstruction looks like in practice, but again the danger inheres—that because we close our investigation with deconstruction, students seize on it as the "correct" reading, at long last. There are at least two reasons students tend to respond this way. One is outside our control; as Scholes argues, students come from their high school literature classes wanting desperately to unlock texts' "hidden meanings"; every work is a detective fiction, with the reader an enterprising Holmes. The second source of students' impulse for easy closure, however, lies with us. As much as we try to be objective in listening to, summarizing, and discussing the arguments made from various critical perspectives, we cannot help being influenced by our own deeply ingrained critical predilections, and students pick up on these biases. To leave a wide variety of perspectives hovering in the air, with no sense of closure, is difficult work for both students and instructors. What we are trying to create in the classroom, I believe, is close to Bakhtin's notion of dialogue: a dialogue in which the final word has not been spoken, a dialogue that precludes the existence of an authoritative narrative that would reduce our dialogue to a monologue. If we wish to deal honestly with our students, neither Beckett, nor Derrida, nor you, nor I, must be allowed to have the final word.

APPENDIX: A SHORT BIBLIOGRAPHY FOR TEACHING CRITICAL THEORY AND *GODOT*

Psychological Interpretations

Berlin, Normand. "The Tragic Pleasure of *Waiting for Godot*." *Beckett at 80/Beckett in Context*. Ed. Enoch Brater. New York: Oxford UP, 1986. 46–63.

Breuer, Rolf. "The Solution as Problem: Beckett's *Waiting for Godot*." *Modern Drama* 19 (1976): 225–36.

Dukore, Bernard F. "Gogo, Didi, and the Absent Godot." *Drama Survey* 1 (1962): 301–07.

Iser, Wolfgang. "Counter-Sensical Comedy and Audience Response in Beckett's *Waiting for Godot*." *Gestos* 2.4 (1987): 11–35.

Levy, Shimon. "Notions of Audience in Beckett's Plays." *Assaph* 1. 1C (1984): 71–81.

McCray, Judith, and Ronald G. McCray. "Why Wait for Godot?" *Southern Quarterly* 14.2 (1976): 109–15.

Murch, Anne C. "Considérations sur la proxémique dans le théâtre de Samuel Beckett." *Australian Journal of French Studies* 20 (1983): 159–71.

Riggs, Larry W. "Slouching toward Consciousness: Destruction of the Spectator Role in *En attendant Godot* and *Fin de Partie*." *Degré Second: Studies in French Literature* 7 (1983): 57–79.

Sociohistorical Interpretations

Bruck, Jan. "Beckett, Benjamin and the Modern Crisis in Communication." *New German Critique* 26 (1982): 159–71.

Corfariu, Manuela, and Daniela Rovenţa-Frumuşani. "Absurd Dialogue and Speech Acts—Beckett's *En attendant Godot*." *Poetics* 13 (1984): 119–33.

Cormier, Ramona, and Janis L. Pallister. "Communications." *Waiting for Death: The Philosophical Significance of Beckett's* En attendant Godot. Tuscaloosa: U of Alabama P, 1979. 52–79.

Cousineau, Thomas. "*Waiting for Godot* and Politics." *Théâtre et politique*. Ed. Jean-Paul Debax and Yves Peyre. Toulouse: Université de Toulouse-Le Mirail, 1984. 161–67.

Gans, Eric. "Beckett and the Problem of Modern Culture." *Substance* 35 (1982): 3 –15.

Gautam, Kripa K., and Manjula Sharma. "Dialogue in *Waiting for Godot* and Grice's Concept of Implicature." *Modern Drama* 29 (1986): 580–88.

Hewes, Henry. "Mankind in the Merdecluse." *Saturday Review* 5 May 1956: 32. Rpt. in *Casebook on* Waiting for Godot. Ed. Ruby Cohn. New York: Grove, 1967. 67–69.

Mailer, Norman. "A Public Notice on *Waiting for Godot.*" *Village Voice* 9 May 1956: 12. Rpt. in *Advertisements for Myself.* New York: Putnam's, 1959. 320–25. Rpt. in *Casebook on* Waiting for Godot. Ed. Ruby Cohn. New York: Grove, 1967. 69–74.

Mihályi, Gábor. "Beckett's *Godot* and the Myth of Alienation." *Modern Drama* 9 (1966): 277–82.

Suvin, Darko. "Beckett's Purgatory of the Individual: Or, The Three Laws of Thermodynamics." *Tulane Drama Review* 11.4 (1967): 23–36. Rpt. in *Casebook on* Waiting for Godot. Ed. Ruby Cohn. New York: Grove, 1967. 121–32.

Touchard, Pierre-Aimé. "Le théâtre de Samuel Beckett." *Revue de Paris* Feb. 1961: 73–87.

Zaller, Robert. "Waiting for Leviathan." *Critical Essays on Samuel Beckett.* Ed. Patrick A. McCarthy. Boston: Hall, 1986. 160–73.

Mythic Interpretations

Baldwin, Hélène L. "Waiting on God: The Quest of Vladimir and Estragon." *Samuel Beckett's Real Silence.* University Park: Penn State UP, 1981. 107–24.

Bernard, G. C. "The Pseudocouple: *Waiting for Godot.*" *Samuel Beckett: A New Approach.* New York: Dodd, 1970. 89–100.

Brooks, Curtis M. "The Mythic Pattern in *Waiting for Godot.*" *Modern Drama* 9 (1966): 292–99.

Champigny, Robert. "Interprétation de *En attendant Godot.*" *PMLA* 75 (1960): 329–31. Rpt. as "*Waiting for Godot*: Myth, Words, Wait." *Casebook on* Waiting for Godot. Ed. Ruby Cohn. New York: Grove, 1967. 137–44.

Fraser, G. S. "*They Also Serve.*" *Times Literary Supplement* 10 February 1956: 84. Rpt. in *Casebook on* Waiting for Godot. Ed. Ruby Cohn. New York: Grove, 1967. 133–37.

Kolve, V. A. "Religious Language in *Waiting for Godot.*" *Centennial Review* 11 (1967): 102–27.

Metman, Eva. "Reflections on Samuel Beckett's Plays." *Journal of Analytical Psychology* 5.1 (1960): 41–63. Rpt. in *Samuel Beckett: A Collection of Critical Essays.* Ed. Martin Esslin. Englewood Cliffs: Prentice, 1965. 117–39.

O'Brien, William J. "To Hell with Samuel Beckett." *Foundations of Religious Literacy.* Ed. John V. Apczynski. Chico: Scholars, 1983. 165–74.

Rechtien, John. "Time and Eternity Meet in the Present." *Texas Studies in Literature and Language* 6 (1964): 5–21.

Schricker, Gale. "The Antinomian Quest of *Waiting for Godot.*" *CEA Critic* 49.2–4 (1986–87): 124–33.

Webner, Hélène L. *"Waiting for Godot* and the New Theology." *Renascence* 21 (1968): 3–9, 31.

Zeifman, Hersh. "Religious Imagery in the Plays of Samuel Beckett." *Samuel Beckett: A Collection of Criticism.* Ed. Ruby Cohn. New York: McGraw, 1975. 85–94.

Formal Interpretations

Calderwood, James L. "Ways of Waiting in *Waiting for Godot.*" *Modern Drama* 29 (1986): 363–75.

Cohn, Ruby. "Waiting Is All." *Modern Drama* 3 (1960): 162–67.

Francis, Richard Lee. "Beckett's Metaphysical Tragicomedy." *Modern Drama* 8 (1965): 259–67.

Hryniewicz, Ewa. *"Waiting for Godot*: Beckett's *Homo Ludens.*" *Arizona Quarterly* 42 (1986): 261–70.

Iser, Wolfgang. "Samuel Beckett's Dramatic Language." *Modern Drama* 9 (1966): 251–59.

Janvier, Ludovic. "Cyclical Dramaturgy." *Pour Samuel Beckett.* Paris: Editions de Minuit, 1966. Rpt. in *Casebook on* Waiting for Godot. Ed. Ruby Cohn. New York: Grove, 1967. 166–71.

Reiter, Seymour. "The Structure of *Waiting for Godot.*" *Costerus* 3 (1975): 181–95.

Schechner, Richard. "There's Lots of Time in *Godot.*" *Modern Drama* 9 (1966): 268–76. Rpt. in *Casebook on* Waiting for Godot. Ed. Ruby Cohn. New York: Grove, 1967. 175–87.

Trousdale, Marion. "Dramatic Form: The Example of *Godot.*" *Modern Drama* 11 (1968): 1–9.

Webb, Eugene. *"Waiting for Godot."* *The Plays of Samuel Beckett.* Seattle: U of Washington P, 1972. 26–41.

Poststructuralist or Deconstructionist Essays

Lockhart, Kimball. "The Figure of the Ground." *Enclitic* 3.2 (1979): 74–105.

Sherzer, Dina. "De-Construction in *Waiting for Godot.*" *The Reversible World: Symbolic Inversions in Art and Society.* Ed. Barbara A. Babcock. Ithaca: Cornell UP, 1978. 129–46.

———. "Didi, Gogo, Pozzo, Lucky: Linguistes déconstructeurs." *Etudes littéraires* 13 (1980): 539–58.

NOTE

[1]To date, feminist readings of *Godot* have not been conspicuous. The reasons for this "oversight" are not hard to guess; writing in the *Beckett Circle*, Linda Ben-Zvi,

in one of the first pieces to discuss *Godot* from a feminist perspective, says, "*Godot* is far more a play about the *male* human experience than I had previously thought. . . . Beckett may not be using the term generically when he says 'All mankind is us' " (7).

Ben-Zvi has recently edited a group of essays, *Women in Beckett: Performance and Critical Perspectives*; several pieces collected there suggest a feminist approach to *Godot*.

Lecture and *Lecture*: Recitation and Reading in *Waiting for Godot*

Stephen Barker

> A matter that becomes clear ceases to concern us.
>
> Friedrich Nietzsche, *Beyond Good and Evil*

> You think you are inventing, you think you are
> escaping, and all you do is stammer out your lesson,
> the remnants of a pensum one day got by heart and
> long forgotten, life without tears, as it is wept.
>
> Samuel Beckett, *Molloy*

My title, like all Beckett's writing, inhabits the space between two languages, French and English. Were I to announce that my concern here is with Beckett and lecture, I would mean something quite different from an announcement of the topic Beckett *et la lecture*: in English I would be referring to a recitation, a public event, a didactic exercise with a certain decorum; in French, to a private, heuristic event, a reading. This dilemma of language, not merely different languages but layers of a single language as well, is a most suggestive starting point for teaching *Godot*. I engage this layering, which I have schematized as recitation and reading, in the classroom to show how *Waiting for Godot*, in its quest for the significance of action, valorizes and plays with both these strategies of reading.[1] *Godot* unfolds itself in the idea of public and private reading. To interpret and teach *Godot* is to explore Beckett's means of manipulating and confounding this double (manifest and concealed) process of signification.

To teach the play in the way I am suggesting, one must assert that Beckett's view of reading is teleologically disruptive; indeed, it must be seen as consisting of a series of acts (gestures) that signify disruption. Vivian Mercier's claim that *Godot* is a play in which "nothing happens, twice" (*Beckett/Beckett* 74) is, if one considers the act of reading to be *something*, no longer tenable. Indeed, *Godot* must be seen as profoundly and disruptively active, a drama of suspense: like Didi and Gogo,[2] the audience and the reader are suspended in anticipation of Godot's eventual arrival, which can never occur; this impossibility is a central symbolic antiaction of the play's disruption.

My strategy of teaching the play is, then, a double one. First, epistemologically, *Godot* demonstrates the problem of delivering messages. The play evinces this troublesome suspense and is a test of its completion. Second, ontologically, *Godot*'s suspense of listening and reading evokes a series of concealed texts, of which the reader or listener is allowed to perceive only shreds or pieces, but which stand behind those shreds, solid and authoritative. Beckett's own dialogue (i.e., the play itself), which flits across the top of these concealed texts in constant confrontation with the concealed subtext of these layers of language, reveals through language his idea of the fundamental condition and suffering of human beings.[3] Narrative ambivalence, concealed and revealed, is for Beckett the parabolic evidence of suffering; dramatic narrative is its manifestation. For Beckett, though not for his characters, these issues necessarily cause a voluntary and revolutionary estrangement, as Lance Butler points out:

> Beckett seems to be in violent revolt against the nature of this world, and it is clearly not something political or psychological that he is revolting against. It is something ontological. . . . Beckett's works are, in one central aspect, ontological parables.
>
> (151)

The key to Beckett's parables lies in the dialectic of lecture and *lecture*, of the concealed and revealed nature of reading. Parabolic strategies[4] of narrative force move through *Godot* as the dramatic suspense (and as the test or gauge) of a causal series of thematic concerns: memory, time, presence, meaning (Barker). I consider here (briefly) the last of these, meaning, to see how Beckett's reading might be read:

> The memory came faint and cold of the story I might have told, a story in the likeness of my life, I mean without the courage to end or the strength to go on.
>
> (*Stories* 72)

Significance (i.e., Godot, for whom we wait) is always a suspense and a test of meaning, perpetually in crisis. It depends on what narrative can produce: narrative manipulates character. Meaning is as "dark as [it is] in a head before the worms get at it" (*Stories* 82). This production of meaning is generally seen, then, as an illumination, a function of insight.[5] Beckett reverses this dead metaphor of insight—a fundamental cultural metaphor—by showing narrative as a function rather of blindness (Pozzo) or, at best, of partial sight (all five characters), which is Beckett's Platonic metaphor for the interaction of language and meaning. Not only do characters "produce" dialogue in *Godot*, but what I have called the two registers of language produce their own distinct dialogue; indeed, this narrative produces the characters. The lecture, as recitation, and the *lecture*, as reading, separate and interact to suspend and to test meaning. This dialogue of readings characterizes the entire text of *Godot*, which, thus interpreted, might well be introduced through Beckett's other works (some of which have been quoted or mentioned above), as well as through related critical and theoretical texts that can be excerpted; I suggest some of these above and in my notes.

With this concept of the play's language registers (and their power) in mind, I teach *Godot* by discussing pivotal scenes in which this theme is central and clear. The following three minilectures (impossibly condensed) work through three such scenes. All the dialogue quoted in these three examples must be carefully read aloud, a procedure that demonstrates the lecture-*lecture* dichotomy and partakes of the dilemma being discussed. Students can be assigned to read aloud (getting their assignments and being coached in advance) or the teacher can read the dialogue (including Lucky's long speech below, which must be worked through and punctuated for reading).

The Opening Lecture/Lecture

The opening exchange of the play, between Gogo and Didi, is an introduction to and immersion in the confrontation of lecture and *lecture*. Gogo sits, at work on his boot, struggling unsuccessfully against the epistemology of lived experience: he can't get the boot off. He "*gives up, exhausted, rests, tries again. As before*" (7a). Didi enters, as Gogo, abandoning action, resorts to language:

>   ESTRAGON: Nothing to be done.

Didi advances, with great difficulty, since movement (of legs, bladder, etc.) is extraordinarily hard. But in response to Gogo's offhand remark, Didi delivers a lecture, as though he were reading it:

>   VLADIMIR: I'm beginning to come round to that opinion. All my life
>   I've tried to put it from me, saying, Vladimir, be reasonable, you
>   haven't yet tried everything. And I resumed the struggle. (*He
>   broods, musing on the struggle. . . .*)

Didi has not addressed Gogo at all, nor has he addressed the audience or reader outside the play. He has "read" a text here, one that remains concealed from the reader or viewer of *Godot*, an underlying text whose authority is never questioned or revealed. This unrevealed, authoritative text, which gives Didi such weighty and ponderous delivery, is the text of the politician, the philosopher, the rhetorician, and it is utterly unavailable to Gogo.[6] Having delivered his lecture, Didi slips out to Gogo's experiential world:

VLADIMIR: So there you are again.

This transitional remark is itself caught between two kinds of discourse; it marks the emergence and the nonsynthesis of layers of language. Our first lecture has been delivered. Language has split itself and put us into a state of suspense.

Lucky's Great Lecture or Lecture

The centerpiece of Beckett's theme of reading and recitation is, of course, Lucky's speech near the end of act 1. It is the single time in the play when, for Lucky, words suspend physical action but do not supplant it. The speech is itself physical action, as Beckett's stage directions indicate:[7] Pozzo's first instruction, "Think, pig!" (28a) results in a dance since Lucky cannot remember what *think* means (he subsequently "remembers" better than any of the other characters do). *Think* here means "language," and its manifestation is a ritualized recitation. Lucky demonstrates the truth of Didi's enigmatic pronouncement that "[w]hat is terrible is to *have* thought" (41b). It is terrible to have thought because recitation and reading, in their differing ways, are impossible investments in a desire for order as an index of meaning. This idea is a key not only to Beckett's (and Lucky's) language but to the absurd comedy of *Godot*. Camus, in *The Myth of Sisyphus*, argues that the absurd is precisely the suspense and tension, the abyss, in the human being, instigated by the thought of being caught between the arbitrary irrationality of the world and the rage for order in the mind. Just such a rage for order lies behind both Lucky's speech and Beckett's structure of reading and recitation in *Godot*. For Camus, as for Beckett, meaning must be lived to be significant. In the order of the recitation, of Lucky's speech as lecture, meaning is arbitrary, certainly not the product of "lived" thought. The monologue does not break through to a lived meaning for Lucky or anyone else, since his words do not express any kind of conscious or intellectual conviction. Lucky's speech is the most dramatic exemplum of Beckett's treatment of recitation, as the (de)posited presence of textual traces:

LUCKY: Given the existence as uttered forth in the public works of Puncher and Wattmann of a personal God quaquaquaqua with white beard quaquaquaqua outside time without extension who from the heights of divine apathia divine athambia divine aphasia loves us dearly with some exceptions for reasons unknown but time will tell. . . .

(28b)

The speech is a vast compendium of hidden texts, of philosophy, religion, scholarship, scepticism, and more. The speech is exactly what Victor Turner calls "liminal" (at the border, boundary, or threshold of a structure—in this case language structure). Moreover, Lucky's speech does not represent a simple dialogue of order and chaos; for Turner, as for Beckett, the liminal quality of ritual is the acknowledgment of danger: ritual presentation of the concealed texts of order is "a transformative self-immolation of order as presently constituted, even sometimes a voluntary *sparagmos* or self-dismemberment of order, in the subjunctive depths of liminality" ("Social Dramas" 160).[8] The long speech is precisely this, a self-immolation, for Lucky, who presents himself as a ritual sacrifice to interpretation (or to meaning); it becomes the task of Lucky's reader both in and out of the play to interpret (i.e., neutralize) his discourse. But this interpretation is impossible. His recitation moves with its own incestuous power through what Turner calls the "liminal space-time 'pod' created by ritual action"[9] because in this mode, lecture dramatically avoids traditional (rational) formulation: "[I]n liminality what is mundanely bound in sociostructural form may be unbound and rebound" ("Social Dramas" 161). Lucky's speech seems to be a series of quotations from texts that, although enormously substantial, are concealed from both Lucky and the reader/listener ("quaquaquaqua"); the speech appears to be simultaneously struggling from some protean world of language toward "proper text," mechanically running itself at the expense of Lucky's energy and yet receding into greater and greater obscurity. The speech epitomizes Beckett's indeterminacy in recitation; "man" is lost in Lucky's verbiage:

> . . . as a result of the labors left unfinished crowned by the Acacaca-cademy of Anthropopopometry of Essy-in-Possy of Testew and Cunard it is established beyond all doubt . . . that man in Essy that man in short that man in brief in spite of the strides of alimentation and defecation wastes and pines wastes and pines and concurrently simultaneously what is more for reasons unknown in spite of the strides of physical culture the practice of sports such as tennis . . . in the great cold the great dark the air and the earth abode of stones in the great cold alas alas in the year of their Lord six hundred and something the air the earth the sea the earth abode of stones in the great deeps the great cold on sea on land and in the air I resume for reasons unknown in spite of the tennis. . . .
>
> (28b–29b)

Lucky's words are produced to order in a ritual enactment of narrative in which lecture and *lecture* are radically divorced but strive to merge ("I resume"). Seemingly significant phrases and tendentious verbal formulations, recognizable syntactically and separable into discrete units, appear to indicate a kind of poetic metaphorization but do not produce it. A "reading" of Lucky's speech might conclude that it is a fruitless investment of imagination in which no breakthrough to poetic or rational diction occurs, but, as recitation, Lucky's speech is rich and full.[10] This dichotomy itself delineates Beckett's separated registers of language.

The procedure of Lucky's recitation compounds the enigma of its reading. But Lucky's speech is more than enigmatic—its very enigma and disorder demonstrate the serious (though obscure) dangers of disordered recitation or improperly learned speech, as is evidenced by the other characters' reaction to it. During his lecture, Lucky's control (ordering) of his language is absurdly disordered and Pozzo's control of Lucky disintegrates; Pozzo becomes more and more agitated. Finally, all three attack Lucky and drag him to the ground, enervated, on his last word, which is, appropriately, "unfinished" ("Inachevés"). After Pozzo's instruction to nab Lucky's hat, with which Didi complies, Beckett indicates in stage direction, "*Silence of Lucky. He falls. Silence. Panting of the victors*" (29b). Beckett's use of *vainqueurs* (75) is telling here. Lucky has radically altered his identity in this speech, outdoing Pozzo, Gogo, and Didi in his verbal energy but providing a visualization of Turner's "voluntary *sparagmos* or self-dismemberment of order." Lucky demonstrates that repetition is not order, though it is not necessarily disorder; he enacts the rending or sacrifice of order to disembodied language. In this guise of *sparagmos*, Lucky challenges Pozzo, Gogo, and Didi to suppress him. In the play, they are "victorious" over Lucky's speech and, more important, over his violent manifestation of the slippage of language. To Lucky's suppression, Gogo asserts, "Avenged!" (30a), and Lucky is treated as a figure of contempt. For his part, Lucky, conquered, collapses into a comatose apathy ("divine apathia"?), as though his force has been utterly drained. He must, indeed, be taught to feel again.[11]

Didi's Last Lecture/Lecture

Godot's penultimate lecture, Didi's last lecture and indeed a kind of aria, is a parable of the suspense of meaning:[12]

> VLADIMIR: Was I sleeping, while the others suffered? Am I sleeping now? To-morrow, when I wake, or think I do, what shall I say of to-day? That with Estragon my friend, at this place, until the fall of night, I waited for Godot? That Pozzo passed, with his carrier, and that he spoke to us? Probably. But in all that what truth will there be? (*Estragon, having struggled with his boots in vain, is*

dozing off again. Vladimir looks at him.) He'll know nothing. He'll tell me about the blows he received and I'll give him a carrot. (*Pause.*) Astride of a grave and a difficult birth. Down in the hole, lingeringly, the grave-digger puts on the forceps. We have time to grow old. The air is full of our cries. (*He listens.*) But habit is a great deadener. (*He looks again at Estragon.*) At me too someone is looking, of me too someone is saying, He is sleeping, he knows nothing, let him sleep on. (*Pause.*) . . . What have I said?

(58a–58b)

The poignancy of Didi's questioning, undercut and made more intense by his final question, is not in the fact that he has thought but in the fact that his thought, like all thought the instant it becomes language, must be divorced from both experience and human feeling. Didi is indeed sleeping, insofar as his mode of diction and identification is that of recitation. In this last parabolic lecture, Didi invents two "judges" (both within his rhetoric) to stand for this principle of division and to assess his significance: the first is Didi tomorrow; the second is a posited *lecteur* who will "read" Didi and conclude inevitably, as Didi himself has done, that he is blind, asleep. This double interlocutor, as invisible as his texts, is nonetheless the (double) judge of Didi's meaning. Didi's parable of birth and death, "[a]stride of a grave," is a paradigm of overabundant concealment.[13]

Godot enacts in its play of lecture and *lecture*, recitation and reading, a critique of immanence as a textual phenomenon. It suspends the resolution of all struggles for meaning. *Godot*'s characters recite the texts of suspended meaning, blind to the realization that meaning occurs precisely in that suspense. As David Hesla points out:

"Meaning" is the final idol which the poet and the critic in their human weakness are tempted to fall down and worship. It is the last literary absolute, the one the worker in words finds it most difficult to dispense with.

(227)

In Beckett, this absolute is suggested as the mediation of *Godot*'s two texts, the "anterior present" (origin of lecture) and the "stage present" (characters engaged in *lecture*, in reading life). Once the reader/viewer is extracted from the stage present, the anterior present is revealed as a blind spot. Molloy states the manifesto for *Godot*'s uncompromising criticism of experience and reading:

Not to want to say, not to know what you want to say, not to be able to say what you think you want to say, and never to stop saying, or hardly ever, that is the thing to keep in mind, even in the heat of composition.

(28)

Not to want to say, not to *mean*, as the "thing" to "keep in mind" in the "heat of composition" (here Beckett's own composition, of *Godot*)—Beckett's themes of signification gather and concentrate in Molloy's monologue as they do in Didi's last parable and pervasively in *Godot*. For Didi and Gogo, Molloy's negation of *vouloir dire*, of wanting-to-say as meaning, the suspense of words in words, is the source of arrested—stopped, interrupted, and prolonged—action. To teach the play is to engage in this suspense, without canceling it; indeed one must call attention to the ways in which one's own lecture (*lecture*) on (and of) *Waiting for Godot* reenacts Beckett's play.

NOTES

[1]My use of the doubled word lecture/*lecture* indicates this indeterminate act of reading represented in Beckett's drama. The lecture, a recitation, is the order of the disembodied text; the *lecture*, or reading, comes from the subjective individuation of response posited, in Western tradition, in reason. In Beckett, the *lecteur*, the reader, is then caught, like Gogo and Didi, between these views of reading, in a sense both inside and outside "the reading." Traditional readings of *Godot* are generally blind to a central part of Beckett's theatricality: that within *Godot*, in its mise-en-scène, this act of reading (both aloud and "reading the world," silently) is itself problematic. Wolfgang Iser addresses this issue in *The Act of Reading* when he claims that modern texts "invoke expected functions in order to transform them into blanks," to "fulfill 'minus functions' " (208).

[2]The names of Didi and Gogo represent the agencies of enduring and encoding suspense: Gogo, in English (go go), is the doubling, repetition, and suspense of action as movement; Didi, in French (*dit dit*), is the doubling, repetition, and suspense of action as speech. Suspense here is multiple—anticipation, desire, anxiety, excitement, boredom, narrative—but also, as suspension, it is interruption, deferral of action, enclosing, deprivation, excluding. Suspension is the means of balancing an automobile—and a timepiece. Action is then suspended between movement (Gogo) and speech or language (Didi).

[3]Beckett discusses suffering at length in *Proust*, as for example when he says of Proust's narrative that

> periods of transition . . . represent the perilous zones in the life of the individual, dangerous, precarious, painful, mysterious, and fertile, when for a moment the boredom of living is replaced by the suffering of being.

(8)

This suffering is directly linked both to Nietzsche's comment from *Beyond Good and Evil* and to Beckett's comment from *Molloy*, the epigraphs to this discussion. If clarity = rigidity = death and lack of clarity = fluidity = life, then human beings are caught in an eternal desire for that lack in order to live. Beckett learns this principle from Nietzsche, as I explore in "Beckett and Nietzsche: The Linguistic Turn." (I take up the reference to *Molloy* later in this discussion.) The "suffering of being" referred to is not that of Hesla's dialectic, since for him "being" and "nothing" synthesize into a Hegelian-Heideggerian "becoming" whose activity vanishes in the Heideggerian mysticism of Hesla's "chaos."

⁴In this context, see Frank Kermode's brilliant discussion of parables in *The Genesis of Secrecy*, which is dedicated "To Those Outside" and whose epigraph, "ἐκείνοις δὲ τοῖς ἔξω ἐν παραβολαῖς τὰ πάντα γίνεται" 'to those outside everything is in parables,' is cited in the book only in Greek. In Kermode's design, thought and character (διάνοια and ἔθος) are hidden and secret, while their result, action—in this case narrative action—is not. For an example of Beckett's use of parable, see Didi's tombstone song at the opening of act 2, particularly in the light of the second act's desperate and unsuccessful attempt to remember act 1.

⁵See Jacques Derrida, *Of Grammatology* (141–65). Insight here is seen as the ability to read one's own strategies of reading. This strategic insight is the kernel of Paul de Man's argument in *Blindness and Insight*, which takes on Rousseau and Derrida, among others. Central to this interpretation of *Godot* is Derrida's conception of the supplementarity of writing (absent language) to speaking (present language), in which writing (cor)responds to Beckett's recitation and speaking to individual, personal reading. Derrida claims, as does Beckett, that "when speech fails to protect presence, writing becomes necessary," but the necessity of writing operates within the scene (theater) of a break with nature, that is, Gogo (144, 151).

⁶This *gouffre* continues to exist between them throughout, to the final suspended curtain. Gogo, the poet (who is called Adam, the *original*, in Beckett's English translation but Catulle, the enigmatic lyric poet, in the original French), is a creature of dream, imagination, and emotion; Pozzo and Lucky become "Cain" and "Abel," but Didi, who attempts to master hidden texts but will not let Gogo report his dreams, is only the mundane "Mr. Albert," though of course Gogo and Didi play at being Pozzo and Lucky in the recitation of act 1 in act 2 (47a).

⁷Beckett's English text of *Godot* omits the stage directions with which Lucky's speech begins in the French text: "*débit monotone*" 'delivered in monotone' (71). *Débiter*, which has several meanings, indicates a mechanical process. Referring to a machine, it means "to turn out"; referring to poetry, it means "to run off." In its theatrical context, it means "to recite."

⁸The origin and history of the *sparagmos* is vital to an understanding of *Godot*, particularly in the light of its link to theater. Greek theater was dedicated to Dionysus, whose origins enact the dismemberment and rejuvenation associated with the scapegoat. The androgynous god embodies the principle of association and dissociation (see my discussion of Nietzsche's treatment of Dionysus). Dionysus also represents the ritual sacrifice of meaning to force, as Lucky demonstrates in his speech and its aftermath.

⁹Turner then says that this "pod" is produced by "reflexively ritualized theatre"

(161), an excellent definition of *Godot* in its own right, particularly in the light of the concept of recitation.

[10]Beckett's sense of lecture in Lucky's speech is compounded in the French by the fact that the directions to the other three characters on the stage, which are numbered at the beginning of the text in English, appear as marginal paratexts in the French, coordinated with (and seeming to substantiate) the absurd text beside them as though glossing and commenting on it.

[11]This discussion of Lucky's amazing speech merely touches the surface of a few themes at work in it. Each phrase could be analyzed exhaustively, particularly within the context of the themes of memory, time, presence, and meaning, and an order of repetition could be shown to exist within it. In addition, the relation between the speech and the dialogue that precedes and follows it is far richer than suggested here. One is left, no matter how much one does with it, with a feeling of frustrated underachievement in the face of the speech, a predicament that is precisely the intent of the register of language I have termed "lecture."

[12]My interpretation depends on the centrality of parable, for interesting material on which see Frank Kermode's *Genesis of Secrecy* and John D. Crossan's *In Parables* and *Dark Interval*. Parable, a "nugget" concealed in a text, is both straightforwardly and ironically the essence of Beckett. Didi's parable is a terse and somber one, the nugget of his final lecture:

> Astride of a grave and a difficult birth. Down in the hole, lingeringly, the grave-digger puts on the forceps. We have time to grow old. The air is full of our cries. (*He listens.*) But habit is a great deadener.
>
> (58a–58b)

Beckett's word for *deadener* is *sourdine*, a musical term for "mute." Our "cries" at the ineluctable finitude of life do not return to us, Didi says, because muted voices get in the way. One cannot help thinking here of the basso profundo that finally surfaces in "Ping," the murmur that is our only evidence that all is not over. The final parable is what Didi finds to give himself the impression he exists.

[13]This last parable, evocative of Hamlet and his ambivalence concerning action, life, and death, also combines emergent meaning (the forceps are "put on" ["applique"]) and its concealment ("down in the hole" ["du fond du trou"]). Texts exist, Didi suggests, in one state of concealment or another. The forceps, a tool in the same way a pen is, are a means of extraction that serve only to reconceal.

At another level, the parable (which is also reminiscent of *The Waste Land*) shows itself as portentous but elliptical: it is full of contradictions and reversals while seeming to embody revealed meaning, qualities also present in the way Didi delivers this lecture.

A Comparative Approach to *Godot*

J. Terence McQueeny

This comparative reading of the French and English texts of *Godot* analyzes the changes in the English version for what they reveal about Beckett's strategy as self-translator. The approach that I am suggesting may be modified to fit the needs and abilities of students at various levels of the French curriculum. Those instructors who favor teaching language through literature might introduce this approach in place of the customary readings from the foreign media at the end of the intermediate cycle or use it as a segment of more advanced courses in composition, stylistics, and literature. I have attempted to present this material in such a way as to be of interest also to English or theater teachers who may not have studied French.

The play has much to recommend it to students faced with the *corvée* of reading in a foreign language. The text is short, the vocabulary seems easy, and an English translation is provided. (Since there is as yet no bilingual edition available, I recommend the Suhrkamp trilingual edition in which the French and English texts are set side by side on the left, with the German text on the right in larger type. All page references are to this edition.) There is no need at first to point out that the English version is perhaps the most privileged text in the Beckett canon, that he preferred it to the original (Duckworth, *Angels* 16), and that it raises interesting questions about the theoretical implications of self-translation and the literary status of the second version. These topics emerge gradually and can be more profitably discussed after the analysis.

After a brief outline of Beckett's career as a bilingual writer and a review of the particular circumstances surrounding the composition of the play, its unexpected success, and its subsequent translation by the author into English, the work can be broken down into segments and assigned for class discussion and commentary. Students should be warned that Beckett made changes as he translated and that these should be marked according to whether they are additions, deletions, or alterations in meaning or tonality. It is a good idea for instructors to indicate the most significant changes in a segment before the reading begins, along with any recondite allusions, vocabulary difficulties, and untranslatable material. By the end of the play, if one includes differing levels of language or tone, there are well over three hundred changes in the English version. The major task, then, is to identify some sort of pattern that illuminates Beckett's strategy as self-translator. The following are what I consider the most important elements of that strategy.

A number of key changes illustrate Beckett's tendency toward universalizing particulars, a procedure that increases the possible interpretations of the play. In the manuscript version, for example, Vladimir has in his pocket a piece of paper on which Godot has written down the time of the rendezvous:

"Samedi soir et suivants" (Duckworth, "Making" 94). This indicates that Godot is an actual person and that the tramps have a real reason for waiting. In the original French text, the paper has disappeared, but Didi is still looking to Godot for shelter: "Ce soir on couchera peut-être chez lui, au chaud, au sec, le ventre plein, sur la paille. Ça vaut la peine qu'on attende. Non?" (54) (Perhaps tonight we'll be sleeping at his place, warm, dry, stomachs full, on the straw. It's worth waiting for, don't you think?) Here Godot still seems too much a physical reality. Beckett cuts the passage from the English version, making a definitive interpretation more difficult. In a similar vein, the Holy Savior market in which Lucky is to be sold has no particular name in English (84). Estragon refers to himself as Catulle in French, but in English he says he is Adam (96). Once again the symbolic possibilities of the change are richer. Vladimir remembers that they picked grapes for a man named Bonnelly in Roussillon but forgets both name and place in English (154). Estragon dreams of going away to l'Ariège, a *département* in the Pyrenees. In English, however, the *département* disappears and only the mountains remain (200). Finally, when Didi asks Gogo what they were talking about the night before, he replies that they talked about boots. In English, the boots are cut: "Yes, now I remember, yesterday evening we spent blathering about nothing in particular. That's been going on now for half a century" (164). Beckett's natural bent in revision is to pare details back to the essential.

A similar strategy allows Beckett to heighten and intensify the various predicaments in which his characters find themselves. In French, when Vladimir asks Estragon about whether he was beaten during the night, he answers with an emphatic "Si" but immediately qualifies it with "Pas trop." (Not too much.) In English, there is no qualification: "Beat me? Certainly they beat me" (28). When first reminded that they cannot leave because they are waiting for Godot, Estragon says simply, "C'est vrai." (It's true.) In the second version, however, a new stage direction has been added calling for him to deliver the line *"despairingly"* (38). The play often indicates that Didi and Gogo have come before to wait for Godot, but by adding the stage direction when Godot is first mentioned, Beckett leaves no doubt about how he wants the character played. Their waiting is seen to be chronic from the start. Estragon derives some consolation from the taste of his carrot in the French version: "Elle est sucrée." (It's sweet.) But the second version denies him the pleasures of taste: "It's a carrot" (54). A few lines later "Elle est délicieuse, ta carotte" becomes "I'll never forget this carrot" (56). In the first version, Estragon warns Pozzo: "Vous allez attraper froid." (You're going to catch cold.) In the translation, it is more serious: "You'll get pneumonia" (94). Estragon's comment on Lucky's decrepitude, "C'est normal," becomes "It's inevitable" in translation (70).

Additions in the translation make the theme of death more insistent. Vladimir tries to make Estragon understand that the thieves abused Christ because he would not save them from death. "I thought you said hell," replies Estragon. "From death, from death," insists Didi (36). Dying is also added to Lucky's list of sports (112), and "tête" (head) is translated as the less ambiguous "skull" throughout the monologue (116).

Beckett increases the verbal abuse throughout the second version by adding "pig" or "hog" to Pozzo's commands (64, 80, 104, 218). Vladimir likewise adds "imbecile" in referring to Estragon when the latter does not follow Vladimir's thought on the two thieves early in the play and later calls him "pig" when he offers the wrong leg for inspection rather than the one kicked by Lucky (116). Pozzo utters additional cries for help in the second version (194, 196), and Estragon, to emphasize the wretchedness of their condition vis-à-vis Pozzo, replies to Vladimir's suggestion that they help him with an incredulous added line: "*We* help *him*?" (196).

Other exchanges are sharpened with sarcasm. "J'écoute" (I'm listening), says Gogo when asked to comment on Didi's story of the thieves. In the second version, however, he answers "*with exaggerated enthusiasm*: I find this really most extraordinarily interesting" (36). To Pozzo's question about Vladimir's age Gogo replies: "Demandez-lui." (Ask him.) In the second version, he says, "Eleven" (74). Asked to help recall the subject of an earlier conversation, Estragon tells Vladimir, "Ma foi, là tu m'en demandes trop" (well now, there you're asking too much) (162). In the second version he snaps, "I'm not a historian" (162). Beckett also changes Vladimir's "Attention" to the ironic "Make a note of this" as Pozzo finally begins to explain why Lucky does not put down the bags (82). Lines added in act 2 of the translation underscore Estragon's animosity toward Lucky. Estragon refuses to go and see what has happened to him: "After what he did to me? Never!" (214). The final example here is Pozzo's remark about his work force. Lucky, he says, is working hard to be indispensable as a porter: "Comme si j'étais à court d'hommes de peine!" (As though I were short of laborers!). In English it is "As though I were short of slaves!" (82). All these changes seem calculated to heighten individual conflicts and intensify the already stark dramatic situation.

Other changes in the second version seem to reflect Beckett's increasing confidence as a director. A rough count of the stage directions shows eighty-six deletions, forty additions, and twenty-two transformations of meaning. The second version contains many new indicators. Estragon, as I have pointed out, is to speak his lines "*despairingly*" (38, 42, 140, 168). He is to complain "*angrily*" about the turnip he has been handed rather than "*plaintivement*" (54). His questions for Didi about the rendezvous with Godot are marked "*very insidious*" (42). At other times, Estragon is supposed to look "*wildly*" about him (152) or to be "*exasperated*" (166). Vladimir "*indignantly*" tries to stop Estragon from begging (102) and "*triumphantly*" discovers the wound Lucky has inflicted on Estragon's shin (166). Pozzo's reference to his "[p]rofessional worries!" is to be delivered "with *extraordinary vehemence,*" after which he becomes "*calmer*" (86). The translation also includes new instructions about stage movements. "Wait!" says Estragon. "(*He moves away from Vladimir.*) I sometimes wonder if we wouldn't have been better off alone, each one for himself. (*He crosses the stage and sits down on the mound.*) We weren't made for the same road" (136). The added movement visually reinforces the meaning of his lines, as does Didi's movement immediately afterward: "*Vladimir slowly crosses the stage and sits down beside Estragon.* We can still part, if you think it would be better." "It's not worth while now," replies Estragon as the curtain is about to fall on act 1 (137). At one point in the original version, Lucky is instructed simply to pick up "everything" ("*il reprend tout*"). But in English he is specifically told to pick up "*bag, basket, and stool*" (64). In French, Vladimir is told to begin jumping when they start their exercises: "*Il commence à sauter.*" In English, the direction again is more specific: "*Vladimir hops from one foot to the other*" (188). The motif of uncertainty is also reinforced in the stage directions as Vladimir grows "[*l*]*ess sure*" and then "[*s*]*till less sure*" that Pozzo is not Godot (222).

There are many more of these additions, as well as deletions, in the stage directions. Which were dictated by Beckett himself and which were suggested by his first director, Roger Blin, is difficult to resolve. Beckett was still inexperienced in production when *Godot* was first performed in 1953, and he generally deferred to Blin about what was working and what had to be changed. John Fletcher has reported that "all the omissions" in the translation are Blin's (Fletcher, "Roger Blin" 25). However the changes came about, Beckett was a quick study. By the time he finished the translation for the 1954 Grove Press edition, all these additions were in place.

The final problem raised by a comparison of the texts is that of their disparate levels of language. Before dealing with this aspect of the analysis, the teacher might want to review the traditional ordering of the levels of expression or tonality. The hierarchy places slang at the bottom, followed by popular expression, then familiar or colloquial expression, then written, literary, and, finally, poetic usage. Slang and popular expression are considered vulgar, while the other levels qualify as "bon usage" (Vinay and Darbelnet 33). Expression in the French version of *Godot* tends to remain on the familiar level, occasionally dipping into the popular range. It was the colloquial tone, the everyday words, that the early audiences found so riveting. Beckett has no particular affection for slang, it seems, and only rarely aims for the higher reaches of "bon usage." When he repatriates his French, however, he often works in the higher tonal registers, diving into popular vulgarity only occasionally. Standard translation practice is to maintain the level of expression found in the original. This is precisely what Beckett chooses not to do. His English tends to be more specific, more poetic, and more elevated in tone than his French. There is no shortage of examples in the play. Alan Simpson, Beckett's first Irish director, confronted this difference in the very first line of the play, "Rien à faire," which Beckett translated as "Nothing to be done":

> Now this is obviously very important because, for the tramps, there *is* nothing to be done. But in French, this is a colloquialism, and can be thrown away with a sigh as just a little exclamation of tedium. In my original Dublin production I changed it to "It's no good," because I felt that it was more colloquial and less significant. However, I subsequently discussed it with Sam, and he was most emphatic that he wished it to be spoken as "Nothing to be done."
>
> (45)

Other examples in the same vein: Estragon says, "Les gens sont des cons." (People are jerks.) Beckett's translation is "People are bloody ignorant apes" (38). Vladimir tells Estragon, "Pour jeter le doute, à toi le pompon." (At casting doubt you really take the cake.) The translation elevates the tone considerably: "Nothing is certain when you're about" (40). "Là, tu te goures" (you're kidding yourself) in the translation is "There you're mistaken" (40). Observing Lucky in ruins, Estragon says, "Pour moi, il est en train de crever." (Looks to me like he's about to croak.) This becomes "Looks at his last gasp to me" (70). Pozzo loses his watch: "Merde, alors!" (Well, shit!) is translated as "Damnation" (120). Vladimir asks Estragon, "Qui t'a esquinté?" (Who worked you over?) The translation is "Who beat you?" (146). Vladimir and Estragon glare at one another angrily: "Voyons, pas de cérémonie." (Come on now. Let's not stand on ceremony.) This is changed into "Ceremonious ape!" (186). "Ne sois pas têtu, voyons" (Don't be pigheaded) becomes "Punctilious pig!" (186).

The tone of the second version is sometimes raised by turns of phrase more specific and colorful than those in the original. Vladimir exclaims at one point, "On se croirait au spectacle." (It's like being at a show.) This is translated as "Worse than the pantomime" (90). Estragon can remember neither Pozzo nor Lucky, but he does recall "un énergumen qui m'a foutu des coups de pied." (I remember a lunatic who kicked the hell out of me.) In English it becomes "I remember a lunatic who kicked the shins off me" (152). Gogo's "Parle-moi du sous-sol" (Talk to me about being buried) becomes "Tell me about the worms" (152). Didi's "Je me fais au goût au fur et à mesure" (I get used to the taste as I go along) is translated as "I get used to the muck as I go along" (64). Lucky's eyes are described in French as "coming out" of his head: "ils sortent." Vladimir's phrase in the translation has them "goggling out of his head" (70). At the beginning of act 2, we see that the tree now has "quelques feuilles" (some leaves) in the original. In English it has specifically "four or five leaves" (142). Vladimir's phrase "Je ne comprends pas" (I don't understand) becomes "I remain in the dark" (48). Instead of merely looking at the moon as he does in the French version, Estragon intentionally misquotes Shelley in English: "Pale for weariness. . . . Of climbing and gazing on the likes of us" (55). Vladimir mutters to himself that he will get up off the ground "tôt ou tard" (sooner or later). In translation, it is "In the fullness of time" (200). His verdict on the rope, "Elle ne vaut rien" (It's worthless), is changed to "Not worth a curse" (230).

That these differences in the levels of tonality are due, at least in some measure, to the internal dynamics of the two languages can be argued on the basis of comparative stylistics (Vinay and Darbelnet; E. Simpson). First of all, French, with a preponderance of substantives in its active vocabulary, is more abstract than English. It is characterized by a large number of sign words rather than image words, that is, words which appeal to the mind as abstractions rather than to the senses and the imagination. Reliance on sign words leads naturally to concentration on the essential, to clarity in expression, and to a certain lack of concern for information judged unnecessary for comprehension. Reliance on image words leads to concentration on the particular, precision in expression, and a preoccupation with the order of sensations. Gide put it succinctly in terms borrowed from the visual arts: "It belongs to the genius of our language to make line prevail over color" (qtd. in Vinay and Darbelnet 59).

Second, English has greater lexical resources. Notice the variety of English verbs used in the following stage directions:

Pozzo tire sur sa pipe.
Pozzo puffs on his pipe. . . .
(72)

Vladimir tire Estragon vers les coulisses.
Vladimir drags Estragon towards the wings.
(182)

Pozzo tire sur la corde.
Pozzo jerks the rope.
(80)

Though it might be possible to use *pull* in each instance, the natural tendency is to change the verb according to the context. So, in French the lunatic who (literally) "gave me some kicks" in English "kicked the shins off me" (152)—much more precise. The "spectacle" in French becomes a more particular kind of show in English: "Worse than the pantomime" (90). In French, Didi says he gets used to the "taste" as he goes along. But "taste" is too general in English, so he gets used to "the muck" (64). In French, Lucky's eyes are "coming out." In English, they are "goggling out of his head" (70). The tiger "goes his way" in French ("il se sauve"). In English, he "slinks" away (196). Didi and Gogo look at the sunset in French ("*ils regardent*"), but in English they "*scrutinize*" it (210).

Taine talks about the inevitable loss of going from English to French:

> Translating an English sentence into French is like copying a colored figure with a gray pencil. Reducing aspects and qualities of things, the French mind ends up with general ideas, simple ones, which it aligns in a simplified order, that of logic.
>
> (Qtd. in Vinay and Darbelnet 59)

In the French version of *Godot*, the colloquial and sometimes vulgar tone provided the necessary color to supplement Taine's "gray pencil." When Beckett set out to re-create the work in English, he faced the choice of maintaining the colloquial tone of the original or violating the principle of tonal parity. As a poet, how could he resist the opportunity to capitalize on the greater lexical resources and image words available at all levels of *le bon usage* in English? He made many revisions to *Waiting for Godot* in performance (see McMillan and Fehsenfeld), but, in 1965—despite his repeated choice to write in his nonnative French—he did tell Colin Duckworth that he preferred the English text of *Godot* to the French.

This excursus into what Beckett once referred to as the "wastes and wilds of self-translation" (Wolf and Fancher 184) provides students with a unique opportunity to observe an artist re-creating a work as he translates it. The resulting lesson should be twofold. First, they see in detail how, with simple but brilliant adjustments, Beckett improves the dramatic effectiveness of his play. The practical lesson is dramaturgy. Second, in analyzing the divergent levels of language, they see that Beckett intentionally leaves himself open to the charge of false tonality by refusing to reproduce the colloquial idiom of the French text. Instead he finds his color in the higher tonal levels of English and produces a text that is less abstract than the original, more specific and colorful—finally, one that is better suited both to the natural dynamics of English and to his talents as a poet. The theoretical lesson is poetics.

Who Is Godot? A Semiotic Approach to Beckett's Play

Una Chaudhuri

> This is getting really insignificant.
> Samuel Beckett,
> *Waiting for Godot*

The critical fortunes of Beckett's play give Didi the lie. Far from tracking the growing insignificance to which the main characters bear pathetic testimony, the play's many critics have succeeded in unpacking virtually the whole history of Western ideas from *Waiting for Godot*. This central paradox, this almost ludicrous disjunction between the play's impoverished aspect and its wealth of meaning, serves as a point of departure for a semiotic approach to the play, in which, with advanced drama students, I explore *Godot*'s self-reflexive hints on how drama conquers insignificance and achieves signification.

I start the discussion with an overview of the main thematic and theatricalist readings of the play, beginning with Martin Esslin's initial and influential encoding of the play within an absurdist paradigm. I encourage students to excavate the organizing myth of these approaches: the myth of Sisyphus, which *Godot* "reads out" existentially and theatrically (the classic inscription of this reading being Alain Robbe-Grillet's essay "Samuel Beckett: Or, 'Presence' in the Theatre"). To this myth I oppose—or, rather, pose—another (for I propose it as a heuristic device, much as directors sometimes get actors to switch roles in rehearsal, to deepen their understanding of the play). I cast Tantalus in the role of Sisyphus and explore the play as an example of "tantalizing" dramaturgy, a mode of signification by which meaning is rendered both inevitable and impossible.

Waiting for Godot depicts tantalization, of course, in the ceaseless and motivated waiting of its protagonists, but it creates it, too, as an experience for its audience. Or, rather, for "both" its audiences, for *Godot* produces in most vivid form the distinction between the two kinds of audiences all plays, hypothetically, have: the "first-night" audience, a (fantasied?) audience of innocents, and all the subsequent audiences, who play the role of that first innocent audience but are forever excluded from its paradisiacal, unmediated experience of the play.

The first audience of *Waiting for Godot*, tantalized only by the question of whether Godot will come—"Sardoodledom's ultimate question," as Herbert Blau rightly points out (232)—might be imagined as remaining within the response paradigm of traditional theater, wherein desire is gratified and questions are resolved through the mere passage of time. The time of traditional drama is powerfully purposive, its finality inscribed in its every moment in the form of an assurance of closure. No matter how many detours and complications a plot incorporates, no matter how many time schemes it deploys, the audience can negotiate them secure in the certainty that time will have a stop. It is precisely this feature of traditional drama that Beckett's play challenges. The original question—Will Godot come?—once it is answered in the negative, displaces the traditional mechanisms of suspense and replaces their characteristic mode of query with another one. For the subsequent audience, the question is posed not at the level of action but at a level that previously belonged outside the play, to the critical rather than the spectatorial enterprise. The new question—Who or what is Godot?—reconstitutes the audience: no longer mere spectators charged with negotiating a temporalized action and constructing it into a plot, they must now perform as hermeneuticians, endowing a textual item with allegorical or symbolic meaning before that item has taken its place (i.e., achieved signification) within a dramatic action.[1] In other words, the new question inserts itself between the spectator's desire as defined by traditional dramaturgy (a dramaturgy that Beckett's play depends on, if only negatively) and the fulfillment of that desire. In the place of the pleasure of the plot, Beckett inserts the unpleasure of promised meaning, that is, the unpleasure of tantalization.

Once my students have made the conceptual shift from Sisyphus to Tantalus, I point out that the question of Godot's identity does more than tantalize spectators of Beckett's play: it is a paradigm of textual tantalization itself. Its answer appears to lie outside the play, encouraging criticism to return to that realm it once called home: the author's intentions. However, this ancient ground of textual meaning now seems abandoned, most explicitly in Beckett's work, where its vacancy is announced, paradoxically, in the form of a text strongly marked with intentionality: the direct, nonfictional statement of authorial intent. I am referring, of course, to Beckett's notorious riposte to the question of Godot's identity. "If I knew," Beckett said, "I would have said so in the play" (qtd. in Esslin, *Samuel Beckett* 55). The answer has endeared Beckett to theatricalists, who read his remark as a programmatic (and heroic) refusal to betray the free, theatrical experience of his play to those (critics, intellectuals, humanists) who would colonize it in the name of meaning.

But there is at least as much reason to take Beckett at his word, to read his remark as a confession of ignorance, his failure to endow the play with meaning. If indeed Beckett is not deliberately withholding the identity of Godot but really does not know it (a supposition implying that there is something to be known), then he is displacing the traditional notion of textual meaningfulness—displacing it more radically than if he were simply manip-

ulating spectatorial experience by repressing certain dramatic facts. For if
we take Beckett's remark at face value, we are confronted with the incredible
spectacle of a work of art based on expressive deficiency, a work of art that
lacks the one necessary condition of art: mastery. It is surely significant that
critics have generally been unable to accept this feature in Beckett's work
and have preferred to characterize Godot's nonarrival as an effect of Beckett's
authorial power rather than of the impotence and ignorance he himself insists
on.[2]

As my students are now in a position to understand, this paradoxical
empowering of authorial ignorance traces a critical trajectory that moves
from hermeneutics to semiotics or from criticism to metacriticism, a process
which ends up asserting that the play is not about a specific subject or idea
but about "aboutness," that is, about referentiality. Interestingly enough,
the movement from interpretation to metacritical commentary is largely
conducted under the auspices of another Beckett text. This brief text is itself
a commentary, for it is grafted onto a citation, a sentence from Saint Augustine: "Do not despair, one of the thieves was saved; do not presume: one
of the thieves was damned." Beckett's remark, "That sentence has a wonderful shape. It is the shape that matters" (qtd. in Hobson 154), has been
widely construed as an invitation to formalist analysis of his work, even as
an assertion that the play primarily signifies through its structure rather than
its content. Yet the many ensuing analyses of the play's structure, revealing
its extraordinary balancing of opposites, have not, for all their brilliance,
succeeded in erasing the question of the play: Who is Godot? What they
have achieved is to raise a second question: What does it mean to ask the
question Who is Godot?

The answers to this "second-order" question produce many different Godots (and *Godots*), all, however, profoundly theorized. They make the play
a metasemiotic work, one in which the dramatic conflict does not remain on
stage but descends into the auditorium, involving the spectators in a dialogue
with themselves. This reading of the play has been so persuasive (because,
of course, it is so much in tune with these theoretical and ironic times) that
it is not unusual to be informed even by one's undergraduate students that
the question of Godot's identity is finally irrelevant to a "correct" reading
of the play, indeed, that this correctness is a function of refraining from so
naive a procedure as speculation on the absent character's identity. So much
for the innocent audience.

How does a question become a nonquestion? How does this play contrive
to make us strenuously "unask" the question it has always asked and continues to ask? To answer this question, I invite students to retrace their
steps and return to the original question, the one the play posed to its first
audience. They quickly see, however, that the exercise is futile; that origin

is gone, nonexistent. For, on closer inspection, the original audience we have posited is not the integrated, stable starting point of a process that will continue beyond its encounter with the play: rather, it is an audience already in process, divided against itself. The play's repetitious structure is such that it reverses the usual role-playing of audiences: instead of requiring later audiences to play the role of a first audience, *Godot* requires its first audience to play the role of a subsequent audience.

The mechanism of this unorthodox response paradigm is Godot. His non-arrival in act 1 radically alters the relation between the audience and its horizon of expectations, transforming it from a traditional one (hinging on the question Will Godot come?) into a problematic nonrelation (or not-yet relation). Having established Godot's radical absence in the final moments of the first act, the play puts the audience's continued participation in the play into question. The sameness of act 2, challenging the developmental model on which traditional play watching is predicated, creates a fissure in the audience's experience of the play, placing its members in a relation of subsequentiality to themselves. Thus mediation and irony replace direct experience and meaning: a split audience contemplates a split play, and its experience becomes an experience not of the play but of its own "second-ness."

The audience of *Godot* experiences a sense of belatedness. What we witness in act 2 has already been anticipated and adumbrated by the pre-ceding act: thus our "new" and "different" experience comes to us already heavily marked, if not canceled out altogether, by sameness. Students should now realize that the second act exists not as a version of the first but as its betrayal; it comes into being, treacherously, as a result of the nonaccom-plishment of both the structure and the response paradigm evoked in act 1. When traditional dramatic desire is frustrated, the effect is more than a feeling of being let down. It is the creation of a new mode of desire, one that is fully and agonizingly conscious of its nonfulfillment, its nonfulfill-ability. We are back with Tantalus—and ready to move to the semiotics of the tree.

Tantalizing Dramaturgy: An Example

To produce an ironic oscillation between the promise of meaning and its frustration *Godot* simultaneously entertains two realms of reference, one of which is usually actively suppressed in favor of the other. The two realms are the fictional (the universe of discourse that stands for a supposedly real state of affairs) and the actual (which, in drama, is the theatrical situation, including the auditorium, the stage, the actors, and the audience). The primary task of traditional dramaturgy is to erase the actual, obscuring or plunging it into temporary oblivion to establish the fictional. This paradigm is not, as is often thought, peculiar to realistic drama, although realism is certainly its most successful version.[3]

The way in which Beckett alters the traditional relation of drama to stage may be studied in his handling of that signifying system which most literally supports the construction of a fictional world: space. I suggest that the relation between mimetic and diegetic space receives a new formulation in *Waiting for Godot*, one that comes close to obliterating that distinction. For the reader of Beckett's text, the famous set direction *"A country road. A tree. Evening"* indicates a place that is both marked and unmarked or, rather, a place that is partly marked by absence, by a textual signifier that can easily escape theatrical concretization. The road is so minimally evoked in the script, so shorn of the specificity and descriptive embellishment that would allow a reader of the script to visualize it (Is it straight or crooked, broad or narrow, a highway or a mud path, and in what direction does it run?) that it seems not to be *on* the stage but to be the stage itself. If the stage is the road, can we infer that the road (of the play text, of the play's fictional realm) is the stage? This is, in fact, what many critics have done, taking their cue from Robbe-Grillet. It is also what many productions have done, including Beckett's own at the Schiller Theater, Berlin, in 1975.

But the rest of the stage direction contradicts this metatheatrical reading; the potentially unrepresented road is accompanied by a tree that is not only necessarily represented but a kind of supersign of the world-creating capacities of stage setting. The stage tree—any stage tree—brazenly denies that only God can make a tree; it is the sign of the referential potency of the theatrical image, showing us quite literally how an organic world can grow out of artifice.

The tree in *Godot* functions, first, as a link between the audience and just such an organic "other world," a world that includes, among (very few) other things, material nature. One has only to imagine what the play would be without this tree to realize how global its signification is, for without it the stage-road would indeed be the stage only. Thus, the tree is a relational sign, mediating the relation between the stage and the road in such a way as to render that relation asymmetrical (the stage may be the road, but not, thanks to the tree, vice versa).

Students may object that the referential power of the tree fluctuates greatly according to its stage realization, for which Beckett's sparse stage description affords considerable choice and flexibility. Might not a highly stylized rendering of the tree not oppose but instead contribute to the theatricalization of stage space? To function as a relational sign of the sort I describe—one that relates the stage-road to a fictional realm—does not the tree have to look a certain way, namely, realistic?

This kind of question, deemed irrelevant by traditional drama criticism, is crucial to a semiotic approach to drama, which refuses to constitute its subject apart from the medium (theater) for which it is produced. Beckett's metacritical dramaturgy offers an opportunity to study the issue of materiality, that is, of the substance of the signifier and its effect on the signified. As one of the very few signs of the play's setting system (the metacritical force of the play is achieved largely by means of the attenuation of the various available sign systems), the tree raises the question of material realization, which could be formulated simply as "Should the tree be realistic?" However, the normative cast of this question is disturbing, implying, as it does, that there is a "right" way to "do the tree." The play itself indicates otherwise. The episode in which Didi and Gogo attempt to enact the tree is an instructive example of the dialectic of representation and reference. The episode sets up a relay of signification (actors playing characters play a stage tree that is playing a real tree) in which what is dramatized is one of the thorniest and most crucial aspects of dramatic signification: the transformability of signs. Didi and Gogo's mimetic failure stands in contradiction to the principle of transformability, which holds that "any stage vehicle [or material signifier] can stand . . . for any class of signified phenomena: there are no absolutely fixed representational relations" (Elam 13). Their failure is especially remarkable in the context of their otherwise ample theatrical skill and resourcefulness, which has led critics to read them as carriers of the entire tradition of popular entertainment (Blau 232).

As competent as Didi and Gogo are as performers, their inability to relate performatively to the tree is striking. While critics have not failed to read it symbolically, no one, to my knowledge, has addressed its stage dynamic.[4] This dynamic relates the tree, on the one hand, to the potentially unrepresented road—both are signs of the same system—and, on the other, to the actors, who, failing in their attempt to become signs of that system, situate themselves securely in another. In between these two relations a third one intervenes, coded linguistically rather than performatively. This consists of the many discussions of the tree that are scattered throughout the play and that have the effect of foregrounding its significational ambiguity. Not only are the tramps unsure that this is the "right" tree, they are even uncertain about what kind of tree it is, even whether it is a tree at all. Paradoxically, this persistent verbal ambiguating of the tree has the effect of asserting its stage identity, of ostending it as stage tree. Once so established, or (to paraphrase a remark of Beckett's from another context) once so "stated," the tree functions as a sign of a tree, and the question of its materiality becomes irrelevant. In other words, the tree's referentiality (its role in evoking a virtual reality other than that of the stage) is not dependent on the manner of its theatrical realization; rather, it is a function of the relations the play establishes between this signifier and various others (road, actors, dialogue). The stage tree refers to a real tree not because it looks like one (though it may) but because it creates the stage as a road (in a world) and the actors as characters (rather than, as metatheatrical readings insist, as performers).

Thus the function of the tree goes beyond its world-creating capacity. The tree becomes one of the principal mechanisms of the characters' self-constitution, the sign of the area within which their existence might ultimately make sense. It is not so much a question of their "doing" the tree: the tree "does" them. While the theatrically absent road tends to theatricalize the characters, to unravel their characterological existence by placing them on a "mere" stage, the tree (despite its impoverished aspect) richly bestows dramatic identity on the tramps. In this regard, it does not recall the Christian images with which it has been associated as much as it does the sacred post of the voodoo séance, down which the Mystères descend to earth. Here, it is not divinity that the tree attracts like a lightning rod but fictionality: another absent world that constitutes the actors as characters. Within the world thus created, Godot is not merely an absence but a character, however stubbornly diegetic. His literal absence, colliding with the others' literal presence, partakes of their referentiality. The question of his identity, while it can never be answered, cannot be wished away either.

Thus a semiotic approach to the structure and signs of *Waiting for Godot* reveals a constant oscillation between presentation and representation. Within the range of that oscillation lies the play's interpretive arena, a richly hermeneutic space where meanings are compulsively—and tantalizingly—produced.

NOTES

[1]According to Alec Reid, Beckett once made a remark, in conversation, "to the effect that the great success of *Waiting for Godot* had arisen from a misunderstanding: critics and public alike, he said, were seeking to impose an allegorical or symbolic explanation on a play which was striving all the time to avoid definition" ("From Beginning" 64). What interests me about this remark is its unacknowledged assimilation of two separate and very different reception activities, those of the critics and those of the public. While Beckett may, as a reader of his own work, legitimately challenge the findings of the critics, surely those of the public are his responsibility. In other words, is the allegorical quest undertaken by the play's spectators not engendered by the play itself? What else would occasion such a quest?

Beckett's assimilation of the activities of critic and spectator is not at all unusual in traditional drama criticism; indeed, it is very nearly the enabling assumption of that criticism, which tacitly defines the critic as a kind of "superreader." By contrast, the semiotic study of drama depends on making and keeping intact the distinction between critic and spectator and recognizing the profound differences in the reading or decoding procedure employed by these two entities.

[2]Yet, for seekers after authorial sanction, Beckett's own self-characterization supports the opposite view: "The kind of work I do is one in which I'm not master of my own material. The more Joyce knew the more he could. He's tending toward omniscience and omnipotence as an artist. I'm working with impotence, ignorance" (qtd. in Busi epigraph).

[3]This basic model of dramatic signification underlies all drama, including the stylized and presentational modes of pre- and postrealism, for the theatricalism of these modes is invariably put in the service of meaning, which is always, in turn, mediated by the dramatic, that is, fictional, realm. Thus both the metatheatricality of a *Hamlet* and the theatricality of a *Mother Courage* provide perspectives or create viewing effects that are directed exclusively at their dramatic actions. They function, one might say, as hermeneutic guides to those actions and as such are heavily marked with the codes of meaning production required to make that particular universe of discourse intelligible. Thus, far from staging actuality, these modes transform certain selected aspects of that actuality (the theatrical situation) into fictional aids and by so doing subordinate them to the fiction. The frame is always a frame for something.

[4]Hugh Kenner is reminded "of ampler beams which once suspended the Savior and the two thieves, or again of the fatal tree in Eden (and the garden has, sure enough, vanished), or even of the flowering staff in *Tannhäuser*" (*Critical Study* 133). But although Kenner makes a brief comment that relates to the tree's role in the play's response paradigm, he does not follow it up. After mentioning various symbolic meanings that the tree "accretes," Kenner adds, "only in a theatre can we be made to look at a mock tree for that length of time." According to Kenner, the tree's prolonged stage presence produces "mild hallucinations" in the spectators (*Critical Study* 133–34).

PERFORMANCE-ORIENTED APPROACHES

Teaching the Theater, Teaching *Godot*

Stanton B. Garner, Jr.

Most of us, if pressed, would admit that teaching Beckett to undergraduates is often taxing. Trained as readers rather than playgoers, most students approach a play like *Waiting for Godot*—as they do all drama—with an essentially literary sensibility, treating the written text as an end in its own right instead of as a blueprint for performance. When they do consider plays as theater, they import a traditional aesthetic: illusionistic (the stage effaces itself against the "other" world of dramatic representation), actional (the temporal dimension of this world is structured and propelled by vectors of motivated action), and Aristotelian (the resultant narrative consists of a coherent beginning, middle, and end). When students confront Beckett's drama, which is so dependent on the stage and antagonistic to traditional dramaturgical values, their frustration often resembles Gogo's: "Nothing happens, nobody comes, nobody goes, it's awful!" (27b).

These difficulties, of course, present pedagogical opportunities. Most obviously, the instructor is challenged to "theatricalize" *Godot*, to uncover its myriad and particular theatrical energies: the slapstick and cross-talk rhythms of its vaudeville routines; the precise choreography of its movements and gestures; the shifting poetry of its stage language. In-class reading contributes to this end, as do student performances of individual dramatic segments,

and class activities may occasionally be supplemented by outside performances (when local productions are not forthcoming, I have found Alan
Schneider's 1961 film, starring Burgess Meredith and Zero Mostel, both
entertaining and useful).

But if *Waiting for Godot* challenges the teacher of dramatic literature to
locate the play within the theater, it—like all Beckett's dramatic works—
presents another, less obvious opportunity: to locate the theater within the
play and to teach the theatrical medium to students who have thought little
about the stage. More than any other dramatist, Beckett foregrounds this
medium: the conditions of its possibility and the elements of its operation.
This emphasis may not be obvious at first glance, given Beckett's minimalistic
stagecraft. Stripping away the excrescences of language and action, pressing
character toward Lear's "unaccommodated man," Beckett also reduces the
stage, paring away its theatrical inessentials in a denial of conventional "spectacle." Jonas Barish writes: "It is hard to imagine a theater more negative,
more calculatedly eviscerated of everything the world has always thought of
as theater" (458). Ascetic in conception, Beckett's theater stretches toward
the "nothing" that opens this play ("Nothing to be done"), in a gesture that
seems to promise the extinction of theater.

Beckett's theatrical innovation, though, lies in the paradoxical fullness that
charges this bareness, for the rejection of conventional spectacle draws attention to the medium itself. By freeing the stage of inessentials, Beckett
illuminates its phenomenal components: language, silence, movement, stillness, figure, object, space. We can learn much about the theater by looking
not only at what Beckett eliminates but also at what he liberates through
his focus on the medium of performance. Teaching *Godot* from this perspective is a powerful way of teaching the theater—as something physical,
unmediated, felt, an environment of "pure existing" (Wilder 114)—and of
drawing connections between the world represented onstage and the world
experienced in the auditorium. Indeed, I have discovered that Beckett's
drama—and *Waiting for Godot* in particular—can transform student ap-
preciation of theatrical art and can foster the performance literacy that our
students so often lack.

To establish correlations between philosophical issues and theatrical ones,
I structure our exploration of *Godot* in three sections. I have taught *Godot*
in this way to students in drama classes and to students in general literature
courses, with equal success.

Introduction: Existentialism and the Postwar Stage

We begin with general remarks on the intellectual and artistic climate of
postwar Europe, the culmination of a centuries-long attack on Christian and
humanist notions of humanity as part of a divinely ordered creation with es-

tablished social and metaphysical definitions of meaning. We consider the
undermining of this worldview by the Enlightenment; by developments in
science, psychology, social science, and philosophy; by industrialism and two
world wars; and by breakdowns in the conventions of artistic representation
(in terms of its philosophical and artistic contexts, *Godot* is usefully taught in
a modern literature course that has already considered works such as *The
Waste Land* and *The Trial* or in drama courses that have already covered
Ibsen, Pirandello, and the early twentieth-century avant-garde). We consider
philosophical existentialism as a reflection of this historical and cultural milieu:
a radical denial of external meaning, a philosophy of human abandonment in
a world where "existence precedes essence" (Sartre, *Philosophy* 35).

As part of this necessarily vast overview, we consider the following quotations from Wallace Stevens's "Of Modern Poetry" and Albert Camus's
Myth of Sisyphus:

> The poem of the mind in the act of finding
> What will suffice. It has not always had
> To find: the scene was set; it repeated what
> Was in the script.
>   Then the theater was changed
> To something else. Its past was a souvenir.
>   . . . It has
> To construct a new stage. It has to be on that stage
> And, like an insatiable actor, slowly and
> With meditation, speak words that in the ear,
> In the delicatest ear of the mind, repeat,
> Exactly, that which it wants to hear, at the sound
> Of which, an invisible audience listens,
> Not to the play, but to itself, expressed
> In an emotion as of two people, as of two
> Emotions becoming one.
>   (Stevens 239–40)

> A world that can be explained even with bad reasons is a familiar world.
> But, on the other hand, in a universe suddenly divested of illusions
> and lights, man feels an alien, a stranger. His exile is without remedy
> since he is deprived of the memory of a lost home or the hope of a
> promised land. This divorce between man and his life, the actor and
> his setting, is properly the feeling of absurdity.
>   (Camus 5)

I draw the students' attention to the theatrical metaphors in the two passages
and invite discussion concerning the appropriateness of this imagery. The

stage, after all, presents an actor alone, "thrown" onto the stage by a playwright and a director, having to create a play out of nothing, especially on the modern stage. We consider the inscription of cosmological belief within theater structure in the Greek, medieval, and Renaissance stages: the Elizabethan stage, for instance, locates its protagonists between tapestry "heavens" and a trapdoor underworld. Action occurs within an ordered universe, witnessed within the social context of a visible audience. Much postwar theater, by contrast, obscures its audience in darkness and confines its characters to a lighted space within this darkness (for a discussion of the relation between theater structure and worldview, see Kernan). Exploiting the opportunities of theater technology, certain currents of postwar theater constitute a kind of "existential stage," highlighting the essential "thereness" of the theatrical medium in general. As Alain Robbe-Grillet notes in an essay on Beckett's drama, "The condition of man, says Heidegger, is to be *there*. The theatre probably reproduces this situation more naturally than any of the other ways of representing reality. The essential thing about a character in a play is that he is 'on the scene': *there*" (108).

The Unaccommodated Stage

We look at *Godot* as an attempt to heighten the existential quality of theater through its subversion of audience expectations. What are these expectations, I ask, and how does Beckett undermine them? Our discussion raises a number of issues and dramaturgical principles (summarized here in outline form):

Character: Vladimir, Estragon, Pozzo, and Lucky contrasted (for instance) with Othello, Andrew Undershaft, Willy Loman. Beckett's debt to the tradition of Chaplin and other great comics (see *Act without Words I*). The image of humanity presented by Chaplin's tramp: reduced, mechanistic, stylized, a mixture of pathos and humor.

Plot: story reduced to incidents, action reduced to activity. Drama of nonaction announced by opening line of play. Past unclear, subject to disagreement, memory (the cornerstone of dramatic time) debilitated. Interval between acts of unclear duration.

Setting: barren, geographically indeterminate, little more than a stage. Nostalgic locales (the Eiffel Tower, the Rhone, the Pyrenees) that seem discontinuous with this world.

Line between audience and play: rendered unstable through metadramatic allusions to the audience's presence (10a, 10b, 47b, 58b).

The Field of Performance

We conclude from the discussion of the previous points that *Godot* resists the audience's attempts to view the physical stage and its actions in terms of fictional "otherness," as a segment of another world that extends beyond the boundaries of the stage in measurable time and space; we also conclude that *Godot* directs the audience's attention to the actual theatrical moment in its phenomenal complexities (for an excellent introduction to the phenomenology of theatrical performance, see States, *Great Reckonings in Little Rooms*). Turning our attention to this moment, we begin with a segment of dialogue, such as the following exchange between Vladimir and Estragon:

ESTRAGON: And what did he reply?
VLADIMIR: That he'd see.
ESTRAGON: That he couldn't promise anything.
VLADIMIR: That he'd have to think it over.
ESTRAGON: In the quiet of his home.
VLADIMIR: Consult his family.
ESTRAGON: His friends.
VLADIMIR: His agents.
ESTRAGON: His correspondents.
VLADIMIR: His books.
ESTRAGON: His bank account.
VLADIMIR: Before taking a decision.
ESTRAGON: It's the normal thing.
VLADIMIR: Is it not?
ESTRAGON: I think it is.
VLADIMIR: I think so too.
Silence.
ESTRAGON: (*anxious*). And we?
VLADIMIR: I beg your pardon?
ESTRAGON: I said, And we?
VLADIMIR: I don't understand.
ESTRAGON: Where do we come in?
VLADIMIR: Come in?
ESTRAGON: Take your time.
VLADIMIR: Come in? On our hands and knees.
ESTRAGON: As bad as that?
VLADIMIR: Your Worship wishes to assert his prerogatives?
ESTRAGON: We've no rights any more?

Laugh of Vladimir, stifled as before, less the smile.
VLADIMIR: You'd make me laugh if it wasn't prohibited.
ESTRAGON: We've lost our rights?
VLADIMIR: (*distinctly*). We got rid of them.
Silence. They remain motionless, arms dangling, heads sunk, sagging at the knees.

(13a–13b)

We explore the rhythms of a sequence like this and work to unearth its points of crisis: those moments when Didi and Gogo must confront the poverty of their condition ("And we?"), when (in Beckett's words) "for a moment the boredom of living is replaced by the suffering of being" (*Proust* 8). But we address these issues from a perspective not usually taken in literature courses: we approach the segment from beneath and around, as it were, through the silence that punctuates the dialogue and gives it shape. I ask the students to discuss silence: What is the experience of silence, of speechlessness? when one is alone? when one is with others? What is the specific experience of theatrical silence, the quality of being when a roomful of people sit without speaking? We work with this experience, using our own silences in the classroom as analogy, to uncover the particular fullness of theatrical silence, the anxiousness, even the unbearableness of that stillness when language stops. We discuss the physiology of silence—the awareness of heartbeat and respiration, a heightened attention—and we note an acute consciousness of those around us, that awkward and inescapable proximity of others that silence heightens. We note the experience of self that rushes in when the shield of language gives way, the "suffering of being" that seems such an intrinsic part of self-consciousness, and we explore the urge to fill this silence with thought, distraction, *anything*. During such an exercise, it becomes clear that the theater is (in Jean-Louis Barrault's words) an "Art of Sensation" and that Beckett's drama explores the "mystery of Presence" (99) that the theater shares with life. (During a 1961 lecture on the theatrical phenomenon, Barrault himself stopped speaking, forcing the audience to experience "the present instant" [97].) It becomes clear, too, that the language games of Beckett's world—the "little canter[s]" (42a)— are responses to felt urgencies, ways of shielding oneself from the nakedness of exposure. Viewed this way, language in *Waiting for Godot* becomes a way of shaping silence, an almost sculptural act by which the stillness of theatrical space is alternately contained and liberated. The cross talk and routines, even Lucky's torrential monologue, are seen as defensive maneuvers against the perceptual weight of a silence that the audience is made to share. Forced into an awareness of its own responses, Beckett's audience listens, "Not to the play, but to itself, expressed / In an emotion as of two people, as of two / Emotions becoming one."

Extending our investigation of Beckett's theatrical space, we consider movement: the ways in which Didi and Gogo demarcate the area of their waiting, marking it off (like Hamm) with their rectilinear pacing; the odd violence done to this space by the entrances and exits of Pozzo and Lucky; the almost choreographed importance of gesture as a way of filling the emptiness of motionlessness; the solidity of motionlessness when gesture gives way to the inertness of tableau. What image of the human figure do Vladimir and Estragon present as they stand puppetlike, *"arms dangling, heads sunk, sagging at the knees"*? In what ways does their motionlessness mirror the audience's own immobility? We also consider props, which (because of their scarcity) stand forward in *Godot*'s stage world with almost ludicrous physicality. Hat, boots, rope, stick, chicken bone, turnip, carrot—the props of *Godot* receive unusual attention, less as means to ends than as objects in themselves. How do props function as objects of attention for the play's characters? for the audience? In what ways do these objects help constitute the world of *Godot*? A tantalizing gloss on the material "thereness" of Beckett's world comes from Chekhov, in a 1904 letter to Olga Knipper: "You ask: What is life? That is just the same as asking: What is a carrot? A carrot is a carrot, and nothing more is known about it" (Simmons 627).

Teaching *Godot* in the light of performance requires an intense effort to re-create the theatrical environment through whatever means are available: description; the instructor's own gestures, movements, and voice; student reading and scene enactment; a use of the spatial elements of the classroom. An actual turnip or a piece of rope can effect wonders. But the rewards are immediate and considerable for an understanding of the play and its design. No longer a sequence of failed actions, the play becomes a kind of visual, aural, and kinetic poetry, a kind of choreography, its materials the elements of a theatrical presence governed by the pressures of being and evasion. The absent Godot begins to appear less an idea than an urgency, a desire called into being by nakedness and stasis. It is continually remarkable to me how easily *Waiting for Godot* is brought to life in this way and how quickly students abandon their predictable judgments and responses to Beckett's play. They learn to see the play not as an abstruse fable but as an enactment, a shaping of perception and self-awareness.

Just as significant, this kind of analysis illuminates the theatrical experience, especially in those moments when the stage's presence makes itself felt in stillness, silence, and the simplicity of gesture. My students and I have moved in a number of directions after *Godot*: into *Endgame* and the even more theatrically luminous worlds of *Not I* and *Rockaby*; into Pinter,

Stoppard, and Shepard. We have often returned, in discussion, to the silences and stillness of earlier drama: Hamlet's pause with Yorick's skull at arm's length; the lyrical ennui of Chekhov's aristocrats; Shaw's Don Juan, illuminated within the theater's darkness. Whatever the works, though, and wherever we travel within them, we have the sense that *Godot* is guiding us and that Beckett has offered us a map of the theater's terrain.

Teaching *Godot* through Set and Poster Design

Toby Silverman Zinman

Let us not waste our time in idle discourse!
—Samuel Beckett, *Waiting for Godot*

Of all the forms of literature I teach, none comes as such a surprise to art students as drama does. Such spatially oriented readers often find the distillation of poetry and the sustained interiority of novels inaccessible. But because plays happen in space as well as time, because the visual component—two- and three-dimensional—is strong, art students find they have access to the very terms of drama.

Some years ago, I began using a conceptual set and poster assignment and exhibition to teach drama. I have tried the approach with performing arts majors with happy results, and I suspect that it could be generally used to provide students with a sense of the theatrical life of a play. For any teacher who has ever said, with Estragon, "I can't go on like this" (60b), this approach offers the promise of bringing new life to the difficult task of teaching *Waiting for Godot*.

The assignment sheet reads like this: Design a conceptual set for any play we have studied in this course. In other words, create a stage set that conveys your interpretation of the play. It may be presented in two or three dimensions, and it can be in any medium (one student actually sculpted in ice and entered the classroom shouting, "Quick! Quick!"). It can be big or small; living or dead; animal, vegetable, or mineral; indoors or out; here or there. You are not bound by the playwright's stage or set directions, although you may follow them if you wish; the degree of fidelity is your choice, but whatever and however you choose must be justifiable.[1] To further the fun, you are free to ignore all the practical considerations that an actual staging of your design might entail; you need not worry about size or expense, about buildability, about safety, about entrances or exits. The object is to convey your concept of the play.

The challenge here, in theoretical terms, is the challenge to fourth-wall realism. When I provide students with the sort of throwaway, illustrative examples one always needs to accompany an unusual assignment, their eyes widen with possibilities. Ibsen's dramatic realism is a good starting point. I suggest, for instance, doing *A Doll's House* in Ken and Barbie style, with lots of asexual good looks, lots of plastic, lots of shine, lots of vulgar colors. These elements insist on the relevance of the play's themes to contemporary culture—the materialism, the feminist issues, the radical assault on middle-class roles, and the resulting assault on the sanctity of the institution of marriage; further, they prevent the play from becoming the creaky period piece it often is in production. Once the distance of time is no longer there to comfort the audience, the play can take on a new vitality and a renewed capacity to shock. The implications of Ibsen's title (immaturity, artificiality, toy) are clearly expressed by the Ken and Barbie motif. Another good example is *Ghosts*. I suggest to the class the possibility of staging it in a room full of gigantic furniture, creating a noncomic version of Lily Tomlin's little girl who sits in an enormous chair and says, "And that's the truth." Such a set emphasizes the claustrophobia the main characters feel and makes manifest the overwhelming, overstuffed, bourgeois world that Ibsen indicts.

Once the students see the possibilities, they are fearless. One student, responding to the aspect of Ionesco's *Chairs* that addresses the failure of communication, filled a large, undefined space in the building with chairs arranged as if they were an audience, each one with a tape recorder on it talking relentlessly. Another person in the same class, with the same play in mind, designed conceptual costumes—mummy wrappings, covering the entire body and face, rendering the characters mute as well as immobile— and had three friends model them. Although these designs produced opposite results, both worked as valid, exciting interpretations of the absurdist play.[2]

An alternative to the set design is the poster design, which is based on the same interpretive premise but aimed at students whose inclinations are more graphic than sculptural. Since they are *not* allowed to illustrate, this version of the assignment often produces very strong pieces, many of which make sophisticated use of photography. Conveying a theatrical concept in two dimensions may be harder than doing so with the three-dimensional set design. The least interesting work often comes from architecture majors, who seem to be so obsessed with seeing everything in plan that they cannot get beyond literal configuration. Literalness of representation sometimes defeats illustration majors, who have a difficult time resisting the impulse to condescend to their viewers. Often all it takes for students to exceed these limitations is the warning that they might not. Consciousness of their imaginative freedom is one of the goals of this assignment.

All the pieces are exhibited at the last class meeting; for a class of twenty-five to thirty students, the session takes three to four hours, a whole evening. It is very much like a high-wired gallery opening that closes the same night. I provide coffee and doughnuts and give everyone time to look closely at the work assembled before we begin to talk about it. We then move around the room (it seems to be crucial that everyone stand, so first we remove all the furniture). One by one, the students explain their concepts—the rationale behind each set or poster. Sometimes we need to go elsewhere to see a piece—to a studio on another floor, to a film screening room, outside on the college grounds—and we all troop around together.

The group is always willing to talk or ask about the literary and technical aspects of the pieces. Since students often experiment with an unfamiliar medium (one senior charmingly and bashfully announced that this was the first time he had ever tried oils), they are less defensive, less competitive, and more admiring of one another's work than they are in their studio assignments. Further, the assignment allows less verbal students to work from a position of strength, and among undergraduates it creates an element of vigorous exchange and openness that no exam taking or paper writing can. (The course also includes two papers and a final exam.) But most important, the project provides a way of teaching plays that is truer to the genre than the conventional classroom approach is.

It is not sufficient merely to do lip service to drama as a collaborative art. If we are to convince our students that we really believe that plays are written to be performed and not merely studied, we must teach the plays that way, too. And since contemporary theater is becoming more and more interdisciplinary, which is to say postmodernist as well as performance-oriented, we need to find ways to make plays come alive in an interdisciplinary way. Too often students believe that, like fiction, drama is to be left on the page or that, like film, it is to be passively watched and endlessly replicated. The hands-on approach of this assignment forces students to cope with mise-en-scène not for its own sake but as a nonverbal way of speaking meaning. They must work with ideas and give them physical form in the imagined spatiality that is fundamental to theater.

With no playwright is this hands-on approach more necessary or relevant than with Beckett. It seems foolish if not traitorous to Beckett's astonishing revision of the theater, the revolution that was *Waiting for Godot*, to teach that play as if it were a scholarly exercise in allusion-getting. No matter how many biblical allusions we trace, no matter how Cartesian the discussion, the play, if one judges it by these exhibition pieces, never becomes merely an intellectual construct. The students are deeply moved by its palpability, its presence, its theatrical power.

Perhaps the best evidence of the play's presence is revealed by the famous San Quentin story, immortalized by Martin Esslin in *The Theatre of the Absurd*:

> On 19 November 1957, a group of worried actors were preparing to face their audience. The actors were members of the company of the San Francisco Actor's Workshop. The audience consisted of fourteen hundred convicts at the San Quentin penitentiary. No live play had been performed at San Quentin since Sarah Bernhardt appeared there in 1913. Now forty-four years later, the play that had been chosen, largely because no woman appeared in it, was Samuel Beckett's *Waiting for Godot*. . . .

The curtain parted. The play began. And what had bewildered the
sophisticated audiences of Paris, London, and New York was immediately grasped by an audience of convicts.

(19)

The prison newspaper the next day revealed just how accurately and acutely
the inmates "got" it. Esslin reasons that the audience understood the play
not only because it presented a situation analogous to their own—that of
endless, repetitious, and futile waiting—but also because they came to the
play without any preconceived theatrical expectations or theories and so
were not troubled by the lack of plot, action, or realistic behavior. I find
my students today—none of whom are English majors—are much like the
San Quentin prisoners: innocent, at least of theory.

What I try to convey when I teach *Godot* is that the play is about boredom
and friendship, about hope and futility; in other words, it is a play about
being human and how hard it is to cope honorably and imaginatively with
our condition. How honorably and imaginatively the students cope with the
set and poster design assignment may be seen in the following examples.

I describe the posters first, in order of increasing abstraction and difficulty
of concept. It is not merely interesting but crucial to note how the two-
dimensional treatment yearns toward the three-dimensional and how, even
in the flattest of posters, the suggestion of surface texture emerges. The
posters become increasingly three-dimensional as they become increasingly
interpretive. (I have tried to suggest the accuracy and sensitivity of the
students' interpretations by providing appropriate quotations as titles of the
descriptions that follow.)

"Things have changed here since yesterday" (39a)

One straightforward and conventional poster—in size, shape, and
technique—was bright white; the play's title ran across the top in clean black
letters. Below, finely drawn in black and angled in balletic first position,
were two Chaplinesque boots, which, without floor or horizon line, seemed
to float in space. On closer inspection, the white background revealed white
falling leaves. The surprise of this discovery made the sharp black lines
soften as though drawn on an embossed surface. That the leaves were falling
suggested, someone in the class thought, the inevitable unwritten third act
when the tree would return to its bare state and we would all be back on
the country road again, "[n]ext day" (36b).

"We'll hang ourselves to-morrow" (60b)

Another poster was more perceptual than practical since it was mounted on
the ceiling rather than on a wall. The design was based entirely on a radical

tilting of the play's title so that each of the three words seemed to recede into the ceiling; the word *Godot* was smallest and highest, conveying, the student told us, the idea of inaccessibility and remoteness and half-parodying the notion of Godot as God who has withdrawn into a heaven of acoustical tiles. She further intended the visceral component of this poster—as we looked at it, we all got dizzy and our necks hurt—to ensure that viewers were placed in the same uncomfortable position in relation to Godot as Gogo and Didi are.

"in a word I resume alas alas abandoned unfinished" (29b)

Another student completely covered a giant poster (about 4' × 6') in charcoal except for the white, dropped-out shapes of Vladimir, Estragon, Pozzo, and Lucky. The figures were not individualized or distinguishable from one another; they were only recognizably human. Hanging from the ceiling in front of the poster were four harnesslike ropes made of surgical bandages; these were meant to suggest Lucky's leash and, further, to suggest that all four characters are Lucky. That the play's characters rather than Godot himself should be indicated by absence rather than presence provoked considerable comment.[3]

The three-dimensional pieces become paradoxical in a way that seems peculiarly appropriate to Beckett, since as the artworks become less like a stage set and more like sculpture, they become more powerfully physical but simultaneously more abstract, less a narrative concept and more a distillation.

"We should turn resolutely towards Nature" (41b)

The most straightforward of the set designs was a minimalist treatment of a studio used for photography shoots. The upstage wall was created by "seamless," enormous rolls of ten-foot-wide paper that eliminate the line of demarcation between wall and floor and here created a sense of appalling limitlessness. In the center was a nearly dead rhododendron bush, with just a few leaves and the ball of roots and earth exposed. The only other elements were intense orange lights that, the student said, would repeat the already uncomfortably warm temperature of the theater. This discomfort would be intensified by the repetitive sound of a dripping faucet that would continue as background noise throughout the performance. Overall, the student intended to create a tolerable level of annoyance in the audience: "I want them to think, 'God, will Godot please show up so I can go home.' I want them to have to exercise willpower to stay, to respect Estragon and Vladimir's patience in their waiting." This student understood not only the play but Beckett's refusal to cater to passive spectators.

"It is true the population has increased" (22a)

Another student gave us minimalism on a smaller scale in a set that used a little square of cardboard as a base to which he attached, at right angles, a mirror of equal size and shape; this formed the backdrop. On the cardboard base, a semicircular road was delineated by an edge of clay, and a clay tree was stuck onto the center of the mirror. The circularity of the road was, of course, completed by the reflection in the mirror, and when one bent down to look more closely at it, one saw oneself in the mirror. The doubleness, the circularity, and the self-reflexive medium all spoke to the meaning of the play, while the simplicity, the starkness, and the mirrored repetition all spoke to the structure of the play. This student's interpretation was completed by the extraordinarily obvious fact that the viewer's face appears as the only character.

"When you think of the beauty of the way" (11b)

Another student created a huge installation of junk that took up most of an industrial hallway; found objects were arranged in an ornate maze, with crushed plastic bottles that groaned under our weight, as we gingerly, wonderingly, picked our way through it. We realized as we went that we were on a road that went nowhere. The use of tiny things to compose a large whole worked perfectly to reflect the play's meaning, as did the languageless voices of the four characters represented by trash. This conceptual set gave us the world of *Godot* as detritus, tragicomic garbage.

"the grave-digger puts on the forceps" (58a)

The class trekked to a studio to view a rough-hewn wooden box, which the student sculptor wordlessly gave a kick. It started to rock. The "death cradle," as this six-foot-long coffin on rockers was named by the class, was clearly a translation of Pozzo's last speech: "They give birth astride of a grave, the light gleams an instant, then it's night once more" (57b). Someone in the class, discovering that the coffin had no bottom, murmured, "It's the whole play." The sculptor growled back, "It lacks the humor."

"Let's just do the tree, for the balance" (49a)

The sculpture majors have a yard where they throw all the stuff they have already used but might need again: jagged sheets of metal, bricks, an old mattress, chunks of wood with nails sticking out, part of a chain-link fence. In the midst of this rubbish, in front of a ruined brick wall, stood a metal tree. About six feet tall, with one boot at the base of its trunk and a bowler hat on its top branch, it looked heartbreakingly, hilariously forlorn. With considerable delight, the student who had made it inserted two big metal leaves into the ends of its branches. The figure-tree was complete now, with the leaves as open hands in a gesture unmistakably human. The conflation of all the elements of the play—actors and costumes and set, all in a junkyard, giving us both comedy and tragedy, the world and ourselves, all in a work of art—nearly silenced us.[4]

Believing that questions of artistic merit and technical proficiency are better left to the studio faculty, I try to base my judgment of the set and poster designs on the student's level of understanding of the play, on the capacity to conceptualize that understanding, and, then, on the heroic attempt to convey that concept to others. *Waiting for Godot* encourages this enterprise for, as Beckett said, "to be an artist is to fail, as no other dare fail" (Beckett and Duthuit 21). Perhaps this assignment helps students to discover the thrill of intellectual and aesthetic risk taking and to understand the daring intellectual art that is *Waiting for Godot*.

NOTES

[1]There is no intention here to challenge the sanctity of Beckett's stage and set directions or to continue the controversy generated by the American Repertory Theatre's production in which JoAnne Akalaitis set *Endgame* in a subway (Cambridge, Massachusetts, 1984). Further, there is no intention here of raising the genre-jumping controversy taken up by many prominent Beckett scholars and directors. See, for example, Cohn's *Just Play* and Brater's *Beyond Minimalism*.

[2]I thank the two students whose ideas these are: Matthew Jacks and Crystal Daigel.

[3]My gratitude and admiration to all the students who have astonished and delighted my eyes. I particularly thank Patrick Detwiler, Adrienne Syphrett, and Joe Goldfedder, whose poster projects I describe.

[4]I am grateful to Erica Freudenstein, Craig Brown, Kathleen Schimert, David McMahon, and Anand Glaser, whose three-dimensional pieces I describe.

Waiting for Godot: Inmates as Students and—Then—Teachers

Sidney Homan

As I discovered one night several years ago, the design of one's life as a scholar and teacher can sometimes be radically altered by mere chance. I received a call from the warden of Florida State Prison; knowing me through his daughter, who was one of my theater majors, the warden asked if there was "any dramatic entertainment" I might bring to the three thousand inmates of that maximum-security prison. I volunteered the play that I had been involved in for several months, *Waiting for Godot*, which my company, Bacchus Productions, had toured through several cities in the Southeast. "Is there anything radical in this *Godot* thing, anything that might stir up the prisoners?" he asked. "No, I don't think so. Nothing much happens, just two men waiting for a character named Godot who never appears," I replied, knowing nothing of the play's history. I only later found out that after *Godot* had failed with a tourist audience at the Coconut Grove in Miami and then failed again with an intellectual (perhaps pseudointellectual) audience in New York, the Actor's Workshop in San Francisco had taken the production to San Quentin. What would happen, they speculated, if a play about men waiting was performed before an audience of men waiting? There at San Quentin, it succeeded beyond anyone's expectations (Esslin, "Godot at San Quentin").

Two nights later the cast and crew of my production approached the first of three guard towers at the prison, introducing ourselves to some authority figure hidden behind the glare of a spotlight, not unlike the spotlight behind the audience that activates the three characters in Beckett's *Play*. Within thirty minutes, we had put on costumes and makeup; placed one rock and one pathetic, leafless tree onstage; and then rushed backstage just as the inmates, almost all of them "lifers," charged into the cafeteria that had been converted to a theater. The warden, like some army sergeant, dressed down the unruly audience: "You so-and-sos, shut the hell up! We have some visitors from Gainesville who have been good enough to come here this evening to present a play for you slobs. So shut up and give them your attention!" One of the worst warm-up acts I've ever heard, I muttered to myself in the wings. We had performed *Godot* about fifty times before and thus pretty well knew what type of laugh a line would fetch or how an audience would respond to a particular part of the play. But what happened this evening, almost from the opening line, was beyond our wildest imaginings.

Knowing nothing of the stultifying theater etiquette that often characterizes Broadway, the inmates, on every other line it seemed, rose from their seats and shouted out comments or questions to the actors, who were desperately trying to stay in character: "Why did you speak that way to him?" "Hey, what the hell do you mean by that remark?" "You two, come down here [downstage]—I've got a few things to say to you!" At first, these interruptions were frustrating; while always aware of the audience on the periphery, the actors were now being asked—forced—to speak directly to them, during the performance! Soon, however, our frustration turned to exhilaration: here was an audience, these men waiting, who demanded to be part of the production, who took what we said so seriously that they could not remain silent. We were actually performing two plays, the one scripted by Beckett and a complementary one, this extension of the text fashioned by our unique audience. These inmates were Brecht's alert spectator taken to the extreme. They were fully visible in the same light that illuminated our makeshift stage, and their presence and interjections demystified the theatrical experience. By the second act the audience was collaborating with us, both in performing and in thinking about the performance. As a result of these now-productive interruptions, our *Godot* took three rather than two hours to stage. At the end, as we were striking the set and packing our equipment, the warden, furious that our lengthy production had fouled up his bed check, grabbed the microphone and ordered the men to line up for the return to their cells. Suddenly, though, the inmates broke ranks and started racing toward the stage. I was terrified. But my fears were born of ignorance: the inmates simply wanted to talk with us about the play, specifically about the identity of Godot, this absent character whose own author once said that if he knew who Godot was, he would have said so in the play (Schneider, "Waiting" 55). After some hasty negotiations with the warden, we did just that, with each member of the cast and crew handling hundreds of eager "students" who, having commented on specific aspects during the performance, now identified Godot with some aspect of their own prison life. The discussion was informed and eloquent beyond anything I had ever known in the classroom.

Shortly after this extraordinary experience, I received moneys from the Florida Endowment for the Humanities to take our production to Florida's nine other state prisons, this time bringing along students and colleagues so that our discussion groups would be more manageable. In every instance, no matter what type of prison it was (maximum or minimum security, male or female), the experience duplicated that original one at Florida State. From the prisoners' perspectives, the play was a conversation between actor-characters and audience; the line separating offstage from onstage was blurred, even nonexistent. Overwhelmed by the tour, I put my Shakespeare slightly to the side for six years, plunged into acting in and directing everything that Beckett had done, and, at length, wrote a book, *Beckett's Theaters: Interpretations for Performance*, that was, in every sense of the word, coauthored by my inmate friends. Yet if our prison tour altered my scholarship, its effect on my teaching was equally profound.

As someone who works both on campus and in the theater, I am by instinct given to discussing plays with my students through performance: the students alternate between directing and being directed by their peers, staging the text before the class. The class itself resembles a rehearsal where ideas are tested out and interpretations are given form in the specifics of blocking and delivery. After our prison tour ended I purposely stocked my modern drama classes with those students who had volunteered as discussion leaders on the tour. In the fashion of the inmates, they were given the liberty to interrupt the performance at the front of the class and, moreover, to tutor classmates in this "art." Alain Robbe-Grillet, in his brilliant piece "Samuel Beckett: Or, 'Presence' in the Theatre," speaks of *Godot* as being a present-tense collaboration between actor and audience; while there may be tantalizing allegorical overtones to the play, the one thing of which we can be certain is the present moment, what is before us visually and verbally on-stage. Or, as a friend who once directed me as Vladimir observed, "If Godot doesn't come for the characters onstage, he doesn't come for their fellow characters in the audience—the joke, the no-show, works both ways." The play is rife with moments that invite the audience "onstage," and the students quickly took advantage of them.

My experience with the prison tour continues to shape the way I teach *Godot* and, in turn, the way my students respond to it. Students join in with Estragon, for example, when he replies, "Repented what?" to Vladimir's otherwise inexplicable call, "Suppose we repented" (8b). Once the pattern is established—"Let's go." "We can't." "Why not?" (10a)—the students anticipate Vladimir's "We're waiting for Godot," even altering the delivery from, say, an initial factual answer to one increasingly filled with despair, resignation, and then, near the end of act 2, a sort of comic relief. Vladimir's refusal to hear Estragon's dream—"DON'T TELL ME!" (11a)—is challenged by an audience that wants to hear about the dream and about anything that happens outside the time spent together onstage, even as Vladimir himself provokes this curiosity about that nebulous outside world with his inquiry about how "His Highness spent the night" (7a). Conversely, students, like the inmates, are suspicious about attempts to introduce material extraneous to the present task of waiting for Godot, as when Estragon tells the joke about the drunk Englishman in the brothel (11b). "How is this relevant?" one student will cry out. When Vladimir stalks offstage, refusing to hear any more of Estragon's joke, while Estragon, in Beckett's stage direction, mocks his exit with "[g]*estures . . . like those of a spectator encouraging a pugilist*" (11b), the audience inevitably asks Vladimir if he isn't overreacting: why doesn't he let Estragon finish the joke? The students seem to feel a special bond with Estragon, and if he is the body (concerned as he is with his feet) to Vladimir's head (as he flicks imaginary fleas from his hatband), then my otherwise bright students draw close to the anti-intellectual of the two.

Only a few of these audience remarks are shallow or "smart"—and then unintentionally so. Students experience *Godot* beat by beat and respond to the experience of the play. For them, *Godot* is not a topic after the fact of performance. Poems and other literature can surely both "be" and "mean," and although teachers sometimes place more emphasis on the latter now, armed with theories of reader response, among others, we can all attend equally to the former. But for me the "being" or—in Robbe-Grillet's sense—the "presence" of the theater is even more insistent: a play, after all, is a physical entity that takes place in space and time and is witnessed and ratified by a live audience, visible to a degree to the performers. My students' remarks constitute a conversation about *Godot*, but one that is tuned to the way a play really works, chronologically, sequentially, with an audience.

When Pozzo and Lucky make their appearance halfway through the first act, the students, having already carried on an intense conversation with Gogo and Didi, almost resent these two new characters; in their liberalism students deplore Pozzo as some sort of fascist and Lucky—here students agree with the inmates—as "someone who lacks guts, who deserves to be pushed about." Their harsh view of Lucky is aggravated when they learn from Pozzo that Lucky had once been the teacher and Pozzo the student. At the same time, the students feel it to be their responsibility to answer or at least to speculate on the questions asked in the first long sequence among the four characters (such as why Lucky doesn't put down his bags [20a–21a]). In fact, for my students Pozzo parodies the academic mind when he raises several possible reasons that Lucky might hold on to the bags: "He wants to impress me, so that I'll keep him. . . . He wants to mollify me. . . . He wants to cod me. . . ." (21a). When Pozzo effectively renders answers irrelevant or shows that there is no single explanation, saying, "The truth is you can't drive such creatures away" (21b), the students, I believe, receive a very quick, firm lesson in the open-endedness of Beckett's world, one of waiting (questions) without an end (answer), of relativity rather than absolutes. When the boy asks the ultimate question—"What am I to tell Mr. Godot, Sir?" (34a, 59a)—we invariably have to suspend the performance for ten minutes or so while the class takes turns in "speaking" to that invisible character in the wings, represented only by a single boy: What is the meaning of our life if we have only the waiting, only "process," and not the comforting, even elevating, promise of a god, the truth, or an absolute? This issue, which my students usually discuss last, is—revealingly—the very one that the inmates discussed first, after the formal performance. It is also interesting, I think, that whereas the otherwise noisy inmates were respectfully silent during Vladimir's reply to the boy ("Tell him . . . [*he hesitates*] . . . tell him you saw me" [59a]), the students generally find the same lines a cop-out, too reductive, a misreading of the significant presence of these two (otherwise) little men.

With my students onstage performing to their peers, we also look for moments when the actors can reverse the tables by addressing the audience, albeit staying with Beckett's text. *Godot*, of course, is full of such metadramatic acknowledgments of the spectator. Audience members are called "[i]nspiring prospects" and then the "bog" as Estragon advances to the front of the stage and "*halts facing auditorium*" (10a–10b). Pozzo, like some vain actor, plays to the audience offstage no less than to the audience of two onstage with his "Is everybody looking at me?" (20b) and, after his rhapsody on the night, with "How did you find me?" (25b). Vladimir's diplomatic assurance, "Oh very good," and Estragon's "Oh tray bong, tray tray tray bong" are matched with a harsher judgment from the student "characters" offstage who, ironically, are here negative in reverse correlation to the craft of the actor effectively playing the foppish, vain Pozzo. Similarly, Vladimir comments that although "[w]e were beginning to weaken. . . . we're sure to see the evening out" (49b), and his observation that Estragon's insistence on a carrot "is becoming really insignificant" (44a) reminds the audience of the peculiar quality of Beckett's own minimalist stage dialogue. His greeting to Estragon, "Together again at last!" (7a), thus bursts the confines of the stage as it includes those offstage as well. Indeed, this identity between actor and audience, established in the first act, provides a contrastive context for Vladimir's and Estragon's inability at the start of act 2 to recall the events of the night before or for Pozzo's "I don't remember having met anyone yesterday" on his return to the stage (56b). The audience sees itself in numerous audiencelike configurations onstage: at one point Pozzo, Lucky, and Estragon watch Vladimir offstage going to the bathroom, and, supine onstage in act 2, Pozzo and Lucky are not only seen but commented on by Vladimir and Estragon standing like spectators above them.

By playing to their audience, the actors are also audience to themselves. At one point, Vladimir and Estragon imitate the absent Pozzo and Lucky, and since act 2 in many ways duplicates act 1—prompting one spectator at the Coconut Grove premiere to observe as she stalked out of the house: "I paid for two acts and this Beckett fellow only gives me one!"—the actors also play to or against themselves in the previous act. In similar fashion, when *Play* repeats itself, the three characters, no less than the audience, automatically compare two enactments of the same text.

My several invocations of Brecht's name may seem ironic if we think of Beckett and Brecht as defining two very different concepts of theater (private and public, character type and social type). Still, in my class performances, the actors' simultaneous awareness of themselves and of the audience not only cements the bond between offstage and onstage—albeit in a way more formal and artificial than in the prison productions—but, since actors and audience were all students, also allows the students to see a character from a double perspective, as the person both projected by the actor's craft and witnessed and then commented on by the audience. In normal productions, such commentary is inward and silent or confined to the after-theater party; in ours, such analysis is given on the spot.

This focus on the student's role as audience and actor in *Godot*, as inspired by the prison tour, leads to two more conventional but no less significant aspects of teaching the play through performance. Since actor and audience are no longer distinct beings, I have the entire class work on the text the way directors would with their actors. With Beckett, particularly, we pay attention to the relation between and among segments of the play which are most often separated by one of those long Beckettian pauses that point where the dialogue stops and the abyss of silence opens up, an abyss only to be avoided when one of the characters revives the conversation. For example, before the first entrance of Pozzo and Lucky, I count twenty-one such segments, ranging from a few lines (Estragon on his feet or Vladimir on the precise location of the ditch) to longer ones (the business about Christ, the two thieves, and the four biblical commentaries) to segments that conflate earlier ones (as when Estragon lingers on Vladimir's "[d]readful [physical] privation" [8b] while his partner addresses more metaphysical matters). We also work on line, beat, and mood analysis of specific speeches, such as Lucky's long speech in act 1 (is it to be delivered as gibberish? as an "essay" with its distinct paragraphs and evolving logic? as impersonal or as deeply felt?); Pozzo's tentative, even neurotic, thoughts on whether or not to stay longer; and the quiet interchange between Vladimir and Estragon at the end, where the topics range from forgetting Godot to coming back tomorrow. Such discussions, which help students think about the play from its theatrical perspective rather than from an exclusively thematic (and often "literary") perspective, later inform a class performance.

I must confess that my method with *Godot* sometimes sacrifices the larger issues of the play for the specific moment, the forest for the trees. But it allows students to see, to talk about, and to participate in the play as a play and to realize the various, sometimes conflicting, interpretations available to the actor. It also helps them understand the all-important, coequal role of the audience members, who are not and should not be mere passive recipients during a performance. Estragon observes before Pozzo's second entrance, "We don't manage too badly, eh Didi, between the two of us?" (44b). Given my experience of the play with prison audiences and then with students in class, I think the number of those who thus "manage" may be higher.

"Dealing with a Given Space": *Waiting for Godot* and the Stage

S. E. Gontarski

One of the curiosities of modern theater is that some of its stellar characters, like the Bald Soprano in Eugène Ionesco's play of the same name or the condemned man in Brendan Behan's *Quare Fellow*, never appear. As a character, Godot too never appears yet is always present. It is an irony not lost on Beckett, who relished, and was even comforted by, the very concreteness, the physicality, the thereness of theater. In fact, he sought out the medium as a refuge. Beckett began to write *Godot* (a first draft between October 1948 and January 1949) "in search of respite from the wasteland of prose" he had been writing at the time, specifically *Malone meurt* (Beckett, letter to the author). To Michael Haerdter, his directorial assistant at the 1967 Schiller Theater production of *Endspiel* (*Endgame*), Beckett noted, "Theater for me is first of all recreation from work on fiction. We are dealing with a given space and with people in that space. That is relaxing" (Gontarski, *Theatrical Notebooks*). The phrase "people in that space," however, may have been disingenuous, for at least part of Beckett's fascination with theater was to undermine or play against that very concreteness, to sustain as much epistemological and phenomenal ambiguity as the sign systems of theater allow; indeed, Beckett's work often subverts the very senses that we use to confirm theater's concreteness. Beckett makes us question what we think we see and presents characters who are *not there*, like the boy Clov sights in *Endgame* or the pacing May of *Footfalls* or Godot himself. It has become critically commonplace to speak of ambiguity or polyvalence of meaning in Beckett's work and of formal irresolution, but we need to be aware in the classroom as well as in the theater of the ambiguities of presence.

When the French novelist and filmmaker Alain Robbe-Grillet, in his very early assessment of *Godot*, focuses on the two tramps "who do nothing, say practically nothing, have no other property but that of being there" (qtd. in Esslin, *Collection* 110), he is quite perceptive. For Didi and Gogo, the problem is most often their *being there*, in the empty space of the stage, in the empty space of the universe. Robbe-Grillet puts the matter in particularly phenomenological terms: "The condition of man, says Heidegger, is *to be there*. The theatre probably reproduces this situation more naturally than any of the other ways of representing reality. The essential thing about a character in a play is that he is 'on the scene': *there*" (qtd. in Esslin, *Collection* 108). What is easily overlooked in Robbe-Grillet's assessment is that the principal character and *primum mobile* of *Godot* is not on stage at all—or, rather, not phenomenally—and the two characters, the two witnesses to Godot's absence who "have no other property but that of being there" (qtd. in Esslin, *Collection* 110), have serious existential doubts about their own presence and fear not being part of the phenomenal world, fear *not being there*. "You're sure you saw me, you won't come and tell me to-morrow that you never saw me!" (59a) shouts Vladimir to his witness, the boy, disclosing his own doubts.

Played against both the concreteness of theater and the Heideggerian theme of being in the world is the imagery of dream. Vladimir suggests the crisis of being near the end of the play:

> Was I sleeping, while the others suffered? Am I sleeping now? To-morrow, when I wake, or think I do, what shall I say of to-day? That with Estragon my friend, at this place, until the fall of night, I waited for Godot? That Pozzo passed, with his carrier, and that he spoke to us? Probably. But in all that what truth will there be?
>
> (58a)

The lines are remarkable for raising questions about the veracity of what we have just witnessed on stage. Doubt is imbedded in the structure of the play, raising questions that, like Winnie's repetition of Mr. Shower's or Cooker's question "What does it mean? . . . What's it meant to mean?" (*Happy Days* 42–43), embrace the hermeneutical dilemma of audience and readers. The tramps are to meet Godot by "the tree," but is the plant that stands conspicuously midstage a tree at all or rather a shrub or a bush? "What are you insinuating?" Vladimir asks. "That we've come to the wrong place?" "He should be here," Estragon replies, and Vladimir is forced to admit, "He didn't say for sure he'd come" (10a).

In fact, the whole landscape has a phenomenally disruptive or dreamlike quality to it: The moon rises "[i]n *a moment*" (34a); the tree sprouts leaves overnight. Pozzo and Lucky go blind and dumb, respectively, overnight. To Vladimir's insistence that they were in the same spot yesterday, Estragon replies, "I tell you we weren't here yesterday. Another of your nightmares" (42b). If it is a nightmare, however, it is like Stephen Dedalus's history, one from which it is difficult to wake. In act 1, Estragon falls asleep. When Vladimir wakes him, Estragon wants to relate his dream, but Vladimir insists, "DON'T TELL ME!" Estragon's reply as he "*gesture[s] towards the universe*" is "This one [i.e., this dream] is enough for you?" (11a). To Vladimir's "Do you not remember [the tree]?" Estragon replies, "You dreamt it" (39a).

But this dreamworld of *Godot* is no simple hierarchical dichotomy between dream and reality. Neither of those states is privileged. Nor is the dream single: we have dream within dream suggesting an overdetermined reality, an infinite regressus and progressus, as the two acts of the play are only two days of a potentially infinite series. Vladimir, looking again at the sleeping, dreaming Estragon, can say, "At me too someone is looking, of me too someone is saying, He is sleeping, he knows nothing, let him sleep on" (58b). The line echoes Christ's observation of Peter in Gethsemane (Mark 14.41): "Sleep on now and take your rest." Instead of a simple dream-reality dichotomy, we have a multiplicity of interpenetrating dreams, all of which displace our epistemological and, finally, phenomenological certainty.

Moreover, the nightmare motif helps explain the relativity of time, which at times appears almost to have stopped. At other times it races forward so that Pozzo, having lost his watch, can scream,

> Have you not done tormenting me with your accursed time! It's abominable! When! When! One day, is that not enough for you, one day he went dumb, one day I went blind, one day we'll go deaf, one day we were born, one day we shall die, the same day, the same second, is that not enough for you? (*Calmer.*) They give birth astride of a grave, the light gleams an instant, then it's night once more.
>
> (57b)

Shortly thereafter, Vladimir resounds the theme: "Astride of a grave and a difficult birth. Down in the hole, lingeringly, the grave-digger puts on the forceps" (58a). The challenge to any interpreter of this text, classroom teacher or theatrical director, is to maintain that tension between the Heideggerian being there and the Freudian dreamworld, the interplay between presence and absence. To privilege one term in that theatrical dialectic is to reduce the play to synecdoche.

This tension between the concreteness of theater and the ambiguities that language, for one, allows is embodied in the character of Godot, that is, character as physical presence and character as verbal construct. Most critics emphasize the metaphysical in analyzing Godot, a level of abstraction suitable for an absence. Robbe-Grillet lists several possibilities (which he wisely dismisses since each is reductive): Godot as God ("Has not the author borrowed the root 'God' from his native language?"), as earthly ideal of a better social order, as death, as silence, as the inaccessible self (qtd. in Esslin, *Collection* 110). Beckett's own thinking about the question of Godot is, however, much more physical than metaphysical. Beckett has, for instance, confirmed any number of stories about the origin of his most famous creation. One is that the work was suggested by *godillot*, French slang for the word *boot*, since feet figure so prominently in the play. In another, Beckett supposedly stopped to ask a crowd of spectators why they were all looking down the street. The answer was "Nous attendons Godot." All the cyclists had passed except the eldest, whose name was apparently Godeau. A third story has Beckett rejecting the advances of a prostitute on the rue Godot de

Mauroy only to have the prostitute ask if he was saving himself for Godot. Beckett's longtime friend and English publisher John Calder summarizes Beckett's position on the play thus: "He wanted any number of stories circulated, the more there are, the better he likes it" (qtd. in *Waiting for Beckett*).

This is precisely the position the theatrical director, classroom instructor, or any other interpreter of the text needs to adopt in approaching the literary text, that version we read in the classroom and use in preparing to translate the play into the polyvalent sign systems of theater. The presence and the immanence of the most fugitive character in modern theater must be felt on the stage throughout the play; he is as real and present as the void he inhabits. Lamentations 3.26 may outline the fundamental dramatic situation of *Godot*: "[I]t is good that a man should both hope and quietly wait for the salvation of the Lord"; but in Romans 8.24–25 we learn the function of absence: "For we are saved by hope: but hope that is seen is not hope: for what a man seeth, why doth he yet hope for? But if we hope for that we see not, then do we with patience wait for it." Godot must never arrive and yet he must always be there, for Didi and Gogo are tied to him as tightly as Lucky is tied to Pozzo.

The tramps' suffering is spiritual and physical. Psalm 40 begins, "I waited patiently for the Lord; and he inclined unto me, and heard my cry. He drew me up from the desolate pit, out of the miry bog and set my feet upon a rock, making my steps secure." The fulfillment of that prophecy in the New Testament was the rock, Simon Peter, the foundation of the Christian church and the first in line of the apostolic succession. Beckett parodies this imagery in the iconography of the stage and in the imagery of Lucky's speech where the labors of two rocks, Steinweg ("stone road" in German) and Peterman (Rockman), are lost. The rock on which the hope of the world was to be built has become a wasteland. In the third section of Lucky's speech, the theme "earth abode of stones" (29a) is repeated four times and alluded to at least twice more. The phenomenal stone we see onstage is the one on which Estragon rests to relieve the suffering not of his soul but of his feet, of which, like the two thieves, one is damned, the other saved. The play is built around such simultaneity of echoes and opposites, such dialectical tensions, and it is the interpreter's task to sustain as many of those as possible. The very physically present Vladimir and Estragon may be the issue of a dreaming mind. The very absent Godot must be as present as the tree.

One can "real-ize" the absent Godot, for instance, by taking seriously the possibility that Pozzo may be Godot; after all, it was a possibility that Beckett himself entertained in an early draft of the play (see Duckworth, "Making"). But even in the completed, published text we see that, when Pozzo first appears, his name sounds sufficiently like Godot's for Estragon to say, "He said Godot" (15b). And once Pozzo and Lucky leave, Vladimir notes, as if he knew them, "How they've changed!" and insists to Estragon, "Yes you do know them. . . . We know them, I tell you. You forget everything. . . . Unless they're not the same." Estragon is curious why Pozzo and Lucky did not recognize them. "That means nothing," Vladimir replies, "I too pretended not to recognize them. And then nobody ever recognizes us" (32a). After their second encounter with Pozzo and Lucky, in act 2, Estragon asks, "Are you sure it wasn't [Godot]?" Vladimir answers, "Not at all! (*Less sure.*) Not at all! (*Still less sure.*) Not at all!" (58a).

The surest way to diminish the play's multiplicity is to foreground one of its hermeneutical possibilities. The temptation to conceptualize the play, to impose the director's reading onto the text, is a danger difficult to resist. The first impulse of Beckett's first director approaching the first performance of a Beckett play was to do precisely that, to impose a concept onto the play. Roger Blin received little conceptual help from the author in those early days. All Beckett could tell Blin about the play was that the characters wore bowler hats. That is, Beckett himself had not fully visualized his work. That would come when he finally brought his director's eye to the text for the Schiller Theater production in December 1974, over twenty years after the Paris opening. Blin's first thought was to stage the play as a three-ring circus with characters made up as clowns. "So I imagined it taking place in a circus ring," added Blin. "That idea lasted for about a week. I realized that the second act could not be situated in the circus idiom. And also, if the circus was certainly there, it should remain in the background. It had to be felt within the play" (qtd. in Bishop 228). Like Godot, the circus had to be there and not be there. Blin resisted the directorial trap, a highly conceptualized production, which is finally a synecdochic reduction, the emphasis on one or two iconographic images at the expense of the play's visual plurality. Not all directors have resisted the temptation: we have had proletariat *Godots* that emphasized the Hegelian master-slave relation of Lucky and Pozzo, feminist *Godots*, interracial *Endgames*, and productions of *Endgame* played on life-size chessboards, with huge black and white squares on the floor and walls of the shelter and Hamm and Clov dressed as harlequins. Not every director has had to confront the stony stare Beckett must have had on his face when Blin proposed his colorful circus imagery, but every director, critic, and teacher should keep that image in mind in developing an interpretation of Beckett's work. The first premise of interpretation is, quite simply, to do as little damage to the original work as possible and certainly to avoid any semblance of synecdochic reduction.

CONTRIBUTORS AND SURVEY PARTICIPANTS

The following scholars and teachers contributed essays or participated in the survey of approaches to teaching Beckett's *Waiting for Godot* that preceded preparation of this book. Their assistance made the volume possible.

Anthony S. Abbott, Davidson College; Teresa R. Amuso, University of Maine, Machias; Ralph Arzoomanian, Lehman College, City University of New York; Helene L. Baldwin, emeritus, Frostburg State College; Stephen Barker, University of California, Irvine; Rosemarie A. Battaglia, Michigan State University; Linda Ben-Zvi, Colorado State University; Enoch Brater, University of Michigan; Katherine H. Burkman, Ohio State University; Lance St. John Butler, University of Stirling, Scotland; James L. Calderwood, University of California, Irvine; Una Chaudhuri, New York University; Claudia Clausius, University of Toronto; Ruby Cohn, University of California, Davis; Michael J. Collins, Georgetown University; Kevin J. H. Dettmar, University of California, Los Angeles; Mary A. Doll, University of Redlands; Lajos Elkan, Long Island University, C. W. Post Campus; Martin Esslin, Stanford University; John Fletcher, University of East Anglia, England; Jack E. Frisch, University of Wisconsin, Green Bay; Steven H. Gale, Kentucky State University; Stanton B. Garner, Jr., University of Tennessee, Knoxville; Irene E. Gnarra, Kean College of New Jersey; S. E. Gontarski, Florida State University, Long Beach; Lois Gordon, Fairleigh Dickinson University, Teaneck; Robert M. Henkels, Jr., Auburn University; David Hesla, Emory University; Sidney Homan, University of Florida; Christopher C. Hudgins, University of Nevada, Las Vegas; William Hutchings, University of Alabama, Birmingham; Leslie Kane, Westfield State College; Katherine E. Kelly, Texas A&M University; James Knowlson, University of Reading, England; Rosette Lamont, Graduate Center, City University of New York; Frederick K. Lang, Brooklyn College, City University of New York; Karen L. Laughlin, Florida State University; Charles R. Lyons, Stanford University; J. Terence McQueeny, Marshall University; Kristin Morrison, Boston College; Darcy O'Brien, University of Tulsa; Julian M. Olf, University of Massachusetts, Amherst; Barry N. Olshen, Glendon College, York University; Lois Oppenheim, Montclair State College; Rubin Rabinovitz, University of Colorado, Boulder; Fred Miller Robinson, University of Massachusetts, Amherst; Robert Sandarg, University of North Carolina, Charlotte; June Schlueter, Lafayette College; Dina Sherzer, University of Texas, Austin; Mary Scott Simpson, Rosary College; Bert O. States, University of California, Santa Barbara; Sharon R. Wilson, University of Northern Colorado; Toby Silverman Zinman, University of the Arts.

WORKS CITED

Abbott, H. Porter. *The Fiction of Samuel Beckett: Form and Effect*. Berkeley: U of California P, 1973.

Abel, Lionel. *Metatheatre: A New View of Dramatic Form*. New York: Hill, 1963.

Abrams, M. H. *A Glossary of Literary Terms*. 5th ed. New York: Holt, 1987.

Abrams, M. H., et al., eds. *Norton Anthology of English Literature*. 5th ed. Vol. 2. New York: Norton, 1986.

Admussen, Richard L. *The Samuel Beckett Manuscripts: A Study*. Boston: Hall, 1979.

Albright, Daniel. *Representation and the Imagination: Beckett, Kafka, Nabokov, and Schoenberg*. Chicago: U of Chicago P, 1981.

Andonian, Cathleen Culotta. *Samuel Beckett: A Reference Guide*. Boston: Hall, 1989.

Artaud, Antonin. *Le théâtre et son double*. Paris: Gallimard, 1938. *The Theater and Its Double*. Trans. Mary C. Richards. New York: Grove, 1958.

Aslan, Odette. *Roger Blin and Twentieth-Century Playwrights*. Trans. Ruby Cohn. Cambridge: Cambridge UP, 1988.

Audiberti, Jacques. "At the Babylone: A Fortunate Move on the Theater Checkerboard." Trans. Ruby Cohn. Cohn, *Casebook* 13–14. Trans. of "Au Babylone et au Lancry, deux coups heureux sur le damier du théâtre." *Arts-Spectacles* 16 Jan. 1953: 3.

Bair, Deirdre. *Samuel Beckett: A Biography*. New York: Harcourt, 1978.

Barale, Michèle Aina, and Rubin Rabinovitz. *A Kwic Concordance to Samuel Beckett's Trilogy:* Molloy, Malone Dies, *and* The Unnamable. 2 vols. New York: Garland, 1988.

Barish, Jonas. *The Antitheatrical Prejudice*. Berkeley: U of California P, 1981.

Barker, Stephen. "Beckett and Nietzsche: The Linguistic Turn." *Beckett and the Idea of Action*. Forthcoming.

Barrault, Jean-Louis. "The Theatrical Phenomenon." Trans. Thomas B. Markus. *Educational Theatre Journal* 17 (1966): 89–100.

Barrett, William. *Irrational Man*. Garden City: Doubleday, 1958.

———. *Time of Need: Forms of Imagination in the Twentieth Century*. New York: Harper, 1972.

Beckerman, Bernard. *Dynamics of Drama: Theory and Method of Analysis*. New York: Knopf, 1970.

Beckett, Samuel. *Act without Words*. [*See* Beckett, *Endgame*]

———. *Breath*. Beckett, *First Love* 89.

———. "Dante . . . Bruno. Vico . . Joyce." *Our Exagmination round His Factification for Incamination of Work in Progress*. Paris: Shakespeare, 1929. 1–22.

————. *Disjecta: Miscellaneous Writing and a Dramatic Fragment.* Ed. Ruby Cohn. London: Calder, 1983; New York: Grove, 1984.

————. "Dream of Fair to Middling Women." MS 1227/7/16/9. Beckett Archives. U of Reading (Eng.).

————. "Eleuthéria." Unpublished ms., 1947.

————. *En attendant Godot.* Paris: Editions de Minuit, 1952.

————. Endgame, *a Play in One Act, Followed by* Act without Words, *a Mime for One Player.* New York: Grove, 1958.

————. *Fin de partie.* Paris: Editions de Minuit, 1957.

————. *First Love and Other Shorts.* New York: Grove, 1974.

————. *Happy Days.* New York: Grove, 1961.

————. Letter to S. E. Gontarski. 1 October 1978.

————. *Malone Dies.* Beckett, *Three Novels* 177–288.

————. *Mercier and Camier.* New York: Grove, 1974.

————. *Molloy.* Beckett, *Three Novels* 7–176.

————. *Molloy, Malone meurt, L'innommable.* Paris: Editions de Minuit, 1951.

————. *Murphy.* New York: Grove, 1957.

————. *Oh les beaux jours.* Paris: Editions de Minuit, 1963.

————. *Ohio Impromptu. Three Plays:* Ohio Impromptu, Catastrophe, What Where. New York: Grove, 1984. 7–19.

————. *Pas moi.* Paris: Editions de Minuit, 1975.

————. "Ping." Beckett, *First Love* 67–72.

————. *Play. Cascando and Other Short Dramatic Pieces.* New York: Grove, 1968.

————. *Proust.* New York: Grove, 1931.

————. *Quad. Collected Shorter Plays of Samuel Beckett.* London: Faber, 1984.

————. *Samuel Beckett: The Complete Dramatic Works.* London: Faber, 1986.

————. *Stories and Texts for Nothing.* New York: Grove, 1967. Trans. of *Nouvelles et textes pour rien.* Paris: Editions de Minuit, 1958.

————. *Three Novels by Samuel Beckett:* Molloy, Malone Dies, The Unnamable. New York: Grove, 1965.

————. *The Unnamable.* Beckett, *Three Novels* 289–414.

————. *Waiting for Godot.* New York: Grove, 1954.

————. *Warten auf Godot. En attendant Godot. Waiting for Godot.* Frankfurt: Suhrkamp, 1971.

————. *Watt.* New York: Grove, 1959.

————. *Worstward Ho.* New York: Grove, 1984.

Beckett, Samuel, and Georges Duthuit. "Three Dialogues." *Transition Forty-nine* 5 (1949): 97–103. Rpt. in Esslin, *Collection* 16–22.

Beerbohm, Max. *Around Theatres.* Vol. 1. New York: Knopf, 1930. 2 vols.

————. "At the Tivoli." Beerbohm, *Around Theatres* 16–20.

————. *Selected Prose.* Boston: Little, 1970.

Beja, Morris, S. E. Gontarski, and Pierre Astier, eds. *Samuel Beckett: Humanistic Perspectives.* Columbus: Ohio State UP, 1983.

Ben-Zvi, Linda. *Samuel Beckett.* Boston: Twayne, 1986.

———, ed. *Women in Beckett: Performance and Critical Perspectives.* Urbana: U of Illinois P, 1990.

———. "Women in *Godot.*" *Beckett Circle* 10.1 (1988): 7.

Bergson, Henri. "Laughter." *Comedy.* Ed. and trans. Wylie Sypher. Garden City: Doubleday, 1956. 61–190.

Berlin, Normand. *The Secret Cause: A Discussion of Tragedy.* Amherst: U of Massachusetts P, 1981.

———. "The Tragic Pleasure of *Waiting for Godot.*" Brater, *Beckett at 80* 46–63.

Bermel, Albert. *Contradictory Characters.* New York: Dutton, 1973.

Bishop, Tom. "Dialogue." Bishop and Federman 141–46. Rpt. as "Blin on Beckett: Interview by Tom Bishop." Trans. James Knowlson. Gontarski, *On Beckett* 226–35.

Bishop, Tom, and Raymond Federman, eds. *Cahiers de l'Herne: Samuel Beckett.* Paris: Editions de l'Herne, 1976.

Blau, Herbert. *The Impossible Theater: A Manifesto.* New York: Macmillan, 1964.

Bodkin, Maud. "Archetypal Patterns in Tragic Poetry." Corrigan 159–76.

Bradbury, Malcolm, and James McFarlane, eds. *Modernism 1890–1930.* New York: Penguin, 1976.

Bradby, David. *Modern French Drama 1940–1980.* Cambridge: Cambridge UP, 1984.

Brater, Enoch, ed. *Beckett at 80/Beckett in Context.* New York: Oxford UP, 1986.

———. *Beyond Minimalism: Beckett's Late Style in the Theater.* New York: Oxford UP, 1987.

———. *The Drama in the Text: Beckett's Late Fiction.* New York: Oxford UP, forthcoming.

———, ed. Spec. Beckett issue of *Journal of Modern Literature* 6 (1977): 3–168.

———. *Why Beckett.* London: Thames, 1989.

Brater, Enoch, and Ruby Cohn, eds. *Around the Absurd: Essays on Modern and Postmodern Drama.* Ann Arbor: U of Michigan P, 1990.

Brecht, Bertolt. "Alienation Effects in Chinese Acting." *The Dramatic Moment.* Ed. Eugene M. Waith. Englewood Cliffs: Prentice, 1967. 492–97.

Brienza, Susan D. "Sam No. 2: Shepard Plays Beckett with an American Accent." Friedman et al. 181–95.

———. *Samuel Beckett's New Worlds: Style in Metafiction.* Norman: U of Oklahoma P, 1987.

Brook, Peter. *The Empty Space.* New York: Atheneum, 1968.

Brown, John Russell. "Beckett and the Art of Nonplus." Brater, *Beckett at 80* 25–45.

————, ed. *Modern British Dramatists: A Collection of Critical Essays.* Englewood Cliffs: Prentice, 1968.

————. *Theatre Language.* London: Allen Lane, 1972.

Browne, Joseph. "The 'Crritic' and Samuel Beckett: A Bibliographic Essay." *College Literature* 8 (1981): 292–309.

Brustein, Robert. *The Theatre of Revolt: An Approach to the Modern Drama.* Boston: Little, 1964.

Bryer, Jackson R. "Samuel Beckett: A Checklist of Criticism." Friedman, *Samuel Beckett Now* 219–59.

Burkman, Katherine H. *The Arrival of Godot: Ritual Patterns in Modern Drama.* Madison: Fairleigh Dickinson UP, 1986.

————. *The Dramatic World of Harold Pinter: Its Basis in Ritual.* Columbus: Ohio State UP, 1971.

————, ed. *Myth and Ritual in the Plays of Samuel Beckett.* Madison: Fairleigh Dickinson UP, 1987.

Busi, Frederick. *The Transformations of Godot.* Lexington: UP of Kentucky, 1980.

Butler, Christopher. *After the Wake.* Clarendon: Oxford UP, 1980.

Butler, Lance St. John. *Samuel Beckett and the Meaning of Being.* New York: St. Martin's, 1984.

Calder, John, ed. *As No Other Dare Fail.* London: Calder; New York: Riverrun, 1986.

————, ed. *Beckett at Sixty.* London: Calder, 1967.

Camus, Albert. *The Myth of Sisyphus and Other Essays.* Trans. Justin O'Brien. New York: Knopf, 1955.

Carpenter, Charles A. *Modern Drama Scholarship and Criticism, 1966–1980.* Toronto: U of Toronto P, 1986.

Cavell, Stanley. *Must We Mean What We Say?* New York: Scribner's, 1969.

Chabert, Pierre, ed. *Revue d'esthétique: Samuel Beckett.* Paris: privately published, 1986.

Ciardi, John. *How Does a Poem Mean?* Boston: Houghton, 1959.

Clark, T. J. *The Painting of Modern Life: Paris in the Art of Manet and His Followers.* Princeton: Princeton UP, 1984.

Clausius, Claudia. "Bad Habits While Waiting for Godot: The Demythification of Ritual." Burkman, *Myth* 124–43.

————. *The Gentleman Is a Tramp: Chaplin's Comedy.* Berne: Lang, 1989.

Clurman, Harold, ed. *Nine Plays of the Modern Theater.* New York: Grove, 1981.

Cohn, Ruby. *Back to Beckett.* Princeton: Princeton UP, 1973.

————, ed. *Casebook on* Waiting for Godot. New York: Grove, 1967.

————. *Currents in Contemporary Drama.* Bloomington: Indiana UP, 1973.

————. *From* Desire *to* Godot: *Pocket Theater of Postwar Paris.* Berkeley: U of California P, 1987.

————. "Growing (Up?) with Godot." Brater, *Beckett at 80* 13–24.

————. *Just Play: Beckett's Theater*. Princeton: Princeton UP, 1980.

————, ed. *Samuel Beckett: A Collection of Criticism*. New York: McGraw, 1975.

————. *Samuel Beckett: The Comic Gamut*. New Brunswick: Rutgers UP, 1962.

————, ed. *Samuel Beckett: Waiting for Godot: A Casebook*. London: Macmillan, 1987.

————, ed. Spec. Beckett issue of *Modern Drama* 9 (1966): 237–346.

————, ed. Spec. Beckett issue of *Perspective* 11 (1959): 119–96.

Connor, Steven. *Samuel Beckett: Repetition, Theory and Text*. Oxford: Blackwell, 1988.

Cooke, Virginia, comp. *Beckett on File*. London: Methuen, 1985.

Corrigan, Robert W., ed. *Tragedy: Vision and Form*. San Francisco: Chandler, 1965.

Cousineau, Thomas. Waiting for Godot: *Form in Movement*. Boston: Twayne, 1990.

Crossan, John D. *The Dark Interval*. Niles: Argus, 1975.

————. *In Parables*. New York: Harper, 1976.

Davenport, Guy. *The Geography of the Imagination*. San Francisco: North Point, 1981.

Dearlove, J. E. *Accommodating the Chaos: Samuel Beckett's Nonrelational Art*. Durham: Duke UP, 1982.

de Man, Paul. *Blindness and Insight: Essays in the Rhetoric of Contemporary Criticism*. Minneapolis: U of Minnesota P, 1983.

Derrida, Jacques. *Of Grammatology*. Trans. Gayatri Chakravorty Spivak. Baltimore: Johns Hopkins UP, 1980.

————. *Positions*. Paris: Editions de Minuit, 1972.

Dobrez, L. A. C. *The Existential and Its Exits*. London: Athlone; New York: St. Martin's, 1986.

Doll, Mary A. *Beckett and Myth: An Archetypal Approach*. Syracuse: Syracuse UP, 1988.

Donoghue, Denis. *The Arts without Mystery*. Boston: Little, 1983.

Driver, Tom F. "Beckett by the Madeleine." *Columbia University Forum* 4.3 (1961): 21–25.

Duckworth, Colin. *Angels of Darkness: Dramatic Effect in Samuel Beckett with Special Reference to Eugène Ionesco*. London: Allen, 1972.

————. Introduction. *En attendant Godot*. By Samuel Beckett. London: Harrap, 1966. vii–cxxxv.

————. "The Making of *Godot*." Cohn, *Casebook* 89–100.

Duvignaud, Jean. *Le théâtre contemporain: Culture et contre-culture*. Paris: Larousse, 1974.

Easy Street. Dir. Charles Chaplin. With Charles Chaplin. 1917.

Elam, Keir. *The Semiotics of Theatre and Drama*. London: Methuen, 1980.

Eliot, T. S. "The Possibility of a Poetic Drama." 1920. *The Sacred Wood: Essays on Poetry and Criticism.* London: Methuen, 1920. 60–70.

———. *The Waste Land. The Complete Poems and Plays, 1909–1950.* New York: Harcourt, 1971. 37–55.

Ellmann, Richard. *James Joyce.* New York: Oxford UP, 1959.

Ellmann, Richard, and Charles Feidelson, Jr., eds. *The Modern Tradition: Backgrounds of Modern Literature.* New York: Oxford UP, 1965.

Elsom, John, ed. *Post-war British Theatre Criticism.* London: Routledge, 1981.

Empson, William. *Some Versions of Pastoral.* New York: New Directions, 1960.

Esslin, Martin. "Godot and His Children: The Theatre of Samuel Beckett and Harold Pinter." Brown, *Modern British Dramatists* 60–63.

———. "Godot at San Quentin." Esslin, *Theatre* 1–3. Rpt. in Cohn, *Casebook* 83–85.

———. *Mediations: Essays on Brecht, Beckett, and the Media.* Baton Rouge: Louisiana State UP, 1980.

———. *Pinter: The Playwright.* London: Methuen, 1984.

———. "A Poetry of Moving Images." Friedman et al. 65–76.

———, ed. *Samuel Beckett: A Collection of Critical Essays.* Englewood Cliffs: Prentice, 1965.

———. *The Theatre of the Absurd.* Rev. ed. Garden City: Doubleday, 1969.

Federman, Raymond. *Journey to Chaos: Samuel Beckett's Early Fiction.* Berkeley: U of California P, 1965.

Federman, Raymond, and John Fletcher, eds. *Samuel Beckett: His Works and His Critics.* Berkeley: U of California P, 1970.

Fehsenfeld, Martha D., and Lois M. Overbeck. *Letters of Samuel Beckett.* In progress.

Fletcher, Beryl S., and John Fletcher. "Introduction: The Context of Modernism and of the 'Theatre of the Absurd.' " *A Student's Guide to the Plays of Samuel Beckett.* 2nd ed. Ed. Beryl S. Fletcher et al. London: Faber, 1985. 19–33.

Fletcher, Beryl S., John Fletcher, Barry Smith, and Walter Bachen, eds. *A Student's Guide to the Plays of Samuel Beckett.* London: Faber, 1978.

Fletcher, John. *The Novels of Samuel Beckett.* London: Chatto, 1970.

———. "Roger Blin at Work." Cohn, *Casebook* 21–26.

———. *Samuel Beckett's Art.* London: Chatto, 1971.

Fletcher, John, and John Spurling. *Beckett: A Study of His Plays.* London: Methuen; New York: Hill, 1972.

Friedman, Alan W., Charles Rossman, and Dina Sherzer, eds. *Beckett Translating/ Translating Beckett.* University Park: Pennsylvania State UP, 1987.

Friedman, Melvin J., ed. *Configuration critique de Samuel Beckett.* Paris: Minard, 1964.

———. "Crritic!" *Modern Drama* 9 (1966): 300–08.

———, ed. *Samuel Beckett Now.* Chicago: U of Chicago P, 1970.

Frye, Northrop. *Anatomy of Criticism*. Princeton: Princeton UP, 1957.

Gassner, John. "The Possibilities and Perils of Modern Tragedy." Corrigan 405–17.

Gidal, Peter. *Understanding Beckett: A Study of Monologue and Gesture in the Works of Samuel Beckett*. New York: St. Martin's, 1986.

Gilman, Richard. *The Making of Modern Drama: A Study of Büchner, Ibsen, Strindberg, Chekhov, Pirandello, Brecht, Beckett, Handke*. New York: Farrar, 1974.

Girard, René. "Perilous Balance: A Comic Hypothesis." *Modern Language Notes* 87.7 (1972): 811–26.

Goldman, Michael. *The Actor's Freedom: Toward a Theory of Drama*. New York: Viking, 1975.

———. "Vitality and Deadness in Beckett's Plays." Brater, *Beckett at 80* 67–83.

Gontarski, S. E. *The Intent of Undoing in Samuel Beckett's Dramatic Texts*. Bloomington: Indiana UP, 1985.

———, ed. *On Beckett: Essays and Criticism*. New York: Grove, 1986.

———, ed. Spec. Beckett issue of *Modern Fiction Studies* 29 (1983): 3–152.

———, ed. *The Theatrical Notebooks of Samuel Beckett*: Endgame. London: Faber, forthcoming.

Gorjanc, Judy. "Jessie's Choice." Unpublished paper, 1987.

Graver, Lawrence. *Samuel Beckett: Waiting for Godot*. Cambridge: Cambridge UP, 1989.

Graver, Lawrence, and Raymond Federman, eds. *Samuel Beckett: The Critical Heritage*. London: Routledge, 1979.

Grossvogel, David I. *Four Playwrights and a Postscript: Brecht, Ionesco, Beckett, and Genet*. Ithaca: Cornell UP, 1962.

Guggenheim, Peggy. *Out of This Century*. New York: Dial, 1946.

Guicharnaud, Jacques, with June Guicharnaud. *Modern French Theatre: From Giraudoux to Beckett*. Rev. ed. New Haven: Yale UP, 1967.

Hale, Jane Alison. *The Broken Window: Beckett's Dramatic Perspective*. West Lafayette: Purdue UP, 1987.

Harvey, Lawrence E. *Samuel Beckett: Poet and Critic*. Princeton: Princeton UP, 1970.

Hassan, Ihab. "The Literature of Silence." *The Postmodern Term: Essays in Postmodern Theory and Culture*. Columbus: Ohio State UP, 1987. 3–22.

Havel, Václav. "The Anatomy of the Gag." *Modern Drama* 23 (1980): 13–24.

Hayman, David, ed. Spec. Beckett issue of *James Joyce Quarterly* 8 (1971): 275–424.

Heilman, Robert B. "Tragedy and Melodrama: Speculations on Generic Form." Corrigan 245–57.

Henning, Sylvie Debevec. *Beckett's Critical Complicity: Carnival, Contestation, and Tradition*. Lexington: UP of Kentucky, 1987.

Hesla, David. *The Shape of Chaos*. Minneapolis: U of Minnesota P, 1968.

Hobson, Harold. "Samuel Beckett, Dramatist of the Year." *International Theatre Annual*. London: Calder, 1956. 153–54.

Holman, C. Hugh, and William Harmon. *A Handbook to Literature*. 5th ed. New York: Macmillan, 1986.

Homan, Sidney. *Beckett's Theaters: Interpretations for Performance*. Lewisburg: Bucknell UP, 1984.

Hornby, Richard. *Script into Performance: A Structuralist View of Play Performance*. Austin: U of Texas P, 1977.

Horton, Susan R. Response to Robert Scholes. Peterfreund 51–57.

Howe, Irving. *The Idea of the Modern in Literature and the Arts*. New York: Horizon, 1967.

Hughes, Ted. *Poetry Is*. Garden City: Doubleday, 1970.

Hutchings, William. "Abated Drama: Samuel Beckett's Unbated *Breath*." *Ariel: A Review of International English Literature* 17.1 (1986): 85–94.

Ionesco, Eugène. *La cantatrice chauve*. Paris: Gallimard, 1954. *The Bald Soprano*. *Four Plays*. New York: Grove, 1958.

Iser, Wolfgang. *The Act of Reading: A Theory of Aesthetic Response*. Baltimore: Johns Hopkins UP, 1984.

———. *The Implied Reader: Patterns of Communication in Prose Fiction from Bunyan to Beckett*. Baltimore: Johns Hopkins UP, 1974.

Jaspers, Karl. *Man in the Modern Age*. London: Routledge, 1933.

Joyce, James. *The Letters of James Joyce*. Vol. 1. Ed. Stuart Gilbert. London: Faber; New York: Viking, 1957. Corr. ed. 1966. Vols. 2 and 3. Ed. Richard Ellmann. London: Faber; New York: Viking, 1966.

Kalb, Jonathan. *Beckett in Performance*. Cambridge: Cambridge UP, 1989.

Kane, Leslie. *The Language of Silence: On the Unspoken and the Unspeakable in Modern Drama*. Madison: Fairleigh Dickinson UP, 1984.

Kant, Immanuel. *Critique of Pure Reason*. Trans. Norman Kemp Smith. London: Macmillan, 1934.

Kennedy, Andrew. *Samuel Beckett*. Cambridge: Cambridge UP, 1989.

———. *Six Dramatists in Search of a Language: Shaw, Eliot, Beckett, Pinter, Osborne, Arden*. Cambridge: Cambridge UP, 1975.

Kenner, Hugh. *A Reader's Guide to Samuel Beckett*. New York: Farrar, 1973.

———. *Samuel Beckett: A Critical Study*. Berkeley: U of California P, 1968.

Kermode, Frank. *The Genesis of Secrecy: On the Interpretation of Narrative*. Cambridge: Harvard UP, 1979.

Kern, Edith. "Drama Stripped for Inaction: Beckett's *Godot*." *Yale French Studies* 14 (Winter 1954–55): 41–47.

———. *Existential Thought and Fictional Technique: Kierkegaard, Sartre, Beckett*. New Haven: Yale UP, 1970.

Kernan, Alvin B. "The Attempted Dance: A Discussion of the Modern Theater."

The Modern American Theater: A Collection of Critical Essays. Ed. Kernan. Englewood Cliffs: Prentice, 1967. 12–33.

Klapp, Orrin E. "Tragedy and the American Climate of Opinion." Corrigan 302–14.

Knowlson, James. *Light and Darkness in the Theatre of Samuel Beckett.* London: Turret, 1972.

———, gen. ed. Waiting for Godot: *Samuel Beckett's Production Notebooks.* In progress.

Knowlson, James, and John Pilling. *Frescoes of the Skull: The Later Prose and Drama of Samuel Beckett.* London: Calder, 1979.

Kott, Jan. *Shakespeare Our Contemporary.* Garden City: Doubleday, 1964.

Krutch, Joseph Wood. "The Tragic Fallacy." Corrigan 271–83.

Lahr, John. *"Waiting for Godot." Notes on a Cowardly Lion: The Biography of Bert Lahr.* New York: Knopf, 1969. 253–82.

Langer, Susanne. "The Tragic Rhythm." Corrigan 85–98.

Levenson, Michael. *A Genealogy of Modernism.* Cambridge: Cambridge UP, 1984.

Levy, Alan. "The Long Wait for Godot." *Theatre Arts* (Aug. 1956): 33–35, 96. Excerpt rpt. in Cohn, *Casebook* 74–78.

Lyons, Charles R. "Beckett's Major Plays and the Trilogy." *Comparative Drama* 5.4 (1971): 254–68.

———. *Samuel Beckett.* New York: Grove, 1983.

Mailer, Norman. "A Public Notice on *Waiting for Godot.*" *Advertisements for Myself.* New York: Putnam's, 1959. 320–25. Rpt. in Cohn, *Casebook* 69–74.

Marker, Frederick J. "Beckett Criticism in *Modern Drama*: A Checklist." *Modern Drama* 19 (1976): 261–63.

McCarthy, Patrick A. Introduction. *Critical Essays on Samuel Beckett.* Ed. McCarthy. Boston: Hall, 1986. 1–10.

McMillan, Dougald. *Transition: The History of a Literary Era, 1927–38.* New York: Braziller, 1976.

McMillan, Dougald, and Martha Fehsenfeld. *Beckett in the Theatre.* London: Calder, 1988.

Megged, Matti. *Dialogue in the Void: Beckett and Giacometti.* New York: Lumen, 1985.

Mercier, Vivian. *Beckett/Beckett.* New York: Oxford UP, 1974.

———. "Samuel Beckett, Bible Reader." *Commonweal* 105 (1978): 266–68.

———. "The Uneventful Event." *Irish Times* 18 Feb. 1956: 6.

Merleau-Ponty, Maurice. *The Phenomenology of Perception and Other Essays on Phenomenological Psychology, the Philosophy of Art, History, and Politics.* Trans. James M. Edie. Evanston: Northwestern UP, 1964.

Miller, Arthur. "Tragedy and the Common Man." Corrigan 148–51.

Morrison, Kristin. *Canters and Chronicles: The Use of Narrative in the Plays of Samuel Beckett and Harold Pinter.* Chicago: U of Chicago P, 1983.

———. "Neglected Biblical Allusions in Beckett's Plays: 'Mother Pegg' Once More." Beja et al. 91–98.

Nietzsche, Friedrich. *Beyond Good and Evil: Prelude to a Philosophy of the Future.* Trans. Walter Kaufmann. New York: Random, 1966.

Norman, Marsha. *'Night, Mother.* New York: Hill, 1983.

O'Brien, Eoin. *The Beckett Country: Samuel Beckett's Ireland.* Dublin: Black Cat; London: Faber, 1986.

Oldsey, Bernard, ed. Spec. Beckett issue of *College Literature* 8 (1981): 209–312.

Pavis, Patrice. *Languages of the Stage.* New York: PAJ, 1982.

Perloff, Marjorie. *The Poetics of Indeterminacy: Rimbaud to Cage.* Princeton: Princeton UP, 1981.

Peter, John. *Vladimir's Carrot: Modern Drama and the Modern Imagination.* Chicago: U of Chicago P, 1987.

Peterfreund, Stuart, ed. *Critical Theory and the Teaching of Literature.* Proc. of the Northeastern University Center for Literary Studies 3. Boston: Northeastern UP, 1985.

Pilling, John. *Samuel Beckett.* London: Routledge, 1976.

Pountney, Rosemary. *Theatre of Shadows: Samuel Beckett's Drama 1956–76.* Gerrards Cross, Eng.: Colin Smythe; Totowa: Barnes, 1988.

Pronko, Leonard. *Avant-Garde: The Experimental Theater in France.* Berkeley: U of California P, 1962.

Rabinovitz, Rubin. *The Development of Samuel Beckett's Fiction.* Urbana: U of Illinois P, 1984.

Reid, Alec. *All I Can Manage, More Than I Could: An Approach to the Plays of Samuel Beckett.* Dublin: Dolmen, 1968.

———. "From Beginning to Date: Some Thoughts on the Plays of Samuel Beckett." Cohn, *Collection* 63–72.

Robbe-Grillet, Alain. "Samuel Beckett: Or, 'Presence' in the Theatre." *For a New Novel.* Trans. Richard Howard. New York: Grove, 1965. 111–25. Trans. of "Samuel Beckett ou la présence sur la scène." *Pour un nouveau roman.* Paris: Editions de Minuit, 1963. 95–107. Rpt. in Esslin, *Collection* 108–16. Trans. Barbara Bray.

Robinson, Michael. *The Long Sonata of the Dead: A Study of Samuel Beckett.* London: Hart-Davis; New York: Grove, 1969.

Rosen, Steven. *Samuel Beckett and the Pessimistic Tradition.* New Brunswick: Rutgers UP, 1976.

Sartre, Jean-Paul. *Being and Nothingness: An Essay on Phenomenological Ontology.* Trans. Hazel E. Barnes. New York: Philosophical Library, 1956.

———. "Existentialism Is a Humanism." *Existentialism from Dostoevsky to Sartre.* Ed. Walter Kaufmann. Rev. ed. New York: NAL, 1975. 345–69.

———. *The Philosophy of Existentialism.* Ed. Wade Baskin. New York: Philosophical Library, 1965.

Sastre, Alfonso. "Seven Notes on *Waiting for Godot*." Trans. Leonard C. Pronko. *Primer Acto* 1 (Apr. 1957): 46–52. Trans. of "Siete notas sobre *Esperando a Godot*." Rpt. in Cohn, *Casebook* 101–07.

Schlueter, June. *Metafictional Characters in Modern Drama*. New York: Columbia UP, 1979.

Schneider, Alan. *Entrances: An American Director's Journey*. New York: Viking, 1986.

———. "Waiting for Beckett: A Personal Chronicle." *Chelsea Review* 14.2 (1958): 3–20. Excerpt rpt. in Cohn, *Casebook* 51–57.

Scholes, Robert. "Interpretation and Criticism in the Classroom." Peterfreund 35–50.

Shattuck, Roger. *The Innocent Eye: On Modern Literature and the Arts*. New York: Farrar, 1984.

Shenker, Israel. "Moody Man of Letters." *New York Times* 6 May 1956, sec. 2: 1+. Rpt. as "An Interview with Beckett (1956)" in Graver and Federman 146–49.

Sherzer, Dina. "De-Construction in *Godot*." Cohn, *Beckett:* Waiting for Godot 145–49.

Simmons, Ernest J. *Chekhov: A Biography*. Chicago: U of Chicago P, 1962.

Simpson, Alan. "Producing *Godot* in Dublin." *Beckett and Behan*. London: Routledge, 1962. 62–137. Excerpt rpt. in Cohn, *Casebook* 45–49.

Simpson, Ekundayo. *Samuel Beckett: Traducteur de lui-même: Aspects de bilinguisme littéraire*. Saint-Foy, PQ: International Center for Research on Bilingualism, 1978.

States, Bert O. *Great Reckonings in Little Rooms: On the Phenomenology of Theater*. Berkeley: U of California P, 1985.

———. *Irony and Drama: A Poetics*. Ithaca: Cornell UP, 1971.

———. *The Shape of Paradox: An Essay on* Waiting for Godot. Berkeley: U of California P, 1978.

Stevens, Wallace. *Collected Poems*. New York: Knopf, 1955.

Stoppard, Tom. *Jumpers*. New York: Grove, 1972.

———. *Rosencrantz and Guildenstern Are Dead*. New York: Grove, 1967.

Takahashi, Yasunari. "Qu'est-ce Qui Arrive?—Beckett and Noh." Cohn, *Beckett:* Waiting for Godot 142–44.

Tanner, J. F., and J. D. Vann. *Samuel Beckett: A Checklist*. Columbus: Ohio State UP, 1969.

Titterton, W. R. *From Theatre to Music Hall*. London: Swift, 1912.

Tolstoy, Leo. "The Death of Ivan Ilych." Trans. Louise Maude and Aylmer Maude. *Fiction 100: An Anthology of Short Stories*. Ed. James H. Pickering. 4th ed. New York: Macmillan, 1985. 1034–64.

The Tramp. Dir. Charles Chaplin. With Charles Chaplin. 1915.

Turner, Victor. *From Ritual to Theatre: The Human Seriousness of Play*. New York: PAJ, 1982.

———. "Social Dramas and Stories about Them." Mitchell 137–65.

Tynan, Kenneth. Rev. of *Waiting for Godot. Observer* 7 Aug. 1955: 11. Rpt. in Elsom 70.

Ubersfeld, Anne. *Lire le théâtre.* Paris: Editions Sociales, 1977.

Unamuno, Miguel de. *The Tragic Sense of Life.* Ed. J. Flitch. New York: Dover, 1954.

Vinay, J. P., and J. Darbelnet. *Stylistique comparée du français et de l'anglais.* Paris: Didier, 1966.

Waiting for Beckett. Prod. John Reilly. Global Village Video Resource Center. Forthcoming.

Waiting for Godot. Dir. Alan Schneider. With Burgess Meredith and Zero Mostel. 1961. 16mm. 102 min.

Waiting for Godot. Videocassette. Dir. Mike Nichols. With Robin Williams, Steve Martin, F. Murray Abraham, and Bill Irwin. Lincoln Center, New York, forthcoming.

Whitaker, Thomas R. *Fields of Play in Modern Drama.* Princeton: Princeton UP, 1977.

Wilder, Thornton. "Some Thoughts on Playwriting." *Playwrights on Playwriting.* Ed. Toby Cole. New York: Hill, 1961. 106–15.

Willeford, William. *The Fool and His Scepter: A Study of Clowns, Jesters, and Their Audience.* Evanston: Northwestern UP, 1969.

Wilmut, Roger. *Kindly Leave the Stage! The Story of Variety, 1919–1960.* London: Methuen, 1985.

Wimsatt, W. K., Jr., and Monroe C. Beardsley. "The Intentional Fallacy." *The Verbal Icon: Studies in the Meaning of Poetry.* Lexington: U of Kentucky P, 1954. 3–18.

Wolf, Daniel, and Edwin Fancher, eds. *The* Village Voice *Reader.* Garden City: Doubleday, 1962.

Worth, Katharine, ed. *Beckett the Shape Changer: A Symposium.* London: Routledge, 1975.

———. *The Irish Drama of Europe: From Yeats to Beckett.* London: Athlone; Atlantic Highlands: Humanities, 1978.

Young, Jordan R. *The Beckett Actor.* Beverly Hills: Moonstone, 1987.

Zeifman, Hersh. "The Alterable Whey of Words: The Texts of *Waiting for Godot.*" *Educational Theatre Journal* 29.1 (1977): 77–84. Rpt. in Cohn, *Casebook* (1987 ed.) 86–95.

Zilliacus, Clas. *Beckett and Broadcasting.* Ser. A. Humaniora 51.2. Abo, Finland: Acta Academiae Aboensis, 1976.

Zurbrugg, Nicholas. *Beckett and Proust.* Gerrards Cross, Eng.: Colin Smythe; Totowa: Barnes, 1988.

———, ed. Spec. Beckett issue of *Review of Contemporary Fiction* 7.2 (1987): 7–215.

INDEX